FISHING THE
ADIRONDACKS

FISHING THE ADIRONDACKS

SPIDER RYBAAK

BURFORD BOOKS

All photos by Ray Hrynyk

Printed in the United States of America

10 9 8 7 6 5 4 3 2 1

Library of Congress Cataloging-in-Publication Data

Names: Rybaak, Spider.
Title: Fishing the Adirondacks / Spider Rybaak.
Description: Ithaca, NY : Burford Books, 2016. | Includes index.
Identifiers: LCCN 2015039101 | ISBN 9781580801805
Subjects: LCSH: Fishing—New York (State)—Adirondack Park Region.
Classification: LCC SH529 .R934 2016 | DDC 639.209747/5—dc23 LC record available at https://lccn.loc.gov/2015039101

To Susan

CONTENTS

ACKNOWLEDGMENTS

A work of this scope would have been impossible for me to complete by myself at this stage in my life. The following contributed immensely to the project: Susan Douglass, Roger Klindt, Dave Erway, Frank Flack, Rich Preall, Jack Zasada, Dick McDonald, Jonathan Fieroh, Bob Barker, Rob Fiorentino, Gary Fischer, and Best Western Inn of Saranac Lake.

ADIRONDACK PARK AND ENVIRONS

Map References by Site Number

The maps on the following pages show site numbers (listed below) for the principal fishing locations described in this book. Directions for locating any site, including those not identified here, are given in the specific site entry.

ADIRONDACK MOUNTAIN REGION

1. Lake Champlain
2. Champlain Canal
3. Lake George
4. Boquet River
5. Lincoln Pond
6. Taylor Pond
7. Chazy Lake
10. Lower Chateaugay Lake
11. Upper Chateaugay Lake
12. Chateaugay River
14. Schroon Lake
16. Paradox Lake
18. Brant Lake
19. Loon Lake (Warren County)
20. Lake Placid
24. Lake Kushaqua
25. Buck Pond
26. Rainbow Lake
27. Jones Pond
28. Osgood Pond
29. Boy Scout Clear Pond
30. Meacham Lake
34. Lower St. Regis Lake
35. Spitfire Lake
36. Upper St. Regis Lake
37. East Branch, St. Regis River
38. St. Regis River
39. Lake Clear
40. Lake Clear Outlet
41. Bear Pond
42. Little Long Pond (East)
43. Green Pond (St. Regis Canoe Area)
44. St. Regis Pond
45. Ochre Pond
46. Fish Pond
47. Little Fish Pond
48. Little Long Pond (West)
49. Lydia Pond
50. Kit Fox Pond
51. Nellie Pond
52. Bessie Pond
53. Clamshell Pond
54. Grass Pond
55. Turtle Pond
56. Slang Pond
57. Long Pond
58. Mountain Pond (St. Regis Canoe Area)
59. Pink Pond
60. Rat Pond
61. Hoel Pond
75. Upper Saranac Lake
76. Saranac River
77. Middle Saranac Lake
79. Lower Saranac Lake
80. Oseetah Lake
81. Kiwassa Lake
83. Franklin Falls Pond
84. Union Falls Pond (Flow)
85. West Branch Ausable River
87. Main Stem Ausable River
88. Lake Colby
94. Upper Hudson River
99. Lake Pleasant
101. East Branch Sacandaga River
102. Sacandaga River
105. East Caroga Lake
106. West Caroga Lake
115. Blue Mountain Lake
116. Raquette Lake
117. Upper Raquette River
118. Forked Lake
119. Long Lake
120. Tupper Lake
122. Simon Pond
124. Carry Falls Reservoir
127. Rainbow Falls Reservoir
130. Higley Flow Reservoir (Higley Falls Reservoir)
135. Lower Raquette River
136. Lake Ozonia
137. Lake Eaton
141. Stillwater Reservoir
143. Beaver Lake
144. Soft Maple Reservoir
149. Lower Beaver River
152. Big Moose Lake
156. First Lake
157. Second Lake
158. Third Lake
159. Fourth Lake
160. Fifth Lake
161. Sixth Lake
162. Seventh Lake
163. Eighth Lake
166. Cranberry Lake
167. Oswegatchie River
168. Grass River
173. Black River
174. Kayuta Lake
175. Forestport Reservoir

THOUSAND ISLANDS REGION (INDIAN RIVER CHAIN OF LAKES)

216. Star Lake
219. Lake Bonaparte
220. St. Lawrence River (St. Lawrence County)

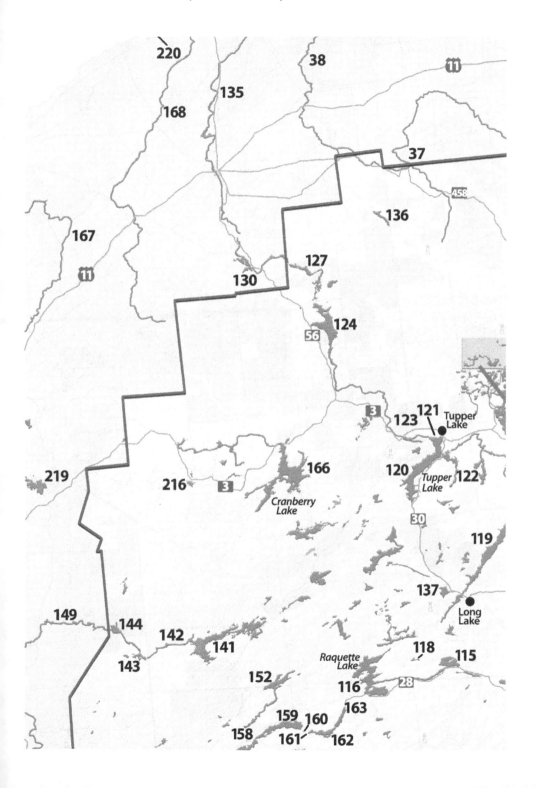

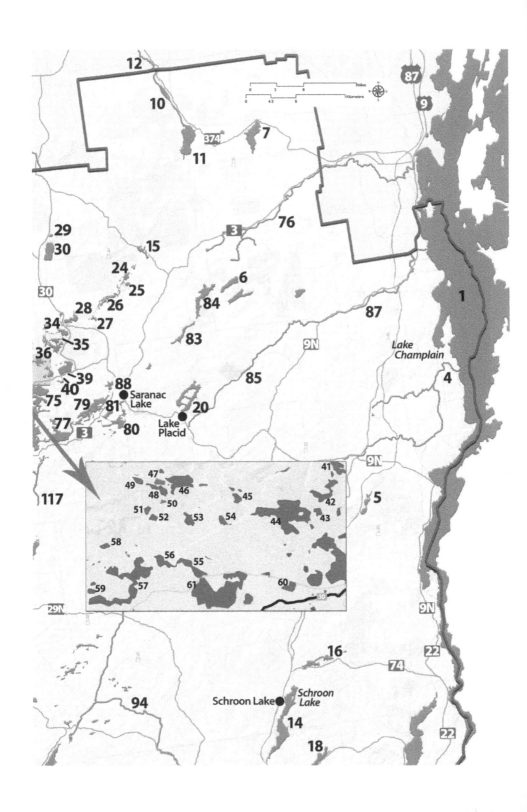

Adirondack Park South: Map References by Site Number

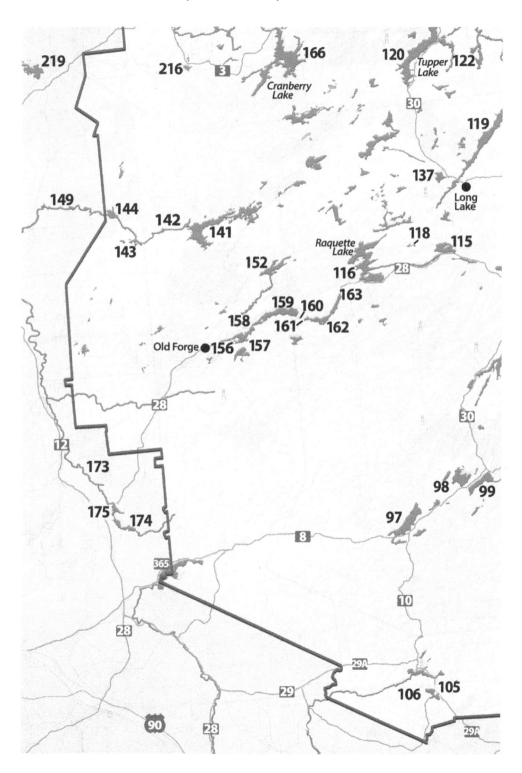

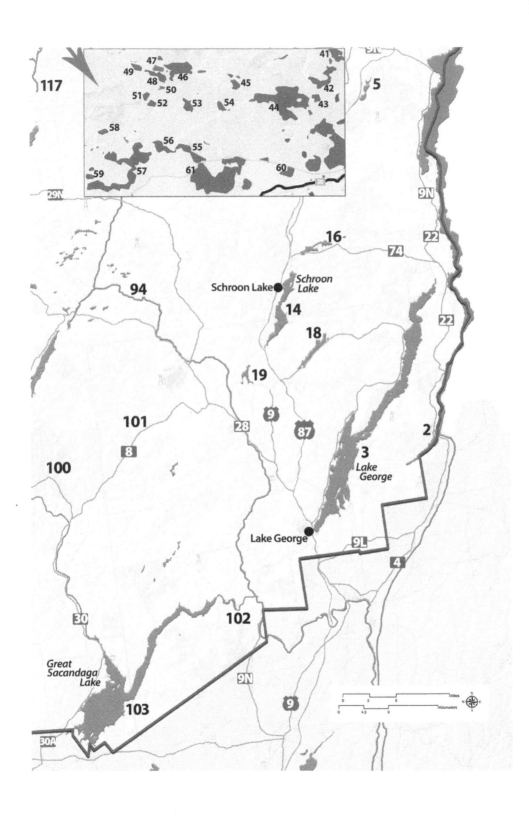

INTRODUCTION

Crowning over 6 million acres of northern New York (nearly 20 percent of the state), the Adirondack Park is the largest state preserve in the Lower 48. Back in the earth's formative days, some of the peaks rose as high as Mount Everest (25,000 feet). Worn down by the winds of time, only 43 reach over 4,000 feet today. Still, veins of garnet flow through the tired old granite, and 100,000 acres of ancient forest complement its expansive new growth. What's more, 2,800 lakes and ponds are set in this fabulous wilderness, and 31,000 miles of rivers and streams run down its face like crooked seams in a baseball cap, offering a fantastic variety of fish habitats in which to cast your dreams.

Just about anything that swims in the temperate waters of the Western Hemisphere can be found here. You can troll for salmon or muskies, fly fish for monster trout, black bass, and northern pike, jig for walleyes and lake trout, target ancient critters like bowfin, burbot, and gars, or simply sit on a dock and dunk worms for bullheads, sunfish, perch . . . you name it.

You name the setting, too. From massive waters like Lake Champlain and city streams where trout chase moths under streetlights, to tiny mountain brooks you can jump across, the top of New York has it all. And while there's no guarantee you'll catch the lunker swimming around in your dreams, you can count on catching limitless memories to hang in your mind for a lifetime.

NEW YORK'S WILDLIFE

While numerous puma sightings have been reported in rural New York over the last couple of decades, their numbers are so small, you have a better chance of catching a smoked fish than of seeing a mountain lion.

About the most dangerous critter you are likely to encounter is a black bear. They can show up just about anywhere in rural New York: I've run into two of them in 45 years of fishing, and both snuck away. Still, if you see one clumsily lumbering down the trail or splashing up-creek toward you, make enough noise to be noticed, then make yourself as big as you can.

The Adirondack Mountains have moose. While they're not particularly violent, their sheer size makes them dangerous. It's probably a good idea to avoid approaching females with calves, especially by canoe.

And then there are coyotes, 11,000 by some estimates. Corrupted by timber wolf genes, they are fully 30 percent larger than the western variety. And though their howls have probably cut some camping trips short, there is no record of one hurting a human. Several have crossed my path over the years but when they winded me, they split so fast I was left wondering if I ever saw one in the first place.

Besides dump ducks (gulls), the friendly skies over the state's waterways are loaded with kingfishers, blue herons, cormorants, wild ducks, and Canada geese. Loons thrive in remote waters and large bodies with swampy areas. Bald eagles are making a comeback; you can expect to see them on popular streams like the Salmon River and Beaver Kill, as well as deep in the Adirondack wilderness.

Insects are plentiful, ubiquitous, and can really bug you. Yellow jackets and bald-faced hornets have sent more than one angler diving for cover. In late spring, blackflies rule the air over backcountry creeks. Some are so aggressive, an old-timer once told me he's seen them chase trout. While that's stretching things a bit, they can swarm in such numbers from mid-May through June, especially in the northern half of the state, they'll drive an unprotected fly fisherman off a stream in the middle of a mayfly hatch. What's more, not all insect repellents discourage them—indeed, some actually seem to sound the dinner bell. Those containing DEET work well. Most roadside streams and lakes are sprayed to keep blackflies in check, but waters in wild forests and wilderness areas are not.

Finally, we have a lot of mosquitoes, establishment attempts at eradication notwithstanding. They've become particularly troublesome lately because some carry West Nile virus, a pathogen known to be fatal to crows and humans. Mosquitoes are especially active at dusk and dawn, near shore around ponds, lakes, canals, and slow-moving rivers. They don't cotton to most insect repellents. Folks wishing to avoid harsh chemicals are encouraged to wear Bug-Out or similar mesh garments over their regular clothes.

NEW YORK'S WEATHER

New York has a temperate climate with an average temperature of about 48 degrees. But that doesn't mean we don't get wild swings. Most winters, temperatures drop below zero. Syracuse, in the heart of the state, averages 120 inches of snow annually, a statistic that earns it the title as one of the snowiest cities in the country. The Tug Hill Plateau Region, stretching from the north shore of Oneida Lake to about Watertown, is blessed with a meteorological phenomenon known as lake effect, in which cold winds blowing over the warmer waters of Lake Ontario generate enough snow to blanket the countryside from the east shore to the Adirondack foothills with an average of 200 inches of snow each winter. The Adirondack village of Old Forge regularly makes it on the national news because its temperatures dip beyond 30 degrees below zero. While most lakes in the northern half of the state develop ice deep enough to drive on most winters, lakes in the southern tier often only have about a month of ice thick enough to walk on, and in some years no ice at all.

Summer is very humid and hot. Temperatures vary with sea level. The Finger Lakes Region sees a lot of days in the high 70s and 80s. The St. Lawrence River lowlands are normally 5 degrees cooler and the Adirondacks as much as 10 degrees cooler.

First snow, often in October, transforms Adirondack streams into winter wonderlands.

Spring and fall are the reason many New Yorkers put up with winter and summer. Temperatures range from 55 to 65. And while many complain it is always cloudy or raining, the truth is, the sun shines about half the time.

FINDING YOUR WAY

The maps in this book were drawn from a variety of sources. In most cases, the mileages given here were recorded by visiting the site. However, odometers aren't created equal, and when combined with factors like weather, rest stops, and garage sales, readings can vary. While every attempt has been made to present accurate distances, please accept them as approximations at best.

CATCH AND RELEASE

One thing all competent anglers with average luck can expect to do in New York is catch fish. So many fish, in fact, that some will have to be released because they're out of season or too small, or you've caught more than you feel like cleaning, or you simply don't feel like killing anymore. And then there are those who practice catch and release religiously. Whatever the reason, it is in the best interest of all concerned for the critter to be released unharmed. Here are some simple pointers to ensure that you release a fish with a future instead of a dead fish swimming.

- Avoid going after big fish with ultralight tackle. The cruel, frustrating struggle for freedom can exhaust them beyond recovery.
- Only use a net when absolutely necessary. Nets tear mouths, rip gills, break fins and teeth, scratch eyes, and remove slime, an important barrier against harmful bacteria.
- Keep the fish submerged in water, even when you're unhooking it.
- If you must remove a fish from the water, particularly a member of the salmonid or pike family, always wet your hands before touching it and place it on something wet.
- If the fish is hooked deep in the tongue, guts, or gills, cut the line. Fish are bleeders, and an internal wound as small as a pinhole can be fatal. By leaving the hook in place, healing will occur around it as it rusts away. No hook is worth a life.
- Never lift a pike by squeezing its eyes with your fingers; always hold it horizontally.
- Keep your fingers out of a fish's gills.

FISH CONSUMPTION ADVISORY

While the doctor may tell you that eating fish is healthy for you, the state advises you eat no more than 0.5 pound of fish per month caught from any of the state's waters, including municipal reservoirs. What's more, the New York State Department of Environmental Conservation *Fishing Regulations Guide* lists three pages of streams and lakes from which you should only eat 0.5 pound per month, or none at all.

BEST TIMES TO FISH

All fish feed most actively around dusk and dawn. Some biologists and successful anglers claim that the moon influences feeding; commercial calendars like Rick Taylor's "Prime Times" list the best days and most productive hours. Still, some fish like catfish, eels, and walleyes feed best at night, especially when there's no moon, while yellow perch and northern pike feed best during daylight. The rest, from trout and bass to salmon, muskies, crappies, and sunfish, feed whenever they feel like it.

REGULATIONS

New York has so many fishing regulations, it takes the DEC *Fishing Regulations Guide* about 40 pages to list them all. While some rules are written in stone—motors and baitfish are prohibited in all wilderness and canoe areas, for instance—it's a good idea to pick up the guide when you buy a license, memorize the general regulations in the front of the book, then check the special regulations by county to see if additional rules apply to the spot you're going to fish.

HOW TO USE THIS GUIDE

The book is broken down into three regions: the Adirondacks, the Tug Hill Plateau, and the St. Lawrence lowlands (also known as the Thousand Islands Region). Every region's major sites will be named, numbered, and described as follows:

KEY SPECIES: This section will include all the fish commonly sought in the spot.

DESCRIPTION: Each site will be summarized. Lake descriptions typically include acreage or square miles, as well as average and maximum depths. Stream summaries contain information on sources, lengths, and mouths.

TIPS: Site-specific tips.

THE FISHING: Details on the fishery, including the typical sizes popular fish species reach, bait and habitat preferences, stocking statistics, and special regulations.

DIRECTIONS: How to get there from the nearest major town. Since one of the main focuses of this book is to introduce traveling anglers to the state's fishing, the directions will be the easiest way to go—not the shortest. In the case of streams, I've listed the major routes paralleling them.

ADDITIONAL INFORMATION: This section will contain on-site camping information, boat launches, campgrounds, bank-fishing access, and other site-specific details.

CONTACT: State and local agencies to contact for information on the site. The complete phone numbers and addresses are listed in the appendix.

Lettered sites listed below the numbered ones include additional features like access points, campgrounds, and—in the case of large waters like Lake Champlain—hot spots.

FISHING ACCESS FOR THE DISABLED

Generally, access for disabled anglers is mentioned in the site's **Additional information** section. However, new facilities crop up all the time. I encourage you to check the NYSDEC website, and search for fishing access for anglers with disabilities.

CAMPING

- Generally, primitive camping is allowed on state land in the Adirondack Park, and in all state forests.
- Groups numbering up to nine can spend up to three nights at any given site. Larger groups and longer stays require a permit from the local forest ranger.
- As a rule, camp must be set up at least 150 feet away from any road, trail, or source of water. Exceptions exist however, in sites designated by a CAMP HERE disk.
- Primitive sites that are not in campgrounds are on a first-come, first-served basis and cannot be reserved.
- Lean-tos are not for exclusive use and must be shared.
- Camping is prohibited above 4,000 feet in the Adirondacks.

The New York State Department of Environmental Conservation operates public campgrounds in the Adirondack Park. Contact the regional office (addresses and phone numbers are listed in the appendix) for informational brochures; online, you can visit www.dec.state.ny.us (click on DEC Camping Information).

Reservations for all campgrounds can be made by contacting the New York State Camping/Cabin Reservation System at 800-456-2267 or online at www.reserveamerica.com.

GLOSSARY

BREAKLINE: A steep drop from shallow to deep water.
BRONZEBACK: Smallmouth bass.

CURLY-TAIL: Soft plastic grub, aka twister tail.

DARTER: A cigar-shaped surface plug.

FLATLINE: Trolling with the lure attached directly to the main line, and without additional weight.

FLATWING STREAMER: A streamer tied so the wing hugs the body and rides horizontally, like a Black Ghost.

FREELINE: Fishing a bait, usually a minnow or stickworm, without added weight.

MINNOWBAIT: A hard, minnow-imitating crankbait like a ThunderStick or Bass Pro Shops XPS Extreme Minnow.

NYSDEC OR DEC: New York State Department of Environmental Conservation.

PANFISH: This category includes bluegills, pumpkinseeds, yellow perch, rock bass, and bullheads; one of these tasty relatively easy-to-catch little critters is usually an angler's first fish.

PIKEASAURUS: Northern pike weighing 10 pounds or better.

ROW-TROLLING: Trolling by paddle power.

SETH GREEN RIG: A system in which up to five lures, usually spoons, each on a leader 5 to 10 feet long, are staggered through the water column at 5- to 10-foot intervals.

STICKWORM: A fat plastic worm like a Senko or YUM Dinger.

WALK-THE-DOG: Jerking a darter so its head swings from side to side.

FISH SPECIES OF NEW YORK

Brook Trout (*Salvelinus fontinalis*)

GENERAL DESCRIPTION: This beautiful fish normally has a deep-olive back decorated with a labyrinth of worm-like markings. Spots on its sides are red and blue, and a white line traces its reddish, lower fins. A member of the char family, its mouth and appetite are greater than your average trout's.

DISTRIBUTION: The state's official fish, brookies are also called natives or speckled trout and can be found in clear, cold brooks, streams, ponds, and lakes throughout the state. They are the fish of choice for anglers hiking into remote Adirondack Mountain ponds and streams.

STUFF WORTH KNOWING: Brookies assume their most striking colors in autumn when they're ready to spawn. Males often have bright-red bellies and large hooked jaws. Their propensity for eagerly taking worms, salted minnows, flies, small spoons and spinners, you name it, has earned them the distinction of being the easiest trout to catch. They're the state's smallest trout, most range from 4 to 10 inches long. Fish around 18 inches long are possible, though, and the state record, caught in the Silver Lake Wilderness Area of Hamilton County by Richard Beauchamp on May 16, 2013, is 6 pounds.

Lake Trout (*Salvelinus namaycush*)

GENERAL DESCRIPTION: Like brookies, this delicious member of the char family isn't exactly the brightest fish in the tank. It has a relatively big mouth and an appetite to match. Its back is generally gray or green; the sides are silvery or gray and speckled with light spots. The belly is white and its tail is forked.

DISTRIBUTION: Another native New Yorker, this species prefers cold, deep water and is often sought in depths exceeding 100 feet. Lakers are present in deep ponds and lakes throughout the Adirondack Mountains.

STUFF WORTH KNOWING: One of the larger trout, lakers easily reach 20 inches, and 30-something inch fish are possible. They spawn in autumn in shallow water over gravel. The state record, caught by Jesse Wykstra in Lake Erie on August 9, 2003, is 41 pounds, 8 ounces.

Brown Trout (*Salmo trutta*)

GENERAL DESCRIPTION: Sporting deep-brown backs, this species' color lightens into golden sides splashed with red and brown spots surrounded by light halos. Sometimes the red spots are so bright they look like burning embers. Mature males sport kypes (curved lower jaws) that are often hooked so extremely, they seem deformed.

DISTRIBUTION: Imported back in the 1830s from Germany, browns found America to their liking and have prospered. Far more tolerant of warm water than brookies or lakers, they do well in every kind of clean, oxygenated water, from deep lakes to shallow streams.

STUFF WORTH KNOWING: Purist fly fishermen consider the brown the savviest of trout. Its propensity for hitting a well-presented dry fly has endeared the species to some of the world's most famous authors—Dame Juliana Berners, Izaak Walton, William Butler Yeats, and Ernest Hemingway, to name a few. Especially colorful when they spawn in autumn, browns assume a brilliance that perfectly complements this colorful season. The state record, caught in Lake Ontario by Tony Brown (no relation) on June 10, 1997, weighs 33 pounds, 2 ounces.

Rainbow Trout (*Oncorhynchus mykiss*)

GENERAL DESCRIPTION: This species has a deep-green back that melts into silvery sides. A pink stripe stretching from the corner of the fish's jaw to the base of its tail is what gives it its name. The upper half of its body, its upper fins, and the entire tail are splattered with black spots.

DISTRIBUTION: Native to the West Coast, rainbows were first introduced to New York in the 19th century and have been here ever since. They can be found in deep, cool lakes and cold streams throughout the state. Relatively easy to catch, they are often stocked in inhospitable urban creeks because biologists know the vast majority will likely be caught way before summer heats the creek to unbearable temperatures. Those that survive the early season's line-dance of anglers seek out spring holes or migrate downstream to cold lakes or the ocean.

STUFF WORTH KNOWING: Rainbows spawn in spring, providing trout enthusiasts with some of the year's most exciting creek action. The state record, caught in Lake Ontario on August 14, 2004, by Robert Wilson, tipped the scale at 31 pounds, 3 ounces.

Splake (Brook Trout–Lake Trout Hybrid)

GENERAL DESCRIPTION: A cross between lake trout and brook trout, these hybrids can look like either one. The only way to identify them exactly is to examine their innards.

DISTRIBUTION: The state stocks splake in Adirondack ponds like Green (**site 64**) and Boy Scout Clear (**site 29**) and lakes like Meacham (**site 30**) and Limekiln (**site 154**).

STUFF WORTH KNOWING: Splake are larger than brookies but generally don't reach the size lakers do. Unlike other hybrids, splake can reproduce, and spawn in autumn. The state record, caught in Limekiln Lake (**site 154**) by Jonathan Simon on June 27, 2004, weighs 13 pounds, 8 ounces.

Atlantic Salmon or Landlocked Salmon (*Salmo salar*)

GENERAL DESCRIPTION: The only salmon native to the state, Atlantic salmon generally have deep-brown backs that quickly dissolve to silvery sides splattered with irregularly shaped spots, which are often crossed.

DISTRIBUTION: At one time, Lake Ontario boasted the greatest population of landlocked Atlantic salmon in the world. A combination of pollution, construction of dams on natal streams, and sterility caused by excessively eating exotic forage (alewives and smelt) wiped them out. Currently, a token presence is maintained in Lake Ontario by stocking. The state releases over 365,000 fingerlings in the lake annually. In addition, local, state, and federal agencies chip in by unloading surplus mature fish from hatcheries and research laboratories.

STUFF WORTH KNOWING: Atlantic salmon are the only salmon that survive the spawning ordeal, often returning to spawn a second time. They're considered the classiest salmon: Catching one, especially on a fly, is many a fly-fishing purist's greatest dream. Atlantic salmon spawn in autumn. The state record, caught in Lake Ontario by Mike Dandino on April 5, 1997, weighs 24 pounds, 15 ounces.

Chinook or King Salmon (*Oncorhynchus tshawytscha*)

GENERAL DESCRIPTION: A silvery fish with a green back, it has black spots along the upper half of its body, including the fins and the entire tail. When they're ready to spawn, they become a dark olive-brown, and the males develop a kype (hooked jaw). The inside of the mouth is entirely black.

DISTRIBUTION: The largest of the Pacific salmon, kings were introduced into Lake Ontario in the late 1960s. Currently, upwards of 1.5 million are stocked annually by the state. Individuals easily reach 35 pounds, and the species has become one of the lake's most important game fish.

STUFF WORTH KNOWING: The most exciting fishing occurs roughly from mid-September through mid-November, when mature, 3½-year-old fish ascend tributaries to spawn. Average size is 25 pounds. However, a few precocious 1½-year-olds (the females are called Jennies, and the males are called Jacks), averaging 8 pounds, are also present. Kings spawn in autumn and die soon afterward. The state record, caught in the Salmon River on September 7, 1991, by Kurtis Killian, weighs 47 pounds, 13 ounces.

Kokanee Salmon (*Oncorhynchus nerka*)

GENERAL DESCRIPTION: The landlocked version of sockeye salmon, this fish is silvery but turns red when spawning.

DISTRIBUTION: The state stopped stocking them at the turn of the century, but naturally reproducing populations are found in some ponds.

STUFF WORTH KNOWING: Among the smaller salmon, kokanees average about 10 inches. Their mouths are very delicate; some anglers actually tie a rubber band onto their line to act as a shock absorber when setting the hook. Two techniques are used to catch them: Chum with oatmeal and then still-fish with a red worm on a tiny (size 14 to 20) hook. Or troll slowly with a red worm about 18 inches behind a Lake Clear Wabbler. They spawn once, in autumn, and die. The state record, caught in Boy Scout Clear Pond (site 29) on June 14, 2002, by Kenneth Shear, is 3 pounds, 6 ounces.

Cisco or Lake Herring (*Coregonus artedi*)

GENERAL DESCRIPTION: This silvery fish has a rounded, cigar-like body and is often described as resembling an oversized smelt.

DISTRIBUTION: They are present in deep, cold lakes like Lake Champlain.

STUFF WORTH KNOWING: Primarily plankton eaters, ciscos will take dry flies, tiny garden worms, small minnows and spoons. They spawn in autumn. The state record, caught in Lake Lauderdale on January 25, 1990, by Albert Baratto, weighs 5 pounds, 7 ounces.

Lake Whitefish (*Coregonus clupeaformis*)

GENERAL DESCRIPTION: These fish generally have brown or blue backs that fade into silvery sides and white bellies.

DISTRIBUTION: Formerly distributed widely throughout the state, lake whitefish have been run out of most of their range by pollution. However, they are still found in cool, deep places like Otsego, Pleasant, and Skaneateles Lakes, along with Lake Ontario.

STUFF WORTH KNOWING: Zebra mussels feed on the same phytoplankton lake whitefish eat, prompting some experts to warn they will wipe out the whitefish in waters occupied by both. Others counter that zebra mussels simply redistribute the biomass by laying their waste on the floor, which will result in explosions of bottom-feeding invertebrates—which whitefish also eat. While the jury is still out on the zebra mussel question, most scientists agree that alewives, which feed heavily on whitefish fry, can send the population into a nosedive. The state record, caught in Lake Pleasant (**site 99**) on August 29, 1995, by Randolph Smith, is 10 pounds, 8 ounces.

Largemouth Bass or Bucketmouth (*Micropterus salmoides*)

GENERAL DESCRIPTION: This is one of two species the New York State Department of Environmental Conservation includes under the heading of black bass in the state *Fishing Regulations Guide*. The largest member of the sunfish family,

The author and a North Country hawg (photo by Susan Douglass).

this fish is dark green on the back; the color lightens approaching the white belly. A horizontal row of large, black splotches runs along the middle of the side, from the gill plate to the base of the tail. Its trademark is its huge head and mouth. The ends of the mouth reach past the eyes.

DISTRIBUTION: Found in lakes, ponds, and sluggish streams throughout the state, except in the highest Adirondack ponds.

STUFF WORTH KNOWING: Occurring in the entire Lower 48 states, inclined to hit artificial lures of every description, the largemouth bass is America's favorite game fish. It'll hit just about anything that moves and is notorious for its explosive, heart-stopping strikes on surface lures. This species spawns in the spring when water temperatures range from 62 to 65 degrees. The state record, caught in Buckhorn Lake on September 11, 1987, by John Higbie, is 11 pounds, 4 ounces.

Smallmouth Bass or Bronzeback (*Micropterus dolomieu*)

GENERAL DESCRIPTION: This is one of two species the New York State Department of Environmental Conservation includes under the heading of black bass in the state *Fishing Regulations Guide*. Brownish in color, it is easily differentiated from the largemouth because the ends of the mouth occur below the eyes. One of America's most popular fish, it is granted equal status with the bucketmouth in most bass tournaments.

DISTRIBUTION: Found in lakes and streams throughout the state.

STUFF WORTH KNOWING: Spawns in late spring and early summer when water temperatures range from 61 to 65 degrees. The state record, caught in Lake Erie on June 4, 1995, by Andrew Kartesz, weighs 8 pounds, 4 ounces.

Muskellunge (*Esox masquinongy*)

GENERAL DESCRIPTION: The largest member of the pike family, this long, sleek species commonly reaches 35 pounds. The back is light green to brownish yellow, and the sides can have dark bars or blotches. Its most prominent feature is its duck-billed mouth filled with razor-sharp teeth. Only the upper halves of the gill covers and cheeks have scales, a fact normally used to differentiate muskies from northern pike and pickerel.

DISTRIBUTION: The Great Lakes, the Susquehanna River watershed, and lakes like Chautauqua, Waneta, and Lamoka.

STUFF WORTH KNOWING: The Ohio and Great Lakes strains occur in the state. Muskies spawn in late April through early May when water temperatures range from 49 to 59 degrees. The state record, caught in the St. Lawrence River on September 22, 1957, by Arthur Lawton, is 69 pounds, 15 ounces.

CAUTION: Keep fingers out of the gill rakers; they are sharp enough to shred human flesh.

Tiger Muskie or Norlunge

GENERAL DESCRIPTION: This species is a cross between a male northern pike and a muskie. Its body is shaped the same as a true muskie's, but its colors are more vivid and its sides have wavy, tiger-like stripes. Its teeth are razor-sharp.

DISTRIBUTION: Tiger muskies occur naturally where muskies and northerns share a range, places like the St. Lawrence River (**site 220**). In addition, they're bred in hatcheries and stocked in lakes and rivers to provide trophy fishing and to control runaway populations of hardy panfish like white perch.

STUFF WORTH KNOWING: These strikingly beautiful hybrids are sterile. The state record, caught in the Tioughnioga River on May 25, 1990, by Brett Gofgosky, is 35 pounds, 8 ounces.

CAUTION: Keep your fingers out of the gill rakers; they are sharp enough to shred human flesh.

Northern Pike, aka Pikeasaurus (*Esox lucius*)

GENERAL DESCRIPTION: A medium-sized member of the pike family, this long, slender fish is named after a spear used in combat during the Middle Ages. Its body is the same as a muskie's, but its color is almost invariably green; it has large, oblong white spots on its sides. Its cheeks are fully scaled, but only the top half of its gill plates are. Its teeth are razor-sharp.

DISTRIBUTION: In large and midsized rivers and lakes throughout the state.

The St. Lawrence River is notorious for large northern pike.

STUFF WORTH KNOWING: Spawns in April through early May, in water temperatures ranging from 40 to 52 degrees. The state record, caught in Great Sacandaga Lake on September 15, 1940, by Peter Dubuc, is 46 pounds, 2 ounces.

CAUTION: Keep your fingers out of the gill rakers; they are sharp enough to shred human flesh.

Chain Pickerel (*Esox niger*)

GENERAL DESCRIPTION: The smallest member of the pike family, the chain pickerel's body is shaped exactly like those of its larger cousins, but its green sides are overlaid in a yellow, chain-mail-like pattern. Its teeth are razor-sharp.

DISTRIBUTION: In ponds and lakes throughout the state.

STUFF WORTH KNOWING: Spawns in early spring, in water temperatures ranging from 47 to 52 degrees. The state record, caught in Toronto Reservoir on February 13, 1965, by John Bosland, is 8 pounds, 1 ounce.

CAUTION: Keep your fingers out of the gill rakers; they are sharp enough to shred human flesh.

Walleye (*Sander vitreus*; Formerly *Stizostedion vitreum*)

GENERAL DESCRIPTION: The largest member of the perch family, the walleye gets its name from its large, opaque eyes. A walleye's back is dark gray to black and fades as it slips down to the sides, which are often streaked in gold. It has two dorsal fins; the front one's last few spines have a black blotch at their base. Its teeth are pointed and can puncture but won't slice. Nocturnal critters, walleyes often enter shallow areas to feed. If the moon is out, their eyes catch and hold the beams, spawning ghost stories and extraterrestrial sightings from folks who see the eerie lights moving around in the water.

DISTRIBUTION: In cool lakes and rivers throughout the state.

STUFF WORTH KNOWING: Walleyes spawn in early spring when water temperatures range from 44 to 48 degrees. The state record, caught by Thomas Reed in Mystic Lake, January 20, 2009, weighs 16 pounds, 9 ounces.

Yellow Perch (*Perca flavescens*)

GENERAL DESCRIPTION: This popular panfish has a dark back that fades to golden-yellow sides overlaid with five to eight dark vertical bands. Sometimes its lower fins are traced in bright orange.

DISTRIBUTION: Found in every type of water throughout the state.

STUFF WORTH KNOWING: Spawns from mid-April through May when water temperatures range from 44 to 54 degrees. The state record, caught in Lake Erie on April 28, 1982, by George Boice, is 3 pounds, 8 ounces.

Crappie (*Pomoxis nigromaculatus*)

GENERAL DESCRIPTION: Arguably the most delicious fish in New York, this member of the sunfish family used to be considered a panfish. Late in the last century, the state imposed a minimum length and daily limit on it, moving its status up a notch. It has a dark-olive or black back and silver sides streaked with gold and overlaid with black spots and blotches. The front of its dorsal fin has seven or eight sharp spines followed by a soft fan.

DISTRIBUTION: Although white and black crappies call the state's waters home, the latter is the more common by far; it thrives in still to slowly moving water.

STUFF WORTH KNOWING: Spawns in late spring when water temperatures range from 57 to 73 degrees. The state record, caught in Duck Lake on April 17, 1998, by Kenneth Kierst, weighs 3 pounds, 12 ounces.

White Crappie (*Pomoxis annularis*)

GENERAL DESCRIPTION: This species looks pretty much the same as its black cousin but is generally lighter and only has six spines on its dorsal fin.

DISTRIBUTION: Found in lakes, ponds, and slow rivers throughout the state.

STUFF WORTH KNOWING: Spawns late spring and early summer when water temperatures range from 57 to 73 degrees. The state record, caught in Sleepy Hollow Lake, June 9, 2001, by James Weinberg, is 3 pounds, 13 ounces.

Bluegill (*Lepomis macrochirus*)

GENERAL DESCRIPTION: One of the most popular sunfishes, its color varies. It has anywhere from five to eight vertical bars running down its sides, a deep-orange breast, and a dark-blue, rounded gill flap.

DISTRIBUTION: Lakes, ponds, and slow-moving rivers throughout the state.

STUFF WORTH KNOWING: Ounce for ounce, bluegills are the sportiest fish. Fly fishing for them with wet flies and poppers is very popular. The species spawns in shallow, muddy areas near vegetation in summer. The state record, caught in Kohlbach Pond on August 3, 1992, by Devin VanZandt, is 2 pounds, 8 ounces.

Pumpkinseed (*Lepomis gibbosus*)

GENERAL DESCRIPTION: This popular sunfish is the most widespread in the state. Its color ranges from bronze to dark green, and its gill flap has an orange/red spot on the end.

DISTRIBUTION: Ponds, lakes, and slow-moving streams throughout the state.

STUFF WORTH KNOWING: Spawns in shallow, muddy areas near vegetation in early summer. The state record, caught in Indian Lake (**site 91**) on July 19, 1994, by R. Kennard Mosher, is 1 pound, 9 ounces.

Rock Bass, aka Redeyes and Googleyes (*Ambloplites rupestris*)

GENERAL DESCRIPTION: Another member of the sunfish family, it's dark brown to deep bronze in color, is heavily spotted in black, and has big red eyes.

DISTRIBUTION: Found in rocky, shallow areas of streams and lakes throughout the state.

STUFF WORTH KNOWING: Spawns over rocky areas in late spring and early summer. The state record, caught in the Ramapo River on May 26, 1984, by Eric Avogrado, is 1 pound, 15 ounces.

Channel Catfish (*Ictalurus punctatus*)

GENERAL DESCRIPTION: The largest indigenous member of the catfish family, it has a dark-brown back, a white belly, a forked tail, and barbels around its mouth. Juveniles up to 24 inches have black spots on their sides. Spines on the dorsal and pectoral fins can inflict a nasty wound.

DISTRIBUTION: Found in deep channels of lakes and large rivers throughout the state, often in heavy current.

STUFF WORTH KNOWING: Spawning takes place in summer, when water temperatures reach between 75 and 85 degrees. The state record, caught in Brant Lake (**site 18**) on July 15, 2001, by Chris Dixon, is 30 pounds.

Brown Bullhead (*Ameiurus nebulosus*)

GENERAL DESCRIPTION: With a dark-brown back and white belly, this member of the catfish family has barbels around its mouth. A relatively square tail distinguishes it from the channel catfish.

DISTRIBUTION: Great variety of habitats. Tolerance for high temperatures and low oxygen levels allows it to live in places other fish can't. Bullheads are found in virtually every type of water, from Adirondack ponds to the old Erie Canal.

STUFF WORTH KNOWING: Spawns in muddy areas from late June through July. Both parents guard the schooling fry for the first few weeks of life. The state record, caught in Lake Mahopac on August 1, 2009, by Glen Collacuro, is 7 pounds, 6 ounces.

White Perch (*Morone americana*)

GENERAL DESCRIPTION: A member of the temperate bass family Moronidae, this species' back can range in color from olive to silvery gray. Its sides are pale olive or silver.

DISTRIBUTION: Common in the Great Lakes drainage. Although they can be found in lakes, white perch are generally a river fish.

STUFF WORTH KNOWING: They spawn from mid-May through mid June, when water temperatures reach 52 to 59 degrees. The state record, caught in Lake Oscaletta on September 21, 1991, by Joseph Tansey, weighs 3 pounds, 1 ounce.

White Bass (*Morone chrysops*)

GENERAL DESCRIPTION: Same as the white perch but with bold, lateral stripes.

DISTRIBUTION: Throughout the Great Lakes drainage. Mainly found in lakes, their populations have boom-and-bust cycles. One year, huge rafts can be seen on the surface in places like Onondaga Lake; the next year they seem as rare as hen's teeth.

STUFF WORTH KNOWING: Spawns in late spring. The state record, caught in Furnace Brook on May 2, 1992, by Robert Hilton, is 3 pounds, 6 ounces.

Burbot, aka Ling and Lawyer (*Lota lota*)

GENERAL DESCRIPTION: Looking like a cross between a bullhead and an eel, this species' color is yellow-brown overlaid with a dark mottled pattern. It has a single barbel on its chin and deeply embedded scales that are so tiny, they are almost invisible.

DISTRIBUTION: Found in cold, deep lakes and rivers in the Great Lakes and Susquehanna River drainages.

STUFF WORTH KNOWING: Found in water up to 700 feet deep, individuals range from 12 to 20 inches. They are the only freshwater fish in the state that spawns in winter. Females lay up to a million eggs. The state record, caught in Black River Bay on February 14, 1991, by Terrance Colwell, weighs 16 pounds, 12 ounces.

Burbot, or freshwater cod—deep-water fish seldom seen by average anglers—spawn in relatively shallow water in winter and are often taken incidentally through the ice on Lake Champlain.

Freshwater Drum or Sheepshead (*Aplodinotus grunniens*)

GENERAL DESCRIPTION: Overall color is silvery with a blue to olive-brown back and a white belly.

DISTRIBUTION: Great Lakes, Mohawk, Hudson, and Susquehanna River drainages.

STUFF WORTH KNOWING: Sheepshead have small, round teeth for crushing snails and have a taste for zebra mussels. They use muscles around their swimming bladders to produce drumming sounds. Spawning takes place in the summer, from July through September. The state record, caught in Lake Ontario's Irondequoit Bay on June 14, 2014, by James VanArsdall, is 26 pounds, 9 ounces.

Rainbow Smelt (*Osmerus mordax*)

GENERAL DESCRIPTION: This long, silvery fish has an olive back and pink or blue iridescence along its sides. It has a large mouth for a small fish, with two large canine teeth on the roof of the mouth. They normally range from 6 to 9 inches but can reach 13 inches.

DISTRIBUTION: Throughout the Adirondacks, especially in large bodies like Lakes Champlain and George, and Great Sacandaga Lake.

STUFF WORTH KNOWING: Smelt are considered a delicacy wherever they are found. They ascend small streams in the spring to spawn and are often taken in large quantities with dip nets. There is no state record.

Carp (*Cyprinus carpio*)

GENERAL DESCRIPTION: A brown-colored, large-scaled fish with orange fins, it has two barbels on each side of its upper jaw. Some are leather-like with no scales or spotted with disproportionately large scales.

DISTRIBUTION: Native to Eurasia, the species was introduced into American waters around 1830 and found the habitat good. They thrive in warm waters, and can be found everywhere from the Great Lakes to abandoned canals, farm ponds, and the lower reaches of creeks and brooks.

STUFF WORTH KNOWING: Like many introduced species, carp suffer an image problem, but they're gaining in popularity. They spawn in late spring when water temperatures reach 62 degrees. The state record, caught in Tomhannock Reservoir on May 12, 1995, by Charles Primeau Sr., is 50 pounds, 6 ounces.

Fallfish (*Semotilus corporalis*)

GENERAL DESCRIPTION: Simply called a chub by many anglers, this long, slender big-eyed fish has a dark-olive to golden-brown back that fades into silver sides armored in large scales. Typically ranging from 4 to 12 inches, this native New Yorker is the largest minnow in the eastern United States.

DISTRIBUTION: Cold streams and lakes throughout the Adirondacks.

STUFF WORTH KNOWING: Willing to strike a dry fly or streamer as eagerly as a worm or egg sac, followed by a respectable fight, the fallfish breaks a lot of anglers' hearts when they discover it's not a trout. Fortunately, fly fishermen with a sense of humor are grateful for its violent strike and valiant fight, and release it unharmed to go feed a trout.

ADIRONDACK MOUNTAIN REGION

Spread over 6 million acres, nearly 20 percent of the state, the Adirondack Park is the largest preserve totally contained within the borders of a single state in the Lower 48. It's one of the earth's oldest mountain ranges; experts claim its peaks towered over 25,000 feet when the world was young. While its summits have been worn smooth by the ages, 43 peaks still reach over 4,000 feet. Geological wonders like veins of garnet flow through its tired old granite, and 100,000 acres of ancient forest crown its expansive new growth. Best of all, this fabulous marriage of public and private forests offers you roughly 2,800 lakes and ponds, 1,500 miles of rivers, and 30,000 miles of brooks and creeks on which to cast your dreams.

1. LAKE CHAMPLAIN

KEY SPECIES: Lake trout, landlocked Atlantic salmon, brown trout, walleyes, largemouth bass, smallmouth bass, muskellunge, northern pike, pickerel, whitefish, smelt, channel catfish, burbot, carp, and panfish.

DESCRIPTION: Bordered by New York, Vermont, and the Canadian providence of Quebec, this international waterway covers 452 square miles (289,280 acres), making it the sixth largest lake in the United States, prompting some to call it—you guessed it—the Sixth Great Lake. Averaging 64 feet deep, with a maximum depth of 403 feet, it has 587 miles of shoreline and 70 islands. Site of major battles during our wars with England, it has a floor littered with shipwrecks.

TIPS: Drift along weed edges atop breaklines and cast spinnerbaits for northerns and bass.

THE FISHING: The state supplements the natural fishery by stocking thousands of salmonids annually; figures and species vary greatly from year to year. Lake trout range from 3 to 12 pounds. From late fall through early spring, they are taken from shore by casting silver crankbaits and spoons, or fishing on bottom with smelt. Come summer, they move into deep water, where they respond to cut bait and spoons trolled slowly anywhere from 50 to 150 feet down. Landlocked Atlantic salmon are stocked most regularly. They range from 2 to 10 pounds and are popularly targeted in tributaries in spring and autumn with egg sacs and streamers, and worms after a rain. In summer, they suspend 5 to 40 feet over deep water and take silver-colored, shallow-diving crankbaits like Rapalas and Jr. ThunderSticks flatlined off planer boards. Lately, the state's been releasing a lot of brown trout. The habitat is good to them, and they typically run from 1 to 5 pounds. They'll hit the same crankbaits the salmon like, trolled near bottom, 5 to 15 feet deep fall through spring, 20 to 50 feet deep in summer.

One of the top 10 bass lakes in the country, Lake Champlain hosts numerous professional events each year. Bucketmouths go from 2 to 7 pounds and are primarily taken in and around weed beds on jig-n-pigs or spinnerbaits, and by slowly dragging Texas-rigged worms around old pilings and cribs. Bronzebacks range from 2 to 5 pounds and take jigs worked off rocky, sandy points from opening day through mid-July and again in the fall. The rest of the summer, they hit Carolina-rigged finesse worms worked along drop-offs and over boulder fields, as well as darters like Zara Spooks walked over 10 to 20 feet of water, especially around dusk and dawn. Let the lure sit on the surface for a minute or two before starting your retrieve.

Walleyes average 3 pounds, but 8-pounders—or even heavier—are available. Trolling and casting crankbaits works well at night. Daylight anglers find that drifting minnows and spinner-rigged worm harnesses on bottom can be productive, especially around the mouths of streams and along drop-offs. Northern pike run from 3 to 15 pounds and are targeted with minnowbaits and spinnerbaits worked along weed edges. The largest pike are caught through the ice on large minnows. Muskies in the 15-pound range are typical, but bruisers stretching the scale at over 25 pounds are taken each year. Most are caught incidentally by anglers targeting northerns. However, they have a small group of fans who target them by throwing large bucktail spinners or trolling spoons and jointed crankbaits. Chain pickerel normally range from 2 to 3 pounds, and take crankbaits, in-line spinners, and worms on spinner harnesses retrieved over weed beds.

Crappies up to 1.5 pounds, yellow perch from 8 to 12 inches, and rock bass up to 10 inches are commonly taken on small minnows, tube jigs, and lures. Bluegills and pumpkinseeds range from 5 to 9 inches and readily take worms, wet flies, and tiny poppers. Bullheads running from 8 to 15 inches congregate on muddy flats in spring, where they eagerly hit worms. White perch averaging 8 inches are so common that icers complain "the fish ain't hittin'" if it takes them longer than two hours to fill a 5-gallon bucket. Channel catfish up to 20 pounds are targeted in the lake's southern narrows with min-nows, cut bait, gobs of worms, and shrimp fished on bottom. Burbot range from 1 to 3 pounds and are mostly taken through the ice on minnows. It is legal to snatch them in Scomotion Creek (Dead Creek on most maps) from December 1 through March 31. Carp grow huge, up to 40 pounds. They like water ranging from 2 to 25 feet deep, and relish kernel corn, bread balls, and baked potato squares still-fished on bottom. Connoisseurs like professional guide Mike McGrath draw them in by chumming an area with a mash made of grains, puffed rice, puffed wheat, and fruit syrup—Pepto-Bismol will do.

Smelt used to be so numerous, and grew so big, ice-shanty villages ap-peared on the lake each winter. According to retired state fisheries biologist Rich Preall, "Alewife appeared in Lake Champlain circa 2004 and dramati-cally altered the smelt fishery. Yellow perch are now less abundant in the lake, too, but their average size has improved."

DIRECTIONS: I-87 parallels the lake.

ADDITIONAL INFORMATION: A New York or Vermont license entitles anglers to fish the main and south lake portions bordered by both states. A New York license is required to fish South Bay in Washington County, and a Canadian license is required in that country's territorial waters.

Lake Champlain offers year-round seasons for more game fish than any other body of water. Muskellunge, northern pike, pickerel, landlocked salmon, and trout can be taken anytime. Black bass season opens the second Saturday in June.

Other differences from statewide regulations include: The minimum length for brown, brook, and rainbow trout is 12 inches, and the daily limit is 3; the daily limit for landlocked salmon is 2; the minimum length for lake trout is 15 inches; for walleyes, 18 inches; for northerns, 20 inches; there is no minimum length for pickerel and the daily limit is 10; the minimum length for black bass is 10 inches.

Sauger, a member of the perch family that's extremely rare in New York and totally protected, closely resemble walleyes. Easily differentiated from walleyes by the spots on the front dorsal fin, they used to be relatively abun-dant in the Lake Champlain and St. Lawrence River watersheds. Only two have been reported caught by anglers since 1978, both from Lake Champlain. Former fisheries biologist Rich Preall says, "Last one seen by DEC or VT fisheries folks was in 2012. If you get one, release it immediately and report the specific location where it was caught (attach a photo if you got it) to fwfish@gw.dec.state.ny.us."

While sour grapes harp about the lake's lampreys, the US Fish and Wildlife Service is controlling their numbers. Currently all eyes are on a couple other invasive species. The alewife, an exotic minnow notorious for its reproductive capability, has a taste for walleye and perch fry, and has been known to wipe out walleye populations and greatly diminish perch numbers in some lakes. And tench (*Tinca tinca*), carp-like minnows native to Eurasia, have escaped from a Canadian fish farm and settled in the Great Chazy River and nearby bays. Averaging around 3 pounds, they taste like a carp and fight like one when hooked.

CONTACT: New York State Department of Environmental Conservation Region 5 and Plattsburgh–North Country Chamber of Commerce.

Lake Champlain on ice.

1A. Rouses Point Municipal Boat Launch and Fishing Pier

DESCRIPTION: This facility offers a paved double-lane ramp, parking for 40 rigs, and toilets. A fishing pier is just south of the launch.

THE FISHING: The pilings crossing the lake here are remnants of an old railroad trestle, and are one of the best largemouth hot spots on the lake. Work Texas-rigged worms around the supports.

DIRECTIONS: Take I-87 north out of Plattsburgh for about 18 miles to Champlain (exit 42), then head east on US 11 for about 4 miles to Rouses Point. The launch is on Montgomery Street.

1B. Great Chazy River State Boat Launch

DESCRIPTION: This launch has two double-wide paved ramps, bulkheads, toilets, loading docks, and parking for 66 rigs.

THE FISHING: The Great Chazy River is stocked regularly with muskies. A few always migrate to the mouth, find the pickings good, and settle in. Drift the area with large minnows while casting big crankbaits or in-line bucktail spinners. King Bay, directly north of the boat launch, is a hot spot for hawg bucketmouths all season long. On calm days, scout weed edges with topwater lures like Hula Poppers and buzzbaits. Then work the mid-layer with spinnerbaits or freelined night crawlers hooked so they form a circle. Finish off the day by throwing wacky-rigged stickworms, or dragging bucktail jigs tipped with Berkley Power Honey Worms and Texas-rigged worms on bottom.

DIRECTIONS: Head north out of Plattsburgh on US 9 for about 15 miles to NY 9B and turn east. A little less than 2 miles later, turn south on Lake Shore Road and travel about a mile.

1C. Point Au Roche State Boat Launch

DESCRIPTION: This facility offers a paved two-lane ramp, bulkheads, parking for 60 rigs, and toilets.

THE FISHING: Work spinnerbaits and crankbaits or drift minnows around this area's weed beds all summer long for scrappy smallmouth bass ranging from 1 to 3 pounds and northern pike up to 8 pounds.

DIRECTIONS: Head north out of Plattsburgh on US 9 for 6 miles, turn east on Point Au Roche Road, and travel for about 2 miles.

1D. Point Au Rouche State Park

DESCRIPTION: This park offers a concrete launch, parking for 20 rigs, and toilets.

THE FISHING: Work the drop-offs of the shoal directly in front of the launch with crayfish for smallmouth bass ranging from 1 to 3 pounds. The drop-off along the east side of Long Point is notorious for holding good numbers of northern pike ranging from 4 to 8 pounds, and walleyes up to 23 inches. The northerns will take spinnerbaits yo-yoed down the drop-off, and walleyes take minnowbaits and worms drifted on harnesses.

DIRECTIONS: Head north out of Plattsburgh on US 9 for about 6 miles, turn right on Point Au Roche Road, and travel a little over a mile to the park entrance.

1E. Cumberland Bay State Park

DESCRIPTION: This 319-acre fee area boasts 134 primitive campsites, 18 with electrical hookups, a bathhouse, a 2,700-foot sand beach, hot showers, picnic facilities, a dumping station, playgrounds, and ball fields. The campground is open from May through Columbus Day. Free day use permitted off-season.

THE FISHING: Cumberland Bay is a popular ice-fishing spot for yellow perch and sunfish.

DIRECTIONS: Head north out of Plattsburgh on US 9 for about a mile, turn east on NY 314, and travel for about a mile.

ADDITIONAL INFORMATION: This area is popular with windsurfers.

1F. Plattsburgh

DESCRIPTION: This site has a hard-surface ramp, plus parking for 12 cars and 31 rigs; 3 sites are handicapped accessible.

THE FISHING: The weed beds out front hold northerns and bass. This site's location ensures it gets a lot of boat traffic so it's best fished early and late in the day. A buzzbait ripped over the tops of vegetation on quiet mornings and evenings can be counted on to rile the pillars of the bass and pike communities to strike with shameless violence.

DIRECTIONS: Off Dock Street, downtown Plattsburgh.

1G. Peru Dock Boat Launch

DESCRIPTION: This site has a hard-surface ramp, parking for 50 rigs, pump-out, and toilets.

THE FISHING: Work the shoals around Valcour Island with soft or hard jerkbaits for smallmouth bass.

DIRECTIONS: Head south out of Plattsburgh on US 9 for about 6 miles.

1H. Ausable Point Public Campground

DESCRIPTION: This fee area is located on the mouth of the Ausable River. There is a cartop launch, parking for 10 cars, shore-fishing access, 115 campsites (43 with electrical hookups), hot showers, a 0.25-mile sand beach, a bathhouse, playgrounds, and a basketball court. Open from mid-May through mid-October. Free day use permitted off-season.

THE FISHING: The upper and lower mouths of the Ausable River attract fish whenever they are swollen with runoff. Schools of landlocked salmon and trout converge on the spot and take flatlined streamers and silver, shallow-diving crankbaits. Walleyes are drawn to the river to spawn and many hang out for a couple of weeks afterward, pigging out on anything from worms drifted on harnesses (spinner-rigged and plain) to crankbaits and jigs.

DIRECTIONS: Take US 9 south out of Plattsburgh for 12 miles.

ADDITIONAL INFORMATION: This area is popular with windsurfers.

1I. Port Douglas Public Boat Launch

DESCRIPTION: This site has a two-lane paved ramp, loading docks and parking for 20 rigs, and 10 additional slots for cars.

THE FISHING: Port Douglas is smack in the middle of a 10-mile stretch of shoreline with a steep drop-off. In spring and fall, salmonids cruise the area within reach of shore anglers fishing smelt off slip bobbers or casting silver spoons and minnowbaits.

DIRECTIONS: Take US 9 south out of Plattsburgh for about 13 miles to Keesville, turn east on CR 16, and travel for about 3 miles.

1J. Willsboro Bay Public Boat Launch

DESCRIPTION: This site offers a hard-surface launch ramp, parking for 100 rigs, toilets, and a pump-out station.

THE FISHING: Landlocked salmon and lake trout enter Willsboro Bay fall through spring. They can be taken by trolling silver spoons and crankbaits, around dawn and dusk, in 25 to 65 feet of water.

DIRECTIONS: From I-87 exit 33, head south on NY 22 for about 7 miles, then north on CR 27 for about 2 miles.

1K. Westport Public Boat Launch

DESCRIPTION: Hard-surface ramp and parking for 35 rigs.

THE FISHING: Northwest Bay's gently sloping floor takes almost 2 miles to reach a depth of 150 feet. This results in ideal lake trout temperatures being present in some part of the bay year-round. From mid-fall through late spring, locals often take them by trolling minnowbaits like ThunderSticks and Rapalas in 5 to 15 feet of water. Come winter, the bay is a popular ice-fishing spot for lake trout.

DIRECTIONS: On NY 22 in the village of Westport.

1L. Port Henry Public Boat Launch

DESCRIPTION: This site has a hard-surface ramp, loading docks, and parking for 45 rigs.

THE FISHING: Locals fish the northwestern part of Bulwagga Bay year-round with spinnerbaits and large minnows for northern pike ranging from 3 to 8 pounds. The ruins of an old railroad bridge at the mouth of the bay make this area one of the hottest bass spots on the lake. Largemouths up to 5 pounds and smallmouths from 1.5 to 3 pounds are commonly taken by dragging Texas- and Carolina-rigged worms around the submerged pilings and cribs. Ice fishing is also hot here.

ADDITIONAL INFORMATION: Champ, Lake Champlain's version of the Loch Ness monster, is sighted in Bulwagga Bay so often it's considered his home.

DIRECTIONS: On Dock Lane, off NY 22, on the north side of Port Henry.

1M. Crown Point Public Campground

DESCRIPTION: This fee area offers 66 sites, coin-operated hot showers, a trailer dumping station, a steel-grate launch ramp, parking for about 10 cars, and shore-fishing access from a pier. The campground is open from April through mid-October. A day-use fee is charged from Memorial Day through Labor Day. Free day use is permitted off-season.

THE FISHING: The pier's concrete pilings hold northern pike and largemouth bass. Cast Carolina-rigged worms for hawg largemouth bass; scented tubes, curly-tailed grubs, and Rat-L-Traps for mixed bags.

ADDITIONAL INFORMATION: This site is partly built on ground hotly contested in the colonial period by the British and French. The old battleground and ruins of its structures are open to the public.

DIRECTIONS: From I-87 exit 31, take NY 9N east for about 16 miles to Bridge Road, turn east, and travel for about 4 miles.

1N. Ticonderoga Ferry Public Boat Launch

DESCRIPTION: This site has a paved ramp, parking for 55 rigs, and a pump-out station.

THE FISHING: This part of the lake is narrow, and clarity is poor all the way to Whitehall. But bass, crappies, and large catfish thrive in the murky water. Ruins of an old pier just south of the launch are a local hot spot for taking large bucketmouths on Texas-rigged worms. Come winter, the spot holds northern pike up to 15 pounds, walleyes averaging 4 pounds, perch ranging from 6 to 12 inches, and black crappies up to a pound. They all hit minnows.

DIRECTIONS: From I-87 exit 28, head east on NY 74 for about 19 miles.

1O. South Bay Public Boat Launch

DESCRIPTION: This site has a paved ramp and parking for 50 rigs.

THE FISHING: This bay is great walleye habitat. The species likes minnows and worms drifted on bottom, and bladebaits yo-yoed and vertically jigged along drop-offs.

ADDITIONAL INFORMATION: The nearby 300-foot-long, handicapped-accessible public fishing pier offers benches, safety railings, a covered pavilion at its deep end, and access to shallow and deep water.

DIRECTIONS: Head north on US 4 out of Hudson Falls for about 20 miles to Whitehall, then go north on NY 22 for about 3 miles.

2. CHAMPLAIN CANAL

KEY SPECIES: Smallmouth bass, walleyes, northern pike, panfish, and catfish.

DESCRIPTION: Stretching for 60 miles, this canal averages 12 feet deep and connects Lake Champlain with the Hudson River.

TIPS: Use brightly colored spinners and plugs.

THE FISHING: Stretching from Whitehall to Waterford, this waterway is mostly a stopgap fishery with anglers waiting to go through locks. It is a great spot to practice bass fishing techniques on smallmouths in the 6- to 12-inch range. Northerns running from 20 to 26 inches are common, hang out on weed edges along the drops, and respond to soft swimbaits, and tube jigs tipped with minnows. Walleyes are plentiful in the channel and hit bucktail jigs tipped with pinched worms. Sunnies, bullheads, and yellow and white perch are abundant and love worms fished on bottom. Crappies up to 13 inches and jack perch up to 12 inches long are available. If you find a school, anchor quietly, fish minnows below bobbers on a couple of rigs, and cast small spinnerbaits like Beetle Spins, 2-inch grubs, and minnows. Catfish in the 12- to 20-inch range are numerous and take worms and commercial pastes fished on bottom.

DIRECTIONS: US 4 parallels the canal.

ADDITIONAL INFORMATION: A hard-surface ramp suitable for cartoppers is at the end of the 1st Street parking lot in Waterford (west bank), and another is on 1st Avenue, on the other side of the canal. Numerous other ramps are scattered along the canal's course and can be found by Googling "Boat Launches NY State Canals."

CONTACT: New York State Department of Environmental Conservation Region 5.

2A. Champlain Canal Lock 1 Launch

DESCRIPTION: Located above the canal's first lock, this site offers a paved launch, floating dock, and parking for five rigs. Overnight docking is permitted.

DIRECTIONS: Off NY 4 (at the NYS Canal Corporation sign), 2.5 miles north of Waterford.

3. LAKE GEORGE

KEY SPECIES: Lake trout, landlocked Atlantic salmon, smallmouth bass, largemouth bass, northern pike, chain pickerel, yellow perch, black crappies, and panfish.

DESCRIPTION: Set in forested mountains, freckled with islands, and boasting water so clean you can drink it right out of the lake, this 28,200-acre body of water averages 50 feet deep and drops to a maximum depth of 200 feet. Known as the Queen of American Lakes, it is divided into north and south basins, separated by an island-choked narrows.

TIPS: In deep summer, jig for smallmouths on bottom in about 50 feet of water.

THE FISHING: This lake has been famed for lake trout ever since the first white man dropped a line into the place. DDT and acid rain all but wiped them out in the 1960s. Environmental protection laws and massive stocking by the state brought them back from the brink. Indeed, the lakers took so well to the restored habitat, the state stopped stocking them in the 1980s. Currently, wild lakers in the 5- to 8-pound range are run-of-the-mill. Natives target them in summer by dragging locally caught ciscos in deep water on Seth Green and Christmas tree rigs, and through the ice on minnows suspended 15 to 20 feet deep below tip-ups. Landlocked Atlantic salmon used to be the lake's most popularly sought coldwater species, but the fishery collapsed, probably due to predation by lake trout. While the state continues to stock Atlantics, retired state aquatic biologist Rich Preall suggests the effort is in vain: "5-pound lakers love snacking on 7-inch salmon . . . Few guys specialize for them now." Still, a few "oops" landlocks are taken each spring and fall on spoons and crankbaits aimed at bass and northerns. Some guys— like Rick Austin, a local guide—fish for them in winter by suspending minnows 6 feet below the ice off tip-ups. Bronzebacks typically range from 1.5 to 3 pounds, but a lot of fish over 4 pounds are available. The squeaky-clean water sends them much deeper than in average lakes, forcing anglers to jig for them vertically with tubes, curly-tailed grubs, bucktail jigs, and bladebaits. Northern pike running from 22 to 30 inches and largemouth bass averaging 2.5 pounds are plentiful in the weedy bays. Both strike floating lures like Zara Spooks when the lake is still; minnowbaits, salted tubes, and live minnows the rest of the time. Chain pickerel up to 30 inches are appearing with increasing regularity. Known for their killer strikes and speed, they're especially fond of nailing minnowbaits like Bass Pro Shops XPS Extreme Minnows twitched on the surface over weeds, and buzzbaits and shallow-diving fat-bodied crankbaits worked along weed lines. Keeper crappies are plentiful and strike minnows and insect larvae through the ice; 2-inch bucktail jigs fished plain or tipped with a minnow during the spring run; and small lures like Beetle Spins and 2-inch tubes from late spring through mid-autumn. Yellow perch averaging 9 inches are popularly sought by ice fishermen jigging insect larvae and minnows. Pumpkinseeds up to 8 inches, rock bass weighing over a pound, and bullheads better than 14 inches are abundant and take worms from early spring through late fall.

The use or possession of smelt, even for human consumption, is prohibited. The minimum length for lakers is 23 inches, and 18 inches for salmon; and the daily limit is two apiece. Trout and salmon can be taken year-round.

DIRECTIONS: NY 9N runs along the entire west bank.

ADDITIONAL INFORMATION: Watercraft must bear a stamp certifying they have been inspected and found free of invasive species before they can launch at any of the local ramps. Free inspection stations are available at local marinas. In addition, all craft propelled by motors 10 horsepower or greater, and human-powered boats 18 feet or longer, must be registered with the

Lake George Park Commission before launching on the lake. For more information, visit www.lgpc.state.ny.us. A free "Fishing and Boating Map" containing all the rules and features is available from the county's tourism office.

CONTACT: New York State Department of Environmental Conservation Region 5 and Warren County Tourism.

Lake George laker on ice.

3A. Million Dollar Beach Boat Launch

DESCRIPTION: Open year-round, this state-operated fee area offers a double-wide hard-surface ramp and parking for 200 rigs; you'll have to go through an underpass with a 7-foot clearance.

THE FISHING: "Ice fishing for yellow perch can be quite good just off the launch area early in the season," advises Preall.

DIRECTIONS: On Beach Road, in the village of Lake George.

3B. Lake George Campgrounds

DESCRIPTION: This state-run fee operation offers 387 beach campsites on 44 islands. These sites are only accessible by boat and are totally primitive with no treated water. Open May 15 through Columbus Day.

DIRECTIONS: The islands are spread out all over the lake and are divided into three groups: the Glen Island Group, set in the narrows east of Bolton Landing; the Long Island Group on the south end; and the Narrow Island Group on the north end.

3C. Hearthstone Point Public Campground

DESCRIPTION: This state-operated fee area offers 251 tent and trailer sites (13 are handicapped accessible), hot showers, swimming, and shore-fishing access. The campground is open mid-May through Labor Day. Free day use allowed off-season.

DIRECTIONS: On NY 9N, 2 miles north of Lake George village.

3D. Norwahl Marina

DESCRIPTION: Offering the easiest access to the lake's islands, this fee area has a two-lane hard-surface ramp and parking for 100 rigs.

DIRECTIONS: Sagamore Road, on the north side of Bolton Landing.

ADDITIONAL INFORMATION: Three different fees are charged; anglers only pay to launch and can park for free.

3E. Rogers Rock State Campground

DESCRIPTION: Located on the west bank, this state-operated fee area offers 332 campsites, a paved boat launch, shore-fishing access, hot showers, picnic areas, a swimming beach, and a trailer dumping station. Open May through Columbus Day. Free day use off-season.

DIRECTIONS: On NY 9N, about 29 miles north of Lake George village.

3F. Mossy Point Boat Launch

DESCRIPTION: This site has a hard-surface ramp, parking for 100 rigs, and a pump-out station.

DIRECTIONS: Head south out of Ticonderoga on CR 3 for about 2 miles.

3G. Lake George Battleground Public Campground

DESCRIPTION: This fee area offers 68 tent and trailer sites, hot showers, and a trailer dumping station. Open mid-May through September.

DIRECTIONS: On US 9N, 0.25 mile south of Lake George village.

4. BOQUET RIVER

KEY SPECIES: Landlocked Atlantic salmon, brown trout, and brook trout.

DESCRIPTION: Tumbling down from the east slopes of the Adirondacks, this river flows for about 38 miles and feeds Lake Champlain east of Willsboro.

TIPS: Use worms in the spring.

THE FISHING: This stream is famed for Atlantic salmon. The state stocks thousands regularly (45,000 averaging 6.5 inches in 2013). They invariably migrate to Lake Champlain but always return. The first run occurs in spring.

Snowmelt swells the river with relatively warm runoff, drawing massive quantities of the lake's emerald shiners to spawn. Atlantics averaging 3 pounds charge the stream hot on their tails, and are generally targeted by anglers flatlining smelt-imitating minnowbaits. Come fall, salmon numbers are smaller but the fish are bigger, averaging 6 pounds. Filled with spawn, they're not into big meals, and respond to small fare like streamers, nymphs, even dry flies. Runoff after a summer rain sometimes spurs minor runs, and the salmon will hit worms. State fisheries biologist Rob Fiorentino says the DEC mans the weir at the dam during the spawning run; salmon that make it into the trap are released upstream, allowing them to reach as far as the headwaters on the north fork, and Wadhams on the south fork.

The state also stocks a lot of browns (10,000 averaging 8.5 inches and 400 12- to 15-inchers in 2014). Released in both branches, throughout the length of the river, they join their naturally spawned and holdover kin, offering anglers opportunities for fish ranging from 8 to 20 inches. They respond well to worms, nymphs, and Woolly Buggers. Finally, thousands of brook trout (5,300 averaging 8.5 inches in 2014) are stocked annually in the upper reaches. They end up ranging from 6 to 15 inches and take worms, minnows, nymphs, and dry flies.

The main river from its mouth to Wadhams Falls, and the North Branch stretching from its mouth to the first barrier impassable by fish, have a mess of special regulations ranging from times you can fish and terminal tackle restrictions to a no-fishing zone, all of which are listed in the special Lake Champlain Regulations section of the New York State Department of Environmental Conservation *Fishing Regulations Guide.*

DIRECTIONS: Head south out of Plattsburgh on NY 22 for about 28 miles to Willsboro. CR 68 parallels about 4 miles of the north branch, and the main stem for a couple of miles upstream of the hamlet. NY 22 parallels the river between the hamlets of Wadhams and Boquet, and US 9 parallels it from Elizabethtown upstream for about 10 miles.

ADDITIONAL INFORMATION: The town plans to remove the dam and fish ladder in Willsboro by 2018. Parking and fishing access are available in Willsboro on School and Mill Streets, which parallel the river downstream of the Main Street (NY 22) bridge. A hard-surface ramp is at the end of School Street. The NYSDEC owns several miles of public fishing rights, and its website offers a map showing the locations.

CONTACT: New York State Department of Environmental Conservation Region 5.

4A. Scriver Lane Public Access

DESCRIPTION: Parking for five cars and access for about 2 miles downstream.

DIRECTIONS: Head south out of New Russia on US 9 for about 3 miles and turn east on Scriver Lane.

4B. Gilligan Lane Public Access

DESCRIPTION: This site offers parking for about five cars.

DIRECTIONS: From **site 4A**, head north on US 9 for about 2 miles and turn right on Gilligan Lane.

5. LINCOLN POND

KEY SPECIES: Norlunge, northern pike, largemouth bass, smallmouth bass, black crappies, and panfish.

DESCRIPTION: Mostly shallow and weedy, this 572-acre pond is 3.25 miles long, up to 0.5 mile wide, averages 12 feet deep, and has a maximum depth of 23 feet.

TIPS: In the spring, work the channel on the east side of the island with bucktail spinners.

THE FISHING: Rich Preall, a retired fisheries biologist formerly assigned to the beat, says a "2012 survey verified that tiger muskie were not surviving" so the DEC discontinued stocking them. Still, norlunge in the 30- to 40-inch range should be available until around 2022. They like in-line bucktail spinners and large minnows. Northern pike aren't too plentiful, but they grow long and fat—as big as the muskies—on the lake's cornucopia of aquatic critters. They like large shiners, jig-rigged stickworms bounced along drops, and Rat-L-Traps. The biggest tigers and northerns are caught through the ice. Largemouth bass ranging from 1.5 to a solid 6 pounds thrive in the lake's copious vegetation. They respond to jig-rigged crayfish dragged along weed edges, wacky-rigged stickworms dropped at the edges of timber and stumps, and poppers and buzzbaits worked around structure, especially windfalls reaching out from shore. Smallmouth bass from 12 to 15 inches are abundant on rock fields in the deeper water and respond to noisy crankbaits, tube jigs, and bucktail jigs fished plain or tipped with minnows or crayfish. Yellow perch running 6 to 12 inches and crappies up to 13 inches hit minnows and small tubes, and bullheads up to 14 inches strike worms on bottom.

DIRECTIONS: From I-87 exit 31, head west on NY 9N for about 4 miles to Elizabethtown, then south on CR 7 for about 6 miles.

ADDITIONAL INFORMATION: Lincoln Pond Public Campground, a fee area that is handicapped accessible, offers 35 campsites, showers, a cartop boat launch, and canoe and rowboat rentals. It's open May through Labor Day. Free day use permitted off-season.

CONTACT: New York State Department of Environmental Conservation Region 5.

6. TAYLOR POND

KEY SPECIES: Lake trout, landlocked Atlantic salmon, and panfish.

DESCRIPTION: Four miles long, completely surrounded by the Taylor Pond Wild Forest, this 856-acre pond averages 44 feet deep and has a maximum depth of 95 feet. It is favored by anglers and campers seeking a wilderness-like setting close to the road.

TIPS: Fish off the inlet on the west end during the spring smelt run.

THE FISHING: A survey conducted in 2013 found good numbers of lake trout and Atlantic salmon. The state periodically stocks 7-inch lakers (1,230 in 2013), but a lot of the fish reported in angler surveys are wild. Smelt are abundant and lakers easily reach the 2-pound average the lake is known for, with many growing to 30 inches and better. In spring—and to a lesser degree in autumn—they respond to spoons worked around the mouths of tributaries, especially on the west side. In summer, they're deeper and take spoons trolled off downriggers or Seth Green rigs. Yearling landlocked Atlantic salmon are also stocked occasionally (600 in 2013). In addition, the Adirondack state hatchery releases 50 to 75 surplus brood stock regularly. They grow big and fat on the smelt, too, and 10-pounders are caught every year. They respond to flatlined minnowbaits and tandem streamers. Sunfish up to 7 inches, yellow perch between 6 and 10 inches, and brown bullheads averaging about a pound are abundant in the relatively shallow northeastern arm and south basin. They like worms still-fished on bottom.

DIRECTIONS: From I-87 exit 34 (Keesville), take NY 9N west for about 9 miles to just before Ausable Forks, turn northwest on Silver Lake Road, and travel 8 miles.

ADDITIONAL INFORMATION: Taylor Pond Public Campground, a primitive operation without flush toilets, only outhouses, offers 25 campsites you can drive to, and 5 "interior sites" you can only reach by boat—3 have lean-tos. It also offers potable water, a hard-surface ramp with parking for 10 rigs, and boat and canoe rentals. A day-use fee is charged to noncampers when the campground is open, mid-May through Labor Day. Free day use off-season. This area is popular with hikers because it has several well-defined trails to the scenic summits (there are two) of Catamount Mountain—allegedly so named because the state's last mountain lion was sighted here.

CONTACT: New York State Department of Environmental Conservation Region 5.

7. CHAZY LAKE

KEY SPECIES: Lake trout, rainbow trout, northern pike, smallmouth bass, and panfish.

DESCRIPTION: Perched high in the northeastern corner of the Adirondacks in the shadow of Lyon, Johnson, and Ellenburg Mountains, this 1,606-acre lake averages 33 feet deep, drops to a maximum depth of 72 feet, and has water so squeaky-clean you can drink it straight.

TIPS: Flatline ⅛- to ¼-ounce spoons, especially off the mouths of tributaries along the west bank in spring and fall for rainbow trout.

THE FISHING: In the past, this lake was famed for wild lake trout and landlocked Atlantic salmon. Both fisheries suffered terribly when local authorities decided lowering water levels each autumn was a good way to control weed growth. The salmon had a habit of following the water out of the place, and the DEC discontinued stocking them in 2011. Currently, the state helps maintain a lake trout presence by stocking roughly 2,500 yearlings annually. Ranging from 2 to 6 pounds, the lakers respond to minnowbaits and spoons trolled below the thermocline (generally deeper than 30 feet) with divers and downriggers. Somewhere in the neighborhood of 7,000 rainbow trout averaging 9 inches are stocked just about every year. They end up ranging from 10 to 20 inches and take worms fished on bottom, near shore, in spring and fall, and spoons flatlined over 20 to 40 feet of water in summer. Savvy locals always pack a fly rod in case they run into a summer hatch. Smallmouth bass ranging from too small to 20 inches rule rocky shorelines and drop-offs, where they hit crayfish, minnows, and rattling plugs. "Chazy Lake produces the occasional trophy northern pike, but the species has eluded DEC netting efforts," says Rich Preall, a retired state fisheries biologist. Pikeasauruses up to 15 pounds are mostly taken incidentally on spinnerbaits and minnows targeting smallmouths during warm weather, and through the ice on minnows and jigging spoons meant for lakers. Yellow perch range from 6 to 12 inches and respond well to 2-inch curly-tailed grubs, small minnows, and worms. Pumpkinseeds averaging 6 inches eagerly take worms, wet flies, and small surface poppers. Both panfish are popularly targeted by ice fishermen using teardrop jigs baited with live grubs.

Trout and salmon season is year-round, and they can be taken through the ice with minnows on tip-ups or by jigging spoons tipped with minnows.

DIRECTIONS: Head west on NY 374 out of Dannemora for about 5 miles.

ADDITIONAL INFORMATION: A paved launch with parking for 20 rigs and eight cars is located on NY 374, at the north end of the lake; and a new cartop launch on the east side, at the end of Wilfred King Road, is on the state's drawing board. Primitive camping is allowed in the Chazy Highlands Wild Forest on the north side NY 374, at the northern tip of the lake, and in the Dannemora State Forest on the southeastern corner of the lake, at the end of Wilfred King Road.

CONTACT: New York State Department of Environmental Conservation Region 5.

8. GREAT CHAZY RIVER

KEY SPECIES: Brown trout, brook trout, walleyes, muskellunge, northern pike, pickerel, black bass, bowfin, and black crappies.

DESCRIPTION: Spawned by Chazy Lake, this stream starts out about the size of an average trout creek and snakes northeast to feed Lake Champlain. On the way, it flows through Miner Lake and grows to river size, swallowing several tributaries including the North Branch.

TIPS: Fish large streamers downstream of Mooers Forks.

THE FISHING: This river is a two-story fishery. Its upper stretch contains prime trout water. Since access isn't great, it doesn't get stocked regularly by the state. A whole lot of natural hanky-panky goes on, however, and it offers good numbers of wild browns averaging 10 inches and brookies ranging from 6 to 10 inches. They'll take worms, nymphs, streamers, and dry flies.

Downstream of Mooers the river becomes warmwater habitat, home to an exciting mix of species. While the fishing is decent up to Champlain—a stretch locals call the Oxbow—it gets really good from Champlain all the way to the mouth. The state stocks hundreds of purebred muskies annually. Typically, they end up ranging from 5 to 15 pounds and provide explosive action for anglers fishing these slow, weedy waters with large minnows, bucktail spinners, minnowbaits, and noisy surface offerings like Jitterbugs. Good numbers of black bass thrive in the river year-round. Resident bucketmouths ranging from 2 to 6 pounds are joined in late spring by waves of lake-run bronzebacks averaging 2.5 pounds. Together, they provide the kind of early-season action fishing dreams are made of. Although most of the smallies beat fins back to the lake after spawning, many stick around, joining the bucketmouths to create one of summer's best bass fishing destinations in the North Country. They strike all the usual suspects, from spinnerbaits and hard plugs to jerkbaits, rubber worms, bucktail jigs, tubes, minnows, and crayfish. While few in number, large northern pike and pickerel are present and, along with monster bowfin, have a habit of surprising—and often upsetting—anglers casting jigs and plugs for relatively harmless bass. In early spring, Lake Champlain's walleyes run the river up to Perrys Mills. After spawning, many in the 2- to 6-pound range stick around in the gentle currents for a couple of weeks—some into late June—to fatten up after their ordeal. They'll take crankbaits like LiveTarget Smelt trolled or cast onto shelves and along breaks, dusk to dawn; and in daylight respond to worms on spinner harnesses trolled along the transitions where drop-offs meet the channel floor. Crappies (local and lake-run) range from 9 to 15 inches and like hanging out around docks, especially in marinas, from ice-out through mid-May. They respond to plain minnows and small tubes tipped with Berkley Honey Worms and fished below tiny bobbers; and to 2-inch scented curly-tailed grubs on spinner forms worked slowly through the slips, tight to dock uprights.

Fishing is prohibited from March 16 through the first Saturday in May from the NY 9B bridge in Coopersville upstream to the Perry Mills dam to protect spawning walleyes.

DIRECTIONS: Take I-87 north out of Plattsburgh for about 19 miles to exit 42 in Champlain and pick up US 11 west, which parallels a long stretch of the river.

CONTACT: New York State Department of Environmental Conservation Region 5.

8A. Great Chazy River State Boat Launch

DESCRIPTION: This launch offers paved ramps, loading docks, parking for 50 rigs, and toilets.

DIRECTIONS: Head north out of Plattsburgh on US 9 for about 15 miles to NY 9B and turn east. A little less than 2 miles later, turn south on Lake Shore Road and travel about a mile.

ADDITIONAL INFORMATION: The most convenient way to fish the Great Chazy River's highly productive lower reaches is by launching a boat here and heading upstream.

9. NORTH BRANCH GREAT CHAZY RIVER

KEY SPECIES: Brown, brook, and rainbow trout.

DESCRIPTION: Springing out of the northeastern corner of the Adirondack Mountains, this stream flows east for about 15 miles and feeds the Great Chazy River in Mooers Forks.

TIPS: Work nymphs at a dead-drift through rifts.

THE FISHING: Wild brook trout running from 3 to 16 inches eke out an existence upstream of Ellenburg Depot. Downstream, closer to the road, the state annually stocks about 3,300 brown trout averaging 8.5 inches, 475 two-year-olds, and 2,010 rainbows averaging 8.5 inches. Habitat is good, fishing pressure moderate, and fish over 12 inches are common. The best bait is a juicy, fat worm after a rain. Fly fishermen do well on sunny summer days by matching the hatch, dead-drifting all-purpose nymphs like March Browns and Hare's Ears, or swinging Woolly Buggers through current.

DIRECTIONS: US 11 parallels the stream from the hamlet of Ellenburg to Mooers Forks, and informal shoulder access is plentiful; in addition, crossroads coming into US 11 from the north offer access at bridges.

CONTACT: New York State Department of Environmental Conservation Region 5.

9A. Public Access

DESCRIPTION: Parking for five cars and public fishing rights on both sides of the stream for about 1.5 miles upstream and about 0.5 mile downstream.

DIRECTIONS: Head west on NY 190 (Star Road) out of Ellenburg for about 1.5 miles to its intersection with Cashamen Road.

10. LOWER CHATEAUGAY LAKE

KEY SPECIES: Northern pike, smallmouth bass, and panfish.

DESCRIPTION: This 545-acre lake averages 12 feet deep and has a maximum depth of 26 feet. The shoreline is heavily developed with private dwellings.

TIPS: Fish along the edges of the weed beds in the north and south basins for monster northern pike.

THE FISHING: Northern pike were illegally introduced into the lake late in the last century, and their population is flourishing. Taking to the place like northerns always do when they're first introduced into waters loaded with trout, pike easily grew to 15 pounds in the early days. DEC stopped stocking trout in 2010. Their free lunch gone, the northerns were brought down to size, typically running from 22 to 28 inches. Casting spinnerbaits, lipless crankbaits like Rat-L-Traps, and shallow-running minnowbaits like Bass Pro Shops XPS Minnows along docks, sunken timber, and any other structure you can find will generally provoke a pike's killer instincts. Smallmouth bass ranging from 1 to 3 pounds thrive along the rocky shoreline. They have a taste for crayfish, salted tubes, and Carolina-rigged 4-inch worms fished on rock beds in 5 to 15 feet of water. Yellow perch ranging from 6 to 10 inches, sunfish the size of saucers, and bullheads up to 14 inches are popular with folks bottom-fishing with worms in summer. The sunnies and perch are also commonly taken by jigging ice dots tipped with grubs through the ice.

Recently, largemouth bass have gotten into the system, particularly in the narrows, a 3-something-mile-long navigable channel connecting Lower and Upper Chateaugay Lakes.

DIRECTIONS: Take US 11 north out of Malone for 12 miles to the village of Chateaugay, turn right (south) on NY 374, and travel for 7.8 miles.

ADDITIONAL INFORMATION: A public boat launch is off NY 374, about 2.5 miles south of the lake. Located on the narrows, it offers a double-wide, paved ramp, parking for about 60 rigs, and toilets. There is no public campground on the lake, but a few private ones are in the area.

CONTACT: New York State Department of Environmental Conservation Region 5 and Plattsburgh–North Country Chamber of Commerce.

11. UPPER CHATEAUGAY LAKE

KEY SPECIES: Northern pike, lake trout, smallmouth bass, yellow perch, and pumpkinseeds.

DESCRIPTION: Roughly four times larger than the lower lake (**site 10**), this wide, windswept, 2,594-acre body of water averages 33 feet deep and has a maximum depth of 72 feet. A small island punctuates its north side; a massive weed bed and wetland skirt its south end. Its east bank is tastefully developed with private residences.

TIPS: Ice fish with minnows.

THE FISHING: Pike were introduced illegally a few years back and took to their new habitat like fire to kindling. The DEC's long-standing landlocked Atlantic salmon and rainbow trout stocking programs were discontinued in 2010 to deny the toothy predators a free lunch. Even without government assistance, though, the lake is good to northerns and big pike are its greatest draw. They respond eagerly and violently to large minnows, their imitations, and just about any other scaly, feathery, fleshy critter that's bite-sized and swims. Lake trout are holding their own, primarily because they usually hang out in depths northerns never stoop to. The laker fishery is totally dependent on stocking, and fisheries biologist Rob Fiorentino says the state's target is to plant 5,000 annually. A good number reach the 21-inch legal size limit. In spring and late fall they cruise near shore and can be taken on crankbaits, spoons, and streamers. Come summer, they go deep and are mostly targeted with silver spoons jigged on bottom. In winter, they'll take live minnows suspended just off bottom and Swedish Pimples tipped with minnows and jigged on the floor. Smallmouth bass range from 12 to 19 inches and like the open lake; bucketmouths grow a few inches bigger and rule in the channel between the lakes. Both bass respond to crayfish fished on bottom, freelined minnows, and surface baits. Yellow perch in the 6- to 12-inch range are typical, enthusiastically hitting small jigs. Pumpkinseeds ranging from 4 to 7 inches hit worms, poppers, and wet flies.

DIRECTIONS: Take US 11 north out of Malone for 12 miles to the village of Chateaugay, turn right (south) on NY 374, and travel for about 11 miles.

ADDITIONAL INFORMATION: A public boat launch is off NY 374, about 0.5 mile north of the lake. Located on the narrows, a 3-something-mile-long navigable channel connecting Lower and Upper Chateaugay Lakes, it offers a double-wide paved ramp, parking for about 60 rigs, and toilets.

CONTACT: New York State Department of Environmental Conservation Region 5.

12. CHATEAUGAY RIVER

KEY SPECIES: Brown, rainbow, and brook trout.

DESCRIPTION: This river drains Lower Chateaugay Lake and runs north for about 13 miles to Canada, cutting a fabulous chasm along the way.

TIPS: Work in-line spinners through pockets.

THE FISHING: Recent DEC surveys confirm this international stream continues to host an impressive population of wild trout. In addition, it gets annual state aid to the tune of roughly 6,700 brookies, 1,700 rainbows, and 1,300 brown trout averaging 8.5 inches; and 400 two-year-old browns. Survival is good in the favorable habitat, and many grow to 20 inches—including the brookies, the Windfall strain known for its fighting spirit and propensity for reaching trophy proportions. Each species is good at using its spots and colors to blend in with bottom in the shallow pockets punctuating the ripples. They take streamers swung through the current, nymphs dead-drifted along undercut banks, and worms cast just about anywhere there's water after a rain. Massive quantities of big trout combined with fabulous scenery make this one of the North Country's most talked-about fly-fishing streams. The fishing is best from High Falls to the Canadian border.

DIRECTIONS: NY 374 parallels the stream.

CONTACT: New York State Department of Environmental Conservation Region 5 and Plattsburgh–North Country Chamber of Commerce.

12A. US 11 Bridge Public Fishing Rights

DESCRIPTION: This mile-long stretch of public fishing rights runs through a gorge, from the US 11 bridge upstream to the high falls. You'll have to park at the shoulder and climb down a steep slope to get to the river.

DIRECTIONS: On the west side of the hamlet of Chateaugay.

12B. CR 35 Bridge Public Access

DESCRIPTION: This bridge crosses the Marble River a few hundred feet upstream of its mouth. The state owns public fishing rights to its last mile; anglers walk downstream to access a mile-something stretch of public fishing on the Chateaugay River. Park at the shoulder.

THE FISHING: The mile of water stretching upstream from the mouth of the Marble River is one of the Chateaugay River's most easily accessible and productive sections.

DIRECTIONS: Take US 11 north out of Malone for about 14 miles, turn north on CR 35 (Chasm Road), and travel for about 2 miles.

ADDITIONAL INFORMATION: The Marble River is a very productive wild trout fishery. Its brook trout range from 6 to 10 inches, rainbow trout run from 8 to 12 inches, and brown trout reach up to 16 inches.

12C. Cooks Mill Public Access

DESCRIPTION: Access at the Sam Cook Road Bridge and shoulder parking.

DIRECTIONS: From **site 12B**, head north on Chasm Road for a few hundred feet to the next intersection, continue straight on Simms Road for a few hundred feet, and turn left on Sam Cook Road.

ADDITIONAL INFORMATION: The state owns public fishing rights on the right bank (looking downstream) to just about the Canadian border. Retired fisheries biologist Rich Preall suggests, "Try the nice pool about 0.25 mile downstream. And if you go any further be sure to wave to the border patrol."

13. SALMON RIVER (FRANKLIN COUNTY)

KEY SPECIES: Brown and rainbow trout.

DESCRIPTION: Tracing its source to the northeastern corner of the Adirondack Mountains, this tributary of the St. Lawrence River flows northeast, crossing into Canada at Fort Covington. Its most popular and productive stretch is downstream of Chasm Falls.

TIPS: Large attractor patterns are productive in summer.

THE FISHING: One of the most famous trout hot spots in the North Country, this large stream is famed for massive quantities of big fish. Some anglers—speaking tongue-in-cheek, of course—complain trout larger than 10 inches are easier to come by than smaller ones. While there are some brook trout in its upper reaches, a combination of warmwater habitat and difficult access discourages most anglers from fishing above Mountain View Lake. The other end is a different story: Groundwater starts cooling it as soon as it pours out of the impoundment, and keeps it at ideal trout temperature for the rest of its length. Pouring out of the lake, it rushes downstream at a good clip for a few miles then tumbles down the mountain, dropping about 900 feet in a spectacular cascade loaded with scenic plunge pools and challenging pocket water. Leveling off a little ways downstream of Chasm Falls, the river runs wide and fairly tame over bedrock, punctuated by a few sets of rapids, all the way to Canada. The state stocks the place annually with up to 20,000 browns and 9,400 rainbows averaging 8.5 inches; and 1,300 two-year-old browns averaging a little over a foot long. Survival is good, and holdovers are plentiful. They take nymphs, caddis and mayfly patterns, attractors like Royal Coachmen and Woolly Worms, streamers, you name it.

DIRECTIONS: CR 25 parallels the river from Chasm Falls to Malone, and NY 37 runs alongside it from Malone to Fort Covington.

ADDITIONAL INFORMATION: The state owns several miles of public fishing rights, about 80 percent of it stretching from Whippleville to Westville Center. A year-round catch-and-release section runs for 2.2 miles, from the Cargin Road bridge to the Flat Rock Road bridge. The stream's mayfly hatches are so legendary, a Henderson Hatch Catch and Release Fly Fishing Tournament is held annually, in late spring.

CONTACT: New York State Department of Environmental Conservation Region 5 and Franklin County Tourism.

13A. Cady Road Public Access

DESCRIPTION: Parking and 0.25 mile of public access on the west side of the stream.

DIRECTIONS: Head north out of Malone on Park Street (it turns into Lower Park Road) for a little over a mile, turn west on Cady Road (some maps list it as Brand Road), and travel a few hundred feet.

13B. Cargin Road Bridge Public Access

DESCRIPTION: Parking and public access for over a mile upstream and 0.5 mile downstream of the bridge.

DIRECTIONS: From **site 13A** above, continue west on Cady Road for several hundred yards, turn right on Bare Hill Road, continue for 0.8 mile, turn right on Cargin Road, and travel a few hundred feet to the bridge.

13C. Lower Flat Rock Road Public Access

DESCRIPTION: Parking areas on both ends of the road where it comes to the stream. The eastern lot offers public access upstream for about a mile on both sides of the stream; the western lot offers access to several miles downstream, on both sides, all the way to Westville Center.

DIRECTIONS: From **site 13B**, head west on Cargin Road for a few hundred yards, turn right on Flat Rock Road, travel about a mile, and turn left on Lower Flat Rock Road. The eastern site will be just beyond the turn; the west site is a few hundred yards farther down the road.

ADDITIONAL INFORMATION: Jack Zasada spent many years fishing this stretch and calls it the meadows. "A weighted Woolly Bugger cast into the willows and windfalls lining the bank is hard to beat," says the Bridgeport resident. This area was local fly-fishing legend Peck Robert's favorite water.

13D. Fireman's Memorial Drive Parking and Access

DESCRIPTION: This site is smack in the middle of the long stretch of public access running from Flat Rock Road to just south of Westville Center.

DIRECTIONS: Head west on Lower Flat Rock Road from **site 13C** for a couple thousand yards, turn right on NY 37, travel about 1.5 miles, and turn right.

14. SCHROON RIVER

KEY SPECIES: Landlocked Atlantic salmon, brook trout, brown trout, rainbow trout, and smallmouth bass.

DESCRIPTION: Formed by the confluence of Crowfoot and New Pond Brooks south of the hamlet of Underwood, this stream starts out averaging 15 feet wide and 10 inches deep. Setting a gentle, southerly, 68-mile course through the eastern Adirondacks, it grows to over 100 feet wide and 4 feet deep by the time it feeds the Hudson River west of Warrensburg.

TIPS: In spring and fall, work Gray Ghosts around the mouth at Schroon Lake.

THE FISHING: Historically, this river has been a spawning ground for landlocked Atlantic salmon. Annually, the state stocks 20,000 fry to supplement natural reproduction. They migrate to Schroon Lake, returning in autumn and spring. According to state aquatic biologist Rich Preall, "Landlocked salmon make late-summer and early-fall runs up to the Palmer Pond dam in the town of North Hudson." Overall, the salmon range from 1 to 4 pounds and hit salmon flies, streamers, and worms. Brook trout occur naturally in the tributaries, migrating to the river when they outgrow their natal haunts. In addition, the state stocks some periodically (1,500 8-inchers in 2013). While they can pop up around the mouth of just about any tributary, they're mostly found in the river's upper reaches above Schroon Lake. Ranging from 6 to 14 inches, these gluttonous members of the trout family will strike just about any worm, minnow, fly, or in-line spinner that's presented naturally. The state also stocks roughly 1,500 browns averaging 8.5 inches annually. They grow to average 12 inches and hit worms, streamers, and spoons. Yearling rainbows (7,000 in 2013, 3,940 in 2014) are stocked into the river below Schroon Lake each year. They end up averaging 10 inches and are mostly taken on worms, salted minnows, nymphs, and wet flies. Smallmouth bass begin appearing below Schroon Lake. While most are small, seldom exceeding 14 inches, the violence with which they strike streamers is worth writing home to Mom about.

Trout, lake trout, and landlocked salmon can be taken year-round from Schroon Lake upstream to Alder Meadow Road; the minimum length for lakers is 18 inches and the daily limit is two. Downstream of Schroon Lake to Starbuckville dam, landlocked salmon, lake trout, and trout can be taken year-round; minimum length for lakers is 18 inches and the daily limit is two. From Starbuckville dam downstream, trout, lake trout and landlocked salmon can be taken year-round, in any size.

DIRECTIONS: I-87 parallels the entire river and US 9 brushes its northern half, from its source to its mouth on Schroon Lake.

ADDITIONAL INFORMATION: Sharp Bridge Public Campground, on US 9, 6 miles south of I-87 exit 30, is a fee area offering 40 no-frills campsites, shore-fishing access, showers, picnic areas, and potable water.

CONTACT: New York State Department of Environmental Conservation Region 5, Lake Placid/Essex County Visitors Bureau, and Warren County Tourism.

14A. Public Access

DESCRIPTION: Parking and access to a couple of miles of public fishing rights (both banks) upstream and downstream of the bridge.

DIRECTIONS: From I-87 exit 28, head east on NY 74 for about 0.5 mile to the bridge.

ADDITIONAL INFORMATION: The PFR section stops a few hundred feet short of the Alder Meadow Road bridge.

14B. Public Access

DESCRIPTION: Parking and public fishing rights on both sides downstream all the way to the Schroon Lake.

DIRECTIONS: From I-87 exit 28, head south on US 9 for about 0.5 mile, turn east on Alder Meadow Road, and travel for a few hundred feet.

14C. Public Access

DESCRIPTION: Parking and access to about 0.8 mile of PFR.

DIRECTIONS: From I-87 exit 24 (Riverbank), head east on Bolton Landing/ Riverbank Road for about 0.25 mile, turn left on East Schroon River Road, and travel about 0.25 mile.

15. SCHROON LAKE

KEY SPECIES: Landlocked Atlantic salmon, lake trout, smallmouth bass, largemouth bass, northern pike, chain pickerel, black crappies, and panfish.

DESCRIPTION: Wearing the Essex and Warren County line in the middle like a belt, this 4,128-acre lake is 9 miles long, averages 56 feet deep, and has a maximum depth of 152 feet. Its shoreline is heavily developed with private cottages.

TIPS: Flatline silver Rapalas in spring and fall for salmon and lake trout.

THE FISHING: Although this lake is stocked with about 3,000 landlocked Atlantic salmon each year, surveys show roughly 10 percent of the population is naturally spawned in the Schroon River and other tributaries. The salmon range from 15 to 20 inches and are commonly taken on smelt-imitating streamers and crankbaits trolled at about 3 miles per hour. Lake trout are the predominant coldwater predator. The state supports the status quo by releasing several thousand annually, averaging 7.5 inches. They easily reach the lake's special, 18-inch minimum length and respond to silver spoons and minnowbaits trolled deep and slow in summer; and minnows, fished plain or tipping jigs, through the ice. The daily limit for lakers is two.

Northern pike ranging from 20 to 30 inches are plentiful. They have a taste for large minnows, spinnerbaits, and Rat-L-Traps. Pickerel ranging from 15 to 22 inches take just about any bite-sized lure ripped rapidly over the heads of weeds and their edges. Largemouth bass in the 1- to 5-pound range are numerous and are commonly targeted with Texas-rigged worms and buzzbaits. While these species can be found around narrow bands of weeds and boat docks anywhere on the lake, they're especially abundant in the weedy north end. Smallmouths running from 12 to 16 inches are also abundant and are mostly taken on bottom in rocky areas with crayfish, minnows, and jigs. Black crappies usually run from 9 to 12 inches and respond to Beetle Spins, tube jigs, poppers, and flies. Yellow perch go from 8 to 13 inches. They have a taste for worms, minnows, and scented 2- and 3-inch curly-tailed grubs and tubes. Bullheads average 1.5 pounds and hit worms fished on bottom, primarily at night.

The lake has high mercury and PCB levels, and the state advises against children and women of child-bearing age eating any of its fish. Men and elderly women are advised not to eat more than one meal per month of lake trout over 27 inches, perch over 13 inches, and smallmouth bass over 15 inches.

DIRECTIONS: Take I-87 north out of the village of Lake George for about 20 miles to exit 26, then head north on US 9, which parallels the lake.

ADDITIONAL INFORMATION: The state launch on the south end of the lake, off CR 62, has a paved ramp and parking for about 45 rigs. Eagle Point Public Campground, a fee area off US 9, 2 miles north of Pottersville, offers 72 no-frills sites, showers, potable water, picnic areas, a swimming beach, a hard-surface ramp, and parking for four rigs. The launch is only accessible when the campground is open, May through Labor Day, and a day-use fee is charged from mid-June through Labor Day.

CONTACT: New York State Department of Environmental Conservation Region 5, Lake Placid/Essex County Visitors Bureau, and Warren County Tourism.

15A. Schroon Lake Public Beach

DESCRIPTION: Hard-surface ramp and parking for 20 rigs.

DIRECTIONS: From I-87 exit 27, head north on US9 about 5 miles to the hamlet of Schroon Lake and turn right onto Dock Street.

15B. Schroon Manor Campground

DESCRIPTION: Built in 2011, this fee area's amenities are handicapped accessible. It offers 60 campsites, hot showers, flush toilets, a fishing pier, boat docks, and a swimming beach.

DIRECTIONS: From I-87 exit 27, hook a right onto Old Schroon Road, travel 0.1 mile, turn right on US 9, and travel 0.8 mile.

16. PARADOX LAKE

KEY SPECIES: Rainbow trout, lake trout, landlocked Atlantic salmon, northern pike, smallmouth and largemouth bass, and panfish.

DESCRIPTION: During spring runoff, this lake's outlet is forced by the swollen Schroon River to flow in reverse, prompting locals to call it Paradox—which, according to some, is Iroquois for "water running backward." Spread over 840 acres, the lake is 4 miles long, averages 25 feet deep, and has a maximum depth of 52 feet.

TIPS: Ice fish with large minnows in the bays on the north end.

THE FISHING: Periodically, the state stocks lake trout (1,120 7-inchers in 2013) to supplement the natural population. Lakers ranging from 2 to 4 pounds are most common but fish up to 20 pounds have been caught. They respond to spoons, streamers, and worms trolled deep and slow, about a foot behind wobblers or dodgers, in the west basin. Up to 5,300 rainbow trout are stocked annually. Averaging 9 inches upon release, they quickly grow to range from 12 to 18 inches, and 8-pounders are taken annually. In spring and fall, and at dusk and dawn during summer, they take small spoons flatlined parallel to shore, in both basins, in 5 to 15 feet of water. Landlocked Atlantic salmon are stocked occasionally (500 averaging 6.5 inches in 2013). Northern pike run from 4 to 8 pounds, but 20-pounders are taken regularly through the ice. They hit large minnows and crankbaits. Smallmouth bass thrive along the lake's drop-offs, where they'll hit Carolina-rigged finesse worms, and 2- to 3-inch worms or scented plastic minnows on dropshot rigs. Largemouth bass up to 6 pounds find the weed beds, especially in the eastern basin, to their liking and can't resist a soft plastic jerkbait or buzzbait ripped violently alongside or through their cover. Yellow perch ranging from 8 to 12 inches and pumpkinseeds averaging 0.75 pound are targeted by ice fishermen with ice jigs tipped with grubs.

Trout season is year-round and the minimum length for lakers is 18 inches.

DIRECTIONS: From I-87 exit 28, head east on NY 74 for about 4 miles.

ADDITIONAL INFORMATION: Paradox Lake State Campground offers 58 no-frills sites, coin-operated showers, a hard-surface launch with parking for 25 rigs, canoe and boat rentals, and picnic areas. A day-use fee is charged for non-campers when the campground is open, from May through Columbus Day. Free day use permitted off-season. The grounds are plowed in winter.

CONTACT: New York State Department of Environmental Conservation Region 5.

17. PUTNAM POND

KEY SPECIES: Northern pike, largemouth bass, black crappies, and panfish.

DESCRIPTION: Set in the east side of the Pharaoh Lake Wilderness, this 185-acre pond averages 10.5 feet deep and has a maximum depth of 34 feet.

TIPS: Cast a spinnerbait to weed edges and timber and yo-yo it back.

THE FISHING: Northern pike in the 18- to 26-inch range and largemouth bass up to 20 inches are plentiful. Both take soft jerkbaits worked in weeds and timber, buzzbaits ripped over water lilies, and spinnerbaits worked along weed edges and breaks. According to retired fisheries biologist Rich Preall, "A 2013 DEC survey found an increasing black crappie population and some huge yellow perch up to 15 inches." Both respond eagerly to small minnows and jigs. Pumpkinseeds averaging 6 inches and brown bullheads ranging from 8 to 12 inches are also plentiful. They'll take worms fished on bottom; and the sunnies provide explosive thrills on poppers and dry flies.

The launch is open year-round.

DIRECTIONS: Take NY 74 west out of Ticonderoga for about 6 miles to CR 39, then head south for about 3 miles.

ADDITIONAL INFORMATION: Putnam Pond Public Campgrounds is a fee area offering 72 campsites, a hard-surface launch ramp, boat rentals, a sand beach, play areas, picnic facilities, and coin-operated showers. Trails striking off from the campground lead to Rock Pond, famed for superb brook trout fishing, and Clear Pond, known for rainbow trout and kokanee salmon ("it's one of the last spots in the state to hold kokanee," says retired fisheries biologist Rich Preall). Open May through Labor Day. Free day use permitted off-season.

CONTACT: New York State Department of Environmental Conservation Region 5.

18. BRANT LAKE

KEY SPECIES: Largemouth bass, smallmouth bass, northern pike, chain pickerel, walleyes, rainbow and brown trout, and panfish.

DESCRIPTION: Set in a mountain valley, this gem is considered one of the prettiest lakes in the North Country. Covering 1,376 acres, averaging 30 feet deep, and dropping to a maximum depth of 65 feet, its shoreline is heavily ringed with cottages. Often the first lake to freeze over, it's one of the most popular ice-fishing destinations in the "Daks."

TIPS: Cast Texas-rigged worms under docks, making sure to hit the stanchions with the lead to attract the fish.

THE FISHING: This lake offers largemouth bass up to 6 pounds and smallmouths over 4 pounds. The bucketmouths hang out in shallow water, specifically around structure like docks, weeds, windfalls, and rock beds, viciously attacking buzzbaits, rattling crankbaits and shallow-diving minnowbaits that come their way. Smallmouths congregate in deeper water, over rocks and boulders, especially off points. They love crayfish, minnows, bucktail jigs tipped with minnows or grubs, and 3-inch worms on dropshot rigs. While not numerous, northerns up to 30 inches are present. They like minnows, crankbaits, and jigs. Pickerel range from 18 to 30 inches and respond to in-line spinners, spoons, and worms rigged on spinner harnesses and ripped over weed edges. The lake used to boast a decent walleye fishery, but their numbers have dropped. Still, some up to 20 inches are taken incidentally on jigs and crankbaits targeting bass and northerns. A state survey conducted in 2005 showed that yellow perch averaging a solid 9 inches are abundant. They're generally targeted through the ice with small minnows and ice jigs tipped with insect larvae. Brown bullheads from 10 to 14 inches are plentiful, especially in the southern basin where they hit worms and stink baits still-fished on bottom. The lake boasts numerous pumpkinseeds and rock bass weighing in at 0.75 pound, or even better; they take worms, wet flies, and tiny surface poppers fished in the shallows. The state stocks thousands of brown and rainbow trout averaging 9 inches annually, and many end up running from 1 to 5 pounds. They generally keep to the deeper north end and respond to flatlined minnowbaits and spoons in spring and fall, live minnows suspended below bobbers in 15 to 30 feet of water in summer, and minnows fished on bottom in winter.

Trout season is open year-round.

DIRECTIONS: Head north on I-87 out of Lake George for about 16 miles to exit 25, then go east on NY 8 for a couple of miles.

ADDITIONAL INFORMATION: The state boat launch on NY 8, on the south tip of the lake, has a hard-surface ramp and parking for 11 rigs. Primitive camping is permitted in the Lake George Wild Forest, which touches NY 8 on the lake's northeastern end.

CONTACT: New York State Department of Environmental Conservation Region 5 and Warren County Tourism.

19. LOON LAKE

KEY SPECIES: Largemouth bass, walleyes, smallmouth bass, northern pike, and panfish.

DESCRIPTION: Covering almost 600 acres, shaped like a crooked, lowercase h, this lake averages 15 feet deep and has a maximum depth of 33 feet. Completely encircled by good roads, what it lacks in silence it more than makes up for with great fishing.

TIPS: Cast spinnerbaits at right angles to weed edges and yo-yo them back.

THE FISHING: Bucketmouths up to 7 pounds are the lake's main draw, mostly targeted in the weedy south end. Serious anglers hit the weedy area first, then circle the lake working its windfalls with everything from poppers, buzzbaits, and fat-bodied crankbaits to crayfish, Texas-rigged worms, and stickworms. Smallmouth bass are abundant and enjoy their own following. They hang out in deeper water, particularly along the transition where drop-offs level off, and strike multicolored (brown and orange, blue and purple) bucktail jigs tipped with worms, minnows, or crayfish and bounced or dragged on bottom, and soft swimbaits worked at a steady clip or yo-yoed around drop-offs. The state has been stocking 12,000 fingerling walleyes annually since 2009. The habitat is good to them, and 20-something-inchers are plentiful. They take minnowbaits swimmed or jerked in water ranging from 5 to 15 feet deep in fall and spring; and, in summer, bucktails tipped with minnows or scented plastic maggots dragged or bounced over rocks. Northern pike range from 3 to 6 pounds. While not huge, these scrappy fighters are notorious for creating heart palpitations by striking at the side of the boat, then getting you all wet by fighting on the surface for a few seconds before taking the battle deep. They like red-and-white spoons and large minnows. Frying-pan-sized sunfish, yellow perch, rock bass, and bullheads are plentiful and very popular. They all like worms fished on bottom, and the perch, sunnies, and rockies will take flies and 2-inch curly-tailed grubs, as well.

DIRECTIONS: Head north out of Lake George on I-87 for about 16 miles to exit 25, then west on NY 8/US 9 for 5 miles.

ADDITIONAL INFORMATION: The town boat launch on NY 8/US 9 has a paved launch and parking for five rigs.

CONTACT: New York State Department of Environmental Conservation Region 5 and Warren County Tourism.

Loon, symbol of the "Daks."

20. LAKE PLACID

KEY SPECIES: Lake trout, rainbow trout, brook trout, smallmouth bass, and yellow perch.

DESCRIPTION: Known for the 1932 and 1980 Olympic Games held in the village stadium and surrounding hills, this scenic, 2,173-acre lake averages 52 feet deep, has a maximum depth of 151 feet, and has two huge islands out in the middle. Its floor is rocky, with little vegetation.

TIPS: Troll spoons for lakers.

THE FISHING: Most of this place is over 40 feet deep. The wild lake trout fishery is legendary. Although 30-something-pound fish have been taken in the past, and 15-pounders are landed each year, the typical laker runs about 2 pounds. Rich Preall, former aquatic biologist with the state, says a 2013 survey resulted in over a dozen fish weighing 8 pounds or better, "and two of those were 22 pounds." Locals normally fish for them by flatlining spoons slowly, near shore, in the spring and fall, and by jigging spoons and fishing minnows on bottom, in deep water, during summer. The state stocks 8,500 rainbow trout averaging 9 inches annually, and many reach between 12 and 18 inches. Preall considers Lake Placid the county's best open water for rainbows. He claims that the legendary "*Hexagenia* hatch is over due to swarms of rock bass . . . [but] anglers pick up rainbows by trolling streamers over deeper water near Pulpit Rock and in the outlet bay." Wild brook trout, some over a foot long, hang out near the mouths of the tributaries they vacated when they outgrew the habitat. They respond to in-line spinners, spoons, and flies. Smallmouth bass running anywhere from 1 to 4 pounds occupy the shallow, rocky areas along the entire shoreline, and hit crayfish and minnows fished on bottom, and tubes and Carolina-rigged worms worked in 5 to 25 feet of water. The lake doesn't have many yellow perch, but when you get one it'll average 12 inches, with some as tall as 14 inches. They take minnows and jigs. A few rock bass, pumpkinseeds, and bullheads manage to scrape a living out of the stingy, rocky shoreline and like worms.

The outlet is stocked with several hundred 9-inch brown trout annually.

The minimum length for lake trout is 15 inches.

DIRECTIONS: Off NY 86, on the north side of the village of Lake Placid.

ADDITIONAL INFORMATION: Hopping Bear Point, on the northeastern corner of the north island, has two lean-tos, available on a first-come, first-served basis. In addition, primitive camping is allowed on state land on both islands, but suitable sites are rare because the banks are steep and heavily wooded. The public launch on Mirror Lake Drive, in the village of Lake Placid, has a hard-surface ramp and parking for 25 rigs.

CONTACT: New York State Department of Environmental Conservation Region 5 and Lake Placid/Essex County Tourism.

21. MIRROR LAKE

KEY SPECIES: Lake trout, rainbow trout, smallmouth bass, perch.

DESCRIPTION: This lake covers 128 acres, averages 14 feet deep, and has a maximum depth of 65 feet. The shoreline is totally developed with marvelous homes, hotels, and the backyards and balconies of Main Street's shops.

TIPS: Jig spoons near bottom for lake trout.

THE FISHING: This lake gets surprisingly little fishing pressure considering it comes right to the road in Lake Placid village, one of New York's most popular resort towns. What's more, its monster lake trout are famous for spawning below the balconies of the main street's restaurants, driving some patrons to the point of wanting to jump in after them with their steak knives in their teeth. Retired state fisheries biologist Rich Preall says, "I haven't heard of anyone catching one of the bruisers but I bet a few canoes have been towed around by them." The state ensures the future of the fishery by stocking several hundred 7-inchers periodically, most recently in 2013. Rainbows are lake's most popularly targeted species. Roughly 1,000 9-inchers are stocked annually. Some years, the state throws in an additional 1,000 13-inchers. They do well, with many reaching 14 inches and better, providing some exciting action for folks casting *Hexagenia* imitations and lures with light tackle. Smallmouth bass ranging from 8 to 14 inches, and perch running from 6 to 8 inches, hang out in the relatively shallow north and south basins and on drop-offs. They take crayfish and worms still-fished on bottom, minnows on dropshot rigs, 2-inch tubes suspended below bobbers, and 3-inch curly-tails dragged on bottom.

Every now and then the state stocks landlocked Atlantic salmon. The minimum length for lake trout is 15 inches.

DIRECTIONS: Located in the heart of Lake Placid village, a stone's throw from NY 86, and just across the highway from the Olympic stadium.

ADDITIONAL INFORMATION: Lake Placid Village Park & Beach, on the southern tip of the lake, allows launching of cartop craft. There's a beach launch on Mirror Lake Drive, on the north shore, with parking for five cars. Only electric motors are allowed on the lake.

CONTACT: Lake Placid/Essex County Visitors Bureau and New York State Department of Environmental Conservation Region 5.

22. CONNERY POND

KEY SPECIES: Brown trout, splake, yellow perch, and largemouth bass.

DESCRIPTION: Nestled in a combination of wilderness, wild forest, and private land, this 83-acre pond averages 17 feet deep and has a maximum depth of 55 feet. Two private camps and a small sandy beach punctuate the forested shoreline.

TIPS: Jig minnows through the ice.

THE FISHING: The state has been stocking splake averaging 7.5 inches into the pond since the 1950s. Growing to between 2 to 5 pounds, most are taken in winter on minnows fished on bottom. While soft-water fishing isn't as popular as ice fishing, summer anglers target splake by trolling streamers or worms behind wobblers, or by drifting and jigging spoons and minnows on bottom. Brown trout were initially stocked in error but took so well, and proved so popular with ice fishermen, that the state now stocks about 1,000 averaging 8 inches annually. They grow to range from 9 to 18 inches, and take worms, minnows, and wet flies. Yellow perch averaging 10 inches are popularly sought through the ice on minnows and teardrop jigs tipped with spikes. Largemouth bass have made it into the system lately. Running anywhere from 12 to 16 inches, they provide explosive action on poppers cast with fly-fishing equipment.

Trout season is year-round. Motors up to 7.5 horsepower are allowed.

ADDITIONAL INFORMATION: Primitive camping is allowed in the McKenzie Mountain Wilderness Area on the pond's north shore.

DIRECTIONS: Head north on NY 86 out of Lake Placid village for about 2.5 miles and turn left on Connery Pond Road, a hard-surface road. Follow it for about 0.5 mile and park in the unpaved lot. You'll have to cross private land to get to the pond but getting permission isn't necessary because of an agreement between the state and the owners.

CONTACT: New York State Department of Environmental Conservation Region 5.

23. MOOSE POND

KEY SPECIES: Brook trout, rainbow trout, lake trout, landlocked salmon, and smallmouth bass.

DESCRIPTION: Set between the Saranac Lake Wild Forest and the McKenzie Mountain Wilderness, this 140-acre pond averages 28.5 feet deep and has a maximum depth of 70 feet. More than half of its shoreline is rocky.

TIPS: Silver crankbaits are productive early in the season.

THE FISHING: Besides supporting wild brook trout, this pond gets an additional 4,000 ranging from 4 to 8 inches from the state in some years. Survival is good and a lot of them reach 12 inches and better. They take wet flies and worms. Naturally spawned lake trout are also present. They range from 2 to 8 pounds and take silver spoons jigged on bottom. Periodically the state stocks rainbow trout averaging 9 inches. Although they're the shiniest trout in these hills, they're not the brightest, and those that survive the first few weeks of freedom often grow to 16 inches and better. They take dry flies and shiny spoons all summer long. Some years the state also releases a couple hundred landlocked Atlantic salmon averaging 6 inches. Their chances of survival are pretty good, and keepers are abundant. They'll hit flatlined tandem streamers and minnowbaits. Smallmouth bass ranging from 4 to 12 inches are so plentiful, their season opens on April 1 and you can keep them in any size and any number. These feisty little guys are a lot of fun to catch on in-line spinners, Berkley Power Grubs, and Atomic Teasers worked on ultralight tackle.

This is one of the few ponds in which the state occasionally stocks spent landlocked Atlantic salmon brood stock up to 30 inches long. Released in autumn, they overwinter, providing challenging sport for anglers the following spring. Try silver Rapalas.

Minimum length for lake trout is only 15 inches. Possession or use of baitfish is prohibited.

DIRECTIONS: From the village of Bloomingdale, head east on River Road (CR 18), then south 1.6 miles later onto Moose Pond Road and continue for about a mile.

ADDITIONAL INFORMATION: The hard-surface ramp at the state boat launch is steep, but small trailers can make it; parking for about 15 rigs. There are several primitive campsites around the pond.

CONTACT: New York State Department of Environmental Conservation Region 5.

24. LAKE KUSHAQUA

KEY SPECIES: Lake trout, largemouth bass, smallmouth bass, walleyes, northern pike, and yellow perch.

DESCRIPTION: This impoundment on the North Branch of the Saranac River covers 377 acres, averages 44 feet deep, and has a maximum depth of 91 feet. Almost totally surrounded by state land, the shoreline is mostly forested.

TIPS: Walk Zara Spooks around emergent vegetation.

THE FISHING: The state stocks about 1,000 lake trout averaging 7 inches about every other year. They hang out in the deep, cold middle and grow to range from 2 to 5 pounds. They do so well, in fact, that the state recently opened the lake to ice fishing. They take worms or tinsel flies trolled behind attractors in 40 to 60 feet of water. In summer, you'll catch more lakers by bumping bottom, but the larger ones suspend. Largemouth bass ranging from 1 to 5 pounds thrive all along the shoreline but are especially numerous in the south end. During hot weather, they seek shade in the shadow of lily pads, weed beds, and under banks and logs. Buzzbaits retrieved quickly over their heads provoke explosive reactions. Smallmouths ranging from 8 to 14 inches can be found over drop-offs in 10 to 20 feet of water. During the heat of day, they respond to bladebaits and diving minnowbaits; violently slam darters like Zara Spooks on calm evenings; and, on choppy days, slam tubes or Carolina-rigged worms dragged on bottom, off points, and along drop-offs. Northern pike like structure in 5 to 15 feet of water and strike spinnerbaits and buzzbaits. Yellow perch ranging from 7 to 10 inches are plentiful, hanging out along weed edges and drop-offs where they hit minnows and tiny bucktail jigs.

DIRECTIONS: From its intersection with NY 30 in Paul Smiths, head east on NY 86 (Easy Street) for 4.5 miles to Gabriels. Turn north on Rainbow Lake Road (CR 60) for 6.3 miles to the Buck Pond Public Campground.

ADDITIONAL INFORMATION: Buck Pond Public Campground, located just across the road from Lake Kushaqua, offers a paved ramp on the lake's southeastern bank and parking for about 10 rigs. A day-use fee is charged noncampers from Memorial Day through Labor Day. The campground offers 116 sites, including several on the beach and a couple on a nearby island, along with hot showers, a dumping station, a sand beach, and boat and canoe rentals.

CONTACT: New York State Department of Environmental Conservation Region 5 and Franklin County Tourism.

25. BUCK POND

KEY SPECIES: Northern pike, largemouth bass, smallmouth bass, yellow perch, pumpkinseeds, and brown bullheads.

DESCRIPTION: This 130-acre pond is connected to Lake Kushaqua (**site 24**) by a channel, averaging 7.5 feet deep and dropping to a maximum depth of 15 feet. The only development on it is the public campground.

TIPS: Cast red-and-white Dardevle spoons over 5 to 15 feet of water.

THE FISHING: This pond boasts a good population of scrappy northern pike in the 18- to 28-inch range. They hit minnows, crankbaits, and spoons. Bronzebacks typically run from 10 to 16 inches, but 20-inchers aren't unheard of. They respond best to crayfish on bottom and 3-inch minnows on dropshot rigs worked around structure. Bucketmouths can go 6 pounds and like floating baits at dusk and dawn when the surface is calm. Yellow perch and bullheads run between 6 and 12 inches and take worms fished on bottom. Perch will also hit wet flies and small lures. Bullheads are most active in the evening.

No motors allowed.

DIRECTIONS: From its intersection with NY 30 in Paul Smiths, head east on NY 86 for 4.5 miles to Gabriels and turn north on Rainbow Lake Road (CR 60) for 6.3 miles to the Buck Pond Public Campground.

ADDITIONAL INFORMATION: Buck Pond Public Campground, a fee area, is on the pond's west bank. It offers 116 sites, hot showers, a cartop boat launch, and boat and canoe rentals. Day use is permitted year-round; a fee is charged noncampers when the campground is open, Memorial Day through Labor Day.

CONTACT: New York State Department of Environmental Conservation Region 5 and Franklin County Tourism.

26. RAINBOW LAKE

KEY SPECIES: Largemouth bass, northern pike, walleyes, yellow perch, and panfish.

DESCRIPTION: This 588-acre lake averages 15 feet deep and drops to a maximum depth of 58 feet. Much of its southern and western shores are bordered by private dwellings. An esker runs most of its north shore, separating it from Clear Pond, a backwater popular with canoeists and campers but not anglers.

TIPS: Cast floating/diving perch-colored crankbaits during low-light conditions.

THE FISHING: Up until just a few years ago, this lake was plagued with stunted yellow perch. Their massive number caused a terrible imbalance, resulting in everything else being stunted, too. In an attempt to manage the perch, the state began stocking walleyes in the 1990s. Richard Preall, an aquatic biologist working with the program, says the plan worked wonderfully. Currently, 25-something-inch walleyes are available, and the perch can go 12 inches and better. Eyes respond to worms drifted on plain or spinner-rigged harnesses by day, and minnow-imitating crankbaits cast near shore around dawn and dusk. The perch respond to minnows, worms, and small lures. Largemouth bass were introduced in the 1940s, followed by northern pike around 1960. The largemouths go anywhere from shorties to a whopping 22 inches. Preall says they like "soft plastics cast tight to bog mats." While not very plentiful, northern pike go from 18 to 32 inches. They're usually caught incidentally on minnowbaits and jigs targeting the walleyes and bass. Panfish also benefited from DEC's wise management. Rock bass and sunfish range from 4 to 9 inches, and bullheads stretch the tape to 14 inches. The rockies and sunnies strike poppers, flies, and 1-inch grubs and, along with the bullheads, like worms, too.

The minimum length for walleyes is 18 inches, and the daily limit is 3.

DIRECTIONS: Head north out of Gabriels for about 2 miles on Rainbow Lake Road.

ADDITIONAL INFORMATION: The south shore is largely on private property, and access from land can be iffy. The easiest way to get here is from Lake Kushaqua (**site 24**), by paddling or motoring up its inlet, through the scenic Rainbow Narrows. You'll need a low-deck craft like a canoe or small motorboat to make it under a bridge. Several primitive beach campsites are on the esker on the north side of the lake.

CONTACT: New York State Department of Environmental Conservation Region 5 and Franklin County Tourism.

27. JONES POND

KEY SPECIES: Northern pike, largemouth bass, yellow perch, and brown bullheads.

DESCRIPTION: Bordered on its west end and southern tip by vast, weedy bays, this 140-acre pond is a warmwater fishery that only averages 4.3 feet deep and has a maximum depth of 8.9 feet. The vast majority of its shoreline is evergreen forest, but there is also some light development.

TIPS: Cast red-and-white Dardevle spoons along the edges of the marshes in early spring and late fall.

THE FISHING: Northern pike are the main predator. They range from 18 to 32 inches and respond well to artificials resembling life-forms ranging from minnows, mice, frogs, and snakes to ducklings and baby muskrats. "Largemouth bass up to 4 pounds are common and floating Rapalas work great on calm evenings," says retired state fisheries biologist Rich Preall. "I watched large bass jumping a foot out of the water to inhale dragonflies this summer [2014]," he adds. Bullheads average 10 inches and hit worms fished on bottom. Perch go from 5 to 10 inches and hit 1- to 2-inch curly-tailed grubs swimmed 1 to 2 feet below the surface and jerked periodically, say every 10 feet or so.

DIRECTIONS: Head east out of Paul Smiths for about a mile on NY 86, turn left on Jones Pond Road (CR 31), and continue for about 1.5 miles.

ADDITIONAL INFORMATION: A couple of informal cartop launches are on CR 31. Adventurers get here by paddling up the outlet from Osgood Pond. If you decide to take this route, be prepared to pull the canoe through shallow spots. Primitive camping is allowed on the state land surrounding three-quarters of the pond.

CONTACT: New York State Department of Environmental Conservation Region 5 and Franklin County Tourism.

28. OSGOOD POND

KEY SPECIES: Northern pike, largemouth bass, and smallmouth bass.

DESCRIPTION: Ringed mostly by woods, this 508-acre pond has a few private residences and two Adirondack Great Camps. It averages 13 feet deep and has a maximum depth of 25 feet. Bald eagles nest in the surrounding forest and are often spotted swooping down for fish.

TIPS: Rattling crankbaits are productive.

THE FISHING: This place is notorious for northerns ranging from 18 to 24 inches. They are mostly targeted by ice fishermen using shiners on tip-ups. Largemouth bass range from 1 to 4 pounds and take Texas-rigged worms tossed into windfalls, weed beds, lily pads, and any other cover you can find. Smallmouths run from 1 to 3 pounds and hang out on the rock fields around the islands. They respond to tubes or curly-tailed grubs dragged on bottom, and Slug-Go-type baits twitched and jerked on the surface.

DIRECTIONS: Head east out of Paul Smiths on NY 86 for 0.6 mile to White Pine Road. Turn left and travel for 0.3 mile.

ADDITIONAL INFORMATION: A beach launch with parking for five rigs is on White Pine Road. An old canal links this pond with Little Osgood Pond and Church Pond, both of which have lean-tos. Two majestic Adirondack Great Camps—massive private estates built in the years between the Civil War and the Great Depression—sit on Osgood Pond's shores: White Pines Camp, built in 1907, served as the White House when President Calvin Coolidge spent the summer in 1926; Northbrook Lodge was built in the 1920s by a colorful character who—depending on whom you talk to—was either a politician or bootlegger.

CONTACT: Franklin County Tourism and New York State Department of Environmental Conservation Region 5.

28A. Church Pond

DESCRIPTION: Crowned with a ring of windfalls, this small pond offers great northern pike, largemouth bass, and perch fishing.

THE FISHING: Rich Preall, a retired DEC fisheries biologist formerly assigned to the beat, says the best largemouth fishing is at the back end, around the mouth of the canal, while the northerns prefer the deeper water close to the road. Perch can be found anywhere. Each species hits jigs tipped with scented plastic trailers.

ADDITIONAL INFORMATION: A hand launch is on Hoffmann Road, just north of its intersection with NY 86, and there's lean-to on its north end.

DIRECTIONS: On the north side of NY 86, about 0.1 mile east of its intersection with NY 30.

29. BOY SCOUT CLEAR POND (CLEAR POND)

KEY SPECIES: Splake.

DESCRIPTION: Almost totally undeveloped, this 81-acre pond is skirted by marsh and woods. It averages 28 feet deep and has a maximum depth of 63 feet.

TIPS: Stay away from the Boy Scout camp on the north end in summer.

THE FISHING: The state stocks splake into this pond periodically, and many reach 10 pounds. A cross between brook trout and lake trout, the species is easy to confuse with one or the other. However, splake are the only trout in the pond. They like to hang out on bottom in relatively deep water and take worms, jigs, and spoons. Black crappies got into the place around 2010 and, according to retired fisheries biologist Rich Preall, "Are now reaching good average size." They take Beetle Spins, Berkley's Atomic Teasers, and 2-inch grubs.

DIRECTIONS: Head north out of Paul Smiths for about 10 miles on NY 30 and turn east at the northern Meacham Road entrance. A beach launch is about 100 yards down the road.

ADDITIONAL INFORMATION: Use of baitfish is prohibited.

CONTACT: New York State Department of Environmental Conservation Region 5 and Franklin County Tourism.

30. MEACHAM LAKE

KEY SPECIES: Northern pike, smallmouth bass, splake, brown trout, landlocked Atlantic salmon, and yellow perch.

DESCRIPTION: This lake covers 1,185 acres, averages 36 feet deep, and has a maximum depth of 80 feet. Its only development is a public campground on the north end.

TIPS: Use large minnows over deep structure in winter for huge northern pike.

THE FISHING: This lake is known for producing northerns of pikeasaurus proportions, and ice fishermen land 15-pounders each year. Summer anglers get in on the action, catching loads of pike ranging from 2 to 10 pounds by throwing spinnerbaits, spoons, and buzzbaits, especially on the weedy south end. Smallmouth bass reach a whopping 5-something pounds. They prefer the rocky east shore between Winnebago Creek and Roaring Brook, and respond to live crayfish, bucktail jigs tipped with minnows, and scented craws dragged slowly on bottom. The state stocks about 2,500 splake averaging 10 inches annually. Typically reaching 2 to 4 pounds, they're bottom-oriented and hang out near shore in spring and fall, responding to streamers and spoons worked deep around the mouths of tributaries. Come summer they seek cool temperatures in 15 to 45 feet of water and will hit deep-diving crankbaits; winter finds splake at the same depths, where they'll take minnows fished on bottom. Wild brown trout up to 20 inches are present and respond to worms in spring and fall, spinners in summer, and shiners suspended below tiny bobbers in winter. Landlocked Atlantic salmon range from 15 to 20 inches and hit small silver spoons and crankbaits, especially near tributary mouths, from mid-April through mid-May. This lake has some of the largest perch in the Adirondack Mountains. Unfortunately, they have high mercury levels; a state health advisory warns against eating any over 12 inches, and recommends only eating one meal per month of smaller ones. They take minnows and curly-tailed grubs.

Trout and salmon can be taken year-round.

DIRECTIONS: Head north out of Paul Smiths on NY 30 for about 8 miles.

ADDITIONAL INFORMATION: Meacham Lake Public Campground, a fee area, has 224 no-frill sites, a paved boat launch, showers, a sand beach, a bathhouse, and canoe and boat rentals. Each of the 25 beach campsites has its own outhouse. A day-use fee is charged noncampers while the campground is open, mid-May through Columbus Day. Free day use off-season. The park road is plowed in winter.

CONTACT: New York State Department of Environmental Conservation Region 5 and Franklin County Tourism.

31. MOUNTAIN POND (PAUL SMITHS)

KEY SPECIES: Brook trout.

DESCRIPTION: Located within the Debar Mountain Wild Forest, this 56-acre pond averages 9 feet deep and has a maximum depth of 29 feet.

TIPS: Use lures with barbless hooks to facilitate easy release.

THE FISHING: This pond is managed for New York's native Windfall strain brook trout. While some natural reproduction occurs, it's not enough to maintain a quality fishery, and the state stocks the place with about 5,000 brookies averaging 4 inches regularly. Past state surveys netted trout over 16 inches long. They'll take wet flies, Mepps spinners, and tiny tube jigs tipped with Berkley Power Wigglers.

This pond is for catch-and-release fishing with artificial lures only. No motors allowed.

DIRECTIONS: Head north out of Paul Smiths on NY 30 for about 2.5 miles and turn right on Mountain Pond Road.

ADDITIONAL INFORMATION: A primitive campsite is located just off the beach on the point reaching out of the northeastern corner of the pond.

CONTACT: New York State Department of Environmental Conservation Region 5 and Franklin County Tourism.

Fishing Mountain Pond, Paul Smiths (site 31).

32. BARNUM POND

KEY SPECIES: Largemouth bass, brook trout, pumpkinseeds, and bullheads.

DESCRIPTION: Averaging about 5 feet deep and having a maximum depth of 10 feet, this pond covers 84 acres and has sprawling wetlands equal in size along the south shore.

TIPS: Work loud surface lures and spinnerbaits to help bass locate your offering.

THE FISHING: A bog on the southwestern corner stains this pond's water almost black. P. T. Barnum's favorite fishing hole when he stayed at Paul Smith's Hotel, a famous Adirondack wilderness lodge in the 19th century, this pond supports good numbers of largemouth bass ranging from 6 to 14 inches (a 6-pounder was caught recently during a state survey). They respond best to crayfish, minnows, and spinnerbaits. Although the pond is shallow, springs keep it cool enough to support wild brookies. Find the spring holes and you'll find squaretails up to 12 inches long. They'll take nymphs and tiny bucktail jigs. Although its cold waters are hard on panfish, there are plenty of 6- to 12-inch bullheads and pumpkinseeds averaging 5 inches. Rich Preall, a former state fisheries biologist assigned to the beat, says the rocky point on the northeastern corner, accessible from NY 30 via a "herd trail," is a great place to take kids for panfish. The sunfish hit flies and poppers and, along with the bullheads, night crawlers and Berkley's Power Honey Worms fished on bottom.

Use or possession of baitfish is prohibited.

DIRECTIONS: From Paul Smiths, head north on NY 30 for about a mile.

ADDITIONAL INFORMATION: This place is a good example of the damage informal stocking can do to native species. Late in the last century, this was one of the best roadside brook trout ponds in Franklin County. Then some "Johnny Basseed" threw in a couple of largemouths and they scarfed down the brookies. Chemical reclamation is out of the question because of the massive wetlands. A beach launch for cartop craft is on NY 30, but it's short and you'll have to launch quickly to avoid a car on the highway slamming your front end. A couple of primitive campsites are located north of the launch.

CONTACTS: New York State Department of Environmental Conservation Region 5 and Franklin County Tourism.

33. BLACK AND LONG PONDS RECREATION AREA

These two ponds are located north of the St. Regis Canoe Area. They are popular destinations with hikers and canoeists. Both were reclaimed with chemicals in 1997 and now support Windfall strain brook trout indigenous to New York.

33A. Black Pond

KEY SPECIES: Brook trout.

DESCRIPTION: This 73-acre pond is completely surrounded by forest and has an esker running its west bank. Its average depth is 20 feet; the maximum is 45 feet deep.

TIPS: If the fish aren't hitting in the main pond, canoe up the east side and try the big bay some call Little Black Pond.

THE FISHING: After being chemically reclaimed in 1997, this pond was stocked twice with Windfall strain brook trout. Currently, the fish are wild and the state feels future stocking probably won't be necessary. Located close to the road, it gets a lot of fishing pressure. Still, it's loaded with brookies typically ranging from 4 to 16 inches; 3-pounders are taken each year. They'll hit most any fly early in the season but clam up as summer progresses. However, a few can be coaxed to hit a black, $\frac{1}{32}$- to $\frac{1}{64}$-ounce bucktail jig, usually striking when it touches bottom right after the cast.

Use or possession of baitfish is prohibited.

DIRECTIONS: Head west out of Paul Smiths on Keese Mills Road for about 2.4 miles.

ADDITIONAL INFORMATION: Located on Paul Smith's College property, this pond's lean-to is for day use only; a permit is required to camp on the property. According to retired fisheries biologist Rich Preall, "DEC takes milt from the males to produce Windfall x domestic hybrids now being tried in the St. Regis Canoe Area, so anglers should return the larger males."

CONTACT: New York State Department of Environmental Conservation Region 5, Paul Smith's College VIC, and Franklin County Tourism.

33B. Long Pond

KEY SPECIES: Brook trout.

DESCRIPTION: Spread over 14 acres, this pond is completely surrounded by forest, shrubs, and wetland. Averaging 9.5 feet deep and dropping to a maximum depth of 20 feet, it feeds Black Pond. A dam halfway down the outlet prevents fish movement between the two.

TIPS: Cast a light-colored fly like a Yellow Humpy near beaver lodges.

THE FISHING: Since being chemically reclaimed in 1997, this pond has been stocked a couple of times with about 550 3-inch brook trout each time. Currently most fish are wild and average 10 inches, but 2-pounders are taken each year. They hit streamers, in-line spinners, and small jigs.

Use or possession of baitfish is prohibited.

DIRECTIONS: Head up Black Pond's inlet (**site 33A**) for about 10.5 miles; you will have to carry for about 0.25 mile.

ADDITIONAL INFORMATION: This pond is located on Paul Smith's College property and the lean-to is for day use only. Camping is prohibited.

CONTACT: New York State Department of Environmental Conservation Region 5, Paul Smiths College VIC, and Franklin County Tourism.

34. LOWER ST. REGIS LAKE

KEY SPECIES: Northern pike, largemouth bass, smallmouth bass, and panfish.

DESCRIPTION: Covering 365 acres and mostly surrounded by forest, this lake averages 17 feet deep and drops to a maximum depth of 38 feet. Paul Smith's College sits on its northeastern corner.

TIPS: Rip jerkbaits around the marshy east and south banks.

THE FISHING: This site has a good warmwater fishery. Northerns ranging from 18 to 30 inches, largemouth bass from 1 to 4 pounds, and smallmouth bass from 0.75 to 2 pounds are plentiful. Each responds to spinnerbaits and crankbaits worked in 5 to 20 feet of water, especially around windfalls, along weed edges, and near shoreline vegetation. In addition, smallmouths hang out on the drop-offs in up to 30 feet of water in summer and take bucktail jigs, scented 3-inch curly-tailed grubs, and salted tubes. Yellow perch running from 6 to 12 inches are common and take small minnows and lures. Pumpkinseeds ranging from 4 to 8 inches and bullheads up to 14 inches are also plentiful and like worms. Retired fisheries biologist Rich Preall reports, "Black crappies were reported by anglers in 2013." This lake is popular with local ice fishermen targeting northern pike and yellow perch with ice dots tipped with insect larvae, minnows dangling off hardware, and live minnows suspended or fished on bottom with tip-ups.

DIRECTIONS: Located on the south side of the hamlet of Paul Smiths.

ADDITIONAL INFORMATION: A small, public cartop launch is located on the campus of Paul Smiths College, north of Essex and Franklin Halls (it's closed when students are out on the lake doing fieldwork), and a waterway access site is above the outlet dam, off Keese Mills Road, 2.4 miles west of its intersection with NY 30. The lean-to at Peter's Rock (the point on the south bank at the outlet's source), and the two farther west, are open to the public.

CONTACT: Franklin County Tourism and New York State Department of Environmental Conservation Region 5.

35. SPITFIRE LAKE

KEY SPECIES: Northern pike, largemouth bass, smallmouth bass, and panfish.

DESCRIPTION: This 254-acre lake averages 16 feet and has a maximum depth of 31 feet. Its banks are heavily developed with cottages.

TIPS: Hungry smallmouths hang around boathouses at dusk.

THE FISHING: Northern pike range from 2 to 5 pounds, bucketmouths run between 1.5 and 4 pounds, and smallmouths go from 1 to 2.5 pounds. Each strikes rattling crankbaits, loud surface lures like Hula Poppers, and minnowbaits twitched around docks at dusk and dawn. The largest northerns are caught through the ice on minnows. Yellow perch averaging 9 inches, pumpkinseeds up to 7 inches, and bullhead up to 12 inches are plentiful and hit worms.

DIRECTIONS: Nestled between Upper and Lower St. Regis Lakes.

ADDITIONAL INFORMATION: Surrounded by private land, the lake has no public access. Most anglers get to it by paddling or motoring up the channels connecting it to the St. Regis Lakes.

CONTACT: Franklin County Tourism and New York State Department of Environmental Conservation Region 5.

36. UPPER ST. REGIS LAKE

KEY SPECIES: Lake trout, landlocked Atlantic salmon, northern pike, largemouth bass, smallmouth bass, and yellow perch.

DESCRIPTION: This 742-acre lake's average depth is 25 feet, and the maximum is 90 feet. One of the world's classiest lakes, its banks are decked in numerous Great Camps like Marjorie Merriweather Post's Topridge and numerous lesser summer mansions.

TIPS: Bump spinnerbaits off the exposed branches of submerged timber.

THE FISHING: The state stocks several hundred Atlantic salmon yearlings periodically. They normally reach 15 to 19 inches and are mostly caught on streamers. Lake trout ranging from 2 to 5 pounds are typical and respond to spoons trolled on Seth Green rigs, mostly in the deep water east of Ward Island. Northern pike run 5 to 10 pounds, and 15-pounders are possible.

Upper St. Regis Lake (site 36) off NY 30.

They hit large minnows and spinnerbaits. Largemouth bass range from 2 to 4 pounds and share the shallow, heavily wooded areas with the northerns where they take the same baits, as well as crayfish. Smallmouths range from 1 to 3 pounds and prefer rocky points where they can be taken on crayfish, Carolina-rigged finesse worms, and 3-inch, soft plastic minnows fished on dropshot rigs. There's a good yellow perch population in the lake, too, but they tend to be grubby, says retired fisheries biologist Rich Preall. Still, locals go after them with minnows and worms in warm weather and ice dots tipped with spikes through the ice.

DIRECTIONS: At the other end of the channel on Spitfire Lake's (**site 35**) south end.

ADDITIONAL INFORMATION: Primitive camping is allowed on the state land midway up the lake's west bank. A beach launch for cartop craft is located on the south end. From its intersection with NY 86 in Paul Smiths, head south on NY 30 for 3.2 miles, turn right onto a gravel road, and keep bearing right, skirting the private club's grounds, to the small launch at the tip of the point; parking for about five cars.

CONTACT: Franklin County Tourism and New York State Department of Environmental Conservation Region 5.

ST. REGIS RIVER

This river has three branches. The west branch is not included because it is difficult to access and runs through a lot of private property.

37. EAST BRANCH ST. REGIS RIVER

KEY SPECIES: Brook trout.

DESCRIPTION: Meacham Lake's outlet, this branch meanders for 11 miles and joins the Main Branch a couple of miles north of the village of Santa Clara. Although it has some rapids, it is mostly mild-mannered. It flows through fabulous forest and is best float-fished in a canoe.

TIPS: Wear hip boots to facilitate carrying around beaver dams.

THE FISHING: Native brook trout rule this stream. They migrate into it when they outgrow their natal waters but seldom stray more than a couple hundred feet beyond the mouths. Although most range from 7 to 10 inches, 14-inchers are possible. Wet flies and worms work best.

DIRECTIONS: Head north out of Paul Smiths on NY 30 for about 8 miles and turn west on NY 458, which parallels the upper half of the river.

CONTACT: New York State Department of Environmental Conservation Region 5 and Franklin County Tourism.

37A. Public Access

DESCRIPTION: This site is owned by The Nature Conservancy. Parking for five cars.

DIRECTIONS: Take NY 458 into the hamlet of St. Regis Falls. Head north on CR 5 for a couple of blocks, turn east on CR 14, and travel for about 6 miles.

38. ST. REGIS RIVER

KEY SPECIES: Brook trout, brown trout, rainbow trout, northern pike, walleyes, smallmouth bass, largemouth bass, and muskellunge.

DESCRIPTION: This river pours out of Lower St. Regis Lake (**site 34**) and meanders north for about 80 miles to feed the St. Lawrence River, gathering the west and east branches along the way. Starting out as good trout habitat, its coldwater environments steadily deteriorate until Nicholville, where it becomes a warmwater fishery.

TIPS: The most productive trout water is from the mill dam in the hamlet of St. Regis Falls downstream for about 2 miles.

THE FISHING: The upper reaches have natural brook trout ranging from 4 to 12 inches. The state annually supplements this fishery by stocking about 4,800 rainbow trout averaging 8.5 inches, 5,400 brown trout averaging 8.5 inches, and 1,700 browns ranging from 12 to 15 inches. They respond to worms, inline spinners, and small crankbaits like Jr. ThunderSticks. This water quickly heats up in summer, and holdover trout concentrate in spring holes and the mouths of tributaries.

Northern pike ranging from 18 to 22 inches, locally called ax handles, are present in the impoundments at Santa Clara and St. Regis Falls. They respond to minnows, streamers, spinnerbaits, and buzzbaits. Smallmouth bass ranging from 0.5 to 1.5 pounds begin appearing in the impoundment at St. Regis Falls. They hit minnows, crayfish, worms, crankbaits, and spinnerbaits. Downstream of St. Regis Falls, both species grow bigger: Northerns range from 20 to 30 inches, and smallies reach up to 18 inches. Walleyes averaging about 20 inches are abundant downstream of Nicholville and have a taste for jigs, along with slowly trolled crankbaits and spinner-rigged worms. In 2014 the state began stocking them above the dam in the hamlet of St. Regis Falls because of the abundant forage, and to take some of the fishing pressure off the northerns and bass.

The stretch flowing through the Akwesasne Nation's (see additional information below) territory downstream of Hogansburg offers tremendous early-season smallmouths averaging 2.5 pounds. Largemouth bass up to 5 pounds, northerns ranging from 24 to 36 inches, and muskies up to 20 pounds are abundant in this stretch summer through fall. They all like

3-inch tubes and bucktail jigs tipped with minnows, spinnerbaits, buzzbaits, and topwater lures like Zara Spooks and Jitterbugs.

Trout can be taken year-round from Fort Jackson upstream to the Franklin County line. In the section flowing through St. Lawrence County, the minimum length for black bass is 10 inches; fishing for bass off-season, even catch and release, is prohibited.

ADDITIONAL INFORMATION: The 3-mile stretch of river below the Canadian border is on the St. Regis Indian Reservation. You need a permit from the tribe ($5 for three days, $10 for the season) to fish it.

CONTACT: New York State Department of Environmental Conservation Regions 5 and 6 and the Mohawk Council of Akwesasne Conservation Department.

38A. Public Access

DESCRIPTION: A low dam at the outlet of Lower St. Regis Lake spawns the Middle St. Regis River. The stream tumbles along the northeastern edge St. Regis Canoe Wilderness for a few hundred yards, a stone's throw from Keese Mills Road, before entering private land.

THE FISHING: This stretch offers good trout habitat.

DIRECTIONS: Head west on Reese Mills Road from Paul Smiths for 2.4 miles. The river is across the road from the Black Pond and Long Pond Recreation Area (**site 33**).

38B. Public Access

DESCRIPTION: In this stretch, the river is littered with huge boulders and flows through spellbinding woods. The area is prime trout water from spring through early summer. Come August, you'll find the fish holing up in spring pools and tributary mouths.

DIRECTIONS: Head north out of Paul Smiths on NY 30 for about 8 miles and turn west on NY 458. Travel for 10.8 miles, bear right on South River Road, and travel about 0.1 mile.

38C. Public Access

DESCRIPTION: This town of Waverly park is located on the impoundment in St. Regis Falls. The grounds offer a paved ramp, a loading dock, formal parking for 3 cars, shoulder parking for about 20 more, shore-fishing access, and picnic facilities.

THE FISHING: This impoundment has trout, northern pike, and smallmouth bass.

DIRECTIONS: From the above site, continue west on South River Road for about 5 miles to the east side of the village of St. Regis Falls.

38D. St. Regis Falls Scenic Campsite

DESCRIPTION: Run by the town of Waverly, this fee area is right at the waterfall, and offers numerous waterfront sites with and without hookups, several cabins, playgrounds, and a museum. Open May 1 through October 15.

THE FISHING: The stretch from the falls, for about 2 miles downstream, is the best trout water on the river.

DIRECTIONS: From the above site, continue west on South River Road for about 100 yards to the stop sign. Turn right, cross the bridge, and turn left.

38E. Brasher Falls State Forest Public Access

DESCRIPTION: This site has an unpaved ramp for cartop craft and parking for five cars.

THE FISHING: The water here is slow and fairly deep, good habitat for bass, northern pike, walleyes, and an occasional muskie.

DIRECTIONS: From the US 11/NY 11B intersection in Pottsdam, head north on US 11 for 10 miles, then turn north on NY 11C for 4 miles. Get on CR 53 in Brasher Falls and head north for 5.5 miles.

ADDITIONAL INFORMATION: Primitive camping is allowed across the road in the state forest.

39. LAKE CLEAR

KEY SPECIES: Landlocked Atlantic salmon, brown trout, lake trout, northern pike, largemouth bass, rainbow smelt, yellow perch, and pumpkinseeds.

DESCRIPTION: This 979-acre lake averages 28 feet deep and has a maximum depth of 60 feet. Its shoreline is partly developed with private homes and camps.

TIPS: Cast streamers around tributary mouths in September.

THE FISHING: A few years back, declining smelt numbers put everyone on alert and many feared the worst. Fortunately, they've rebounded and the state resumed stocking brown trout (1,760 8.5-inchers in 2014) and Atlantic salmon (1,200 yearlings in 2013). Browns end up ranging from 1 to 8 pounds (the big ones are naturally spawned scions of former stocking programs) and are commonly taken by anglers matching hatches on summer evenings, and casting or trolling minnowbaits and spoons spring and fall. A lot of landlocked Atlantic salmon are taken incidentally on lures targeting browns. However, in mid-September (autumn comes early in the Adirondacks) fly fishermen take a lot of salmon by wading out into the surf and casting small spinners and wet flies into the mouth of the little brook just north of the anglers' parking area. According to retired fisheries biologist Rich Preall, authorities were surprised to catch a "half dozen lake trout averaging 5 pounds, which are survivors of a surplus stocking done around 2004. I hear that lakers up to 9 pounds are now [2015] being caught." They're usually taken on minnows targeting northern pike. Largemouth bass range from 1 to 3 pounds and respond hungrily to live minnows, crayfish, and soft jerkbaits. Northern pike run from 2 to 6 pounds and are usually taken through the ice on large minnows. Smelt attract a loyal following of anglers who go for them through the ice by jigging fish bellies hooked 6 to 12 inches below a Swedish Pimple, which acts as an attractor. Yellow perch ranging from 6 to 10 inches and pumpkinseeds from 6 to 8 inches are commonly targeted through the ice with ice flies or tiny jigs baited with grubs and perch eyes.

DIRECTIONS: Take NY 30 south from the hamlet of Paul Smiths for 5.5 miles.

ADDITIONAL INFORMATION: Lake Clear Public Access Site has parking for about 50 cars and a long sandy beach suitable for launching cartop craft. However, a barrier blocks vehicles from driving down to the lake, so you have to carry your craft 80 yards. Primitive camping is allowed in the state forest on the west bank.

CONTACT: Franklin County Tourism and New York State Department of Environmental Conservation Region 5.

40. LAKE CLEAR OUTLET

KEY SPECIES: Northern pike, largemouth bass, and yellow perch.

DESCRIPTION: Also known as Millpond, this 103-acre impoundment averages 3.6 feet deep and has a maximum depth of 8.5 feet. A weedy place with stump fields, its north shore is lightly developed with private residences.

TIPS: Cast stickworms to the edges of submerged stumps.

THE FISHING: This warmwater fishery supports a good population of northern pike ranging between 18 and 24 inches. They hit spinnerbaits and minnow-baits. Largemouth bass in the 0.75- to 3-pound range take the same baits as northerns, but are notorious for violently striking 7- to 10-inch worms dropped in front of their noses. Perch are usually 6 to 9 inches, but larger ones are present. They can be taken on worms and small minnows.

DIRECTIONS: Head south out of Paul Smiths on NY 30 for about 6 miles.

ADDITIONAL INFORMATION: Locals launch canoes at the NY 30 bridge, and at the informal launch on Forest Home Road, off NY 30, about a mile west of the bridge. Forest Home Road offers several bank-fishing sites, as well.

CONTACT: New York State Department of Environmental Conservation Region 5 and Franklin County Tourism.

ST. REGIS CANOE AREA

Spread over 18,400 acres, spotted with ponds, this splendid piece of wilderness is the only area in the state designated exclusively for canoes. Two of its numerous ponds are connected by narrow channels. While the rest are landlocked, they're

normally less than 0.5 mile from neighboring ponds, down well-defined portages. The area's most prominent boundary is the Adirondack Scenic Railroad
skirting its south side.

Motors and the use or possession of baitfish are prohibited.

41. BEAR POND

KEY SPECIES: Brook trout.

DESCRIPTION: This 54-acre pond's shoreline is totally forested and its bottom
is rocky. It averages 22 feet deep and drops to a maximum depth of 60 feet.

TIPS: Use a sinking line to get a Montana nymph to the bottom. Run it at least
100 feet behind the boat and troll slowly by paddling around in a figure-eight
pattern.

THE FISHING: State fisheries biologist John Fieroh describes this pond as "a
snappy little brook trout water that's doing well. In the last survey, we took
24 brookies ranging from 7 to 16 inches." Retired fisheries biologist Rich
Preall claims, "Bear Pond can produce brookies in the 4–5 pound range, but
1–2 pounders are the common catch." Preall adds, "The key to the big boys
is to imitate the thousands of small pumpkinseeds that swarm the shoreline,
dredging the deep with sunfish-color/shade jigs and flies." The water is exceptionally clear and if one trout spots you, it's almost as if word gets out,
because they all clam up. It is essential you work the bait as far away from the
boat as possible and make no unnecessary moves. Wearing camo helps, too.

DIRECTIONS: Located about 0.5 mile due west of the bottom of Upper St. Regis
Lake (**site 36**). Take the portage on the southwestern corner of the lake for a
couple hundred yards to Bog Pond, paddle its length, and take the portage
on the west side for 150 yards to Bear Pond.

ADDITIONAL INFORMATION: The St Regis Canoe Wilderness borders roughly 75
percent of the pond, from the southeastern corner west to the northeastern
corner. Primitive camping is allowed.

CONTACT: New York State Department of Environmental Conservation Region 5.

42. LITTLE LONG POND (EAST)

KEY SPECIES: Brook trout, rainbow trout, and splake.

DESCRIPTION: The larger of the St. Regis Canoe Area's two Little Long Ponds,
this body of water covers 82 acres, averages 19 feet deep, and has a maximum
depth of 60 feet.

TIPS: Cast small crankbaits like Bass Pro Shops 3/16-ounce XPS Extreme Minnows
around the islands at dusk.

THE FISHING: This pond is managed as a coldwater fishery. Extensive stocking by
air and good habitat make it one of the St. Regis Canoe Area's top producers

of large trout. The state periodically stocks fingerling brook trout averaging 4.5 inches. Those that survive the drop from the airplane end up ranging from 8 to 12 inches. They'll hit worms and flies. Roughly 1,000 rainbow trout averaging 8 inches are stocked each year, too. They end up growing to between 12 and 16 inches and provide good sport all summer long on dry flies and in-line spinners. Several hundred yearling splake are thrown into the mix regularly. They end up 2 to 4 pounds and are targeted with streamers trolled deep, 8 inches or so behind attractors like Lake Clear Wabblers.

DIRECTIONS: Take the 0.25-mile portage on the south end of Bear Pond (**site 41**).

ADDITIONAL INFORMATION: Hardened campsites can be found at the portages on both ends, and several others ring the pond.

CONTACT: New York State Department of Environmental Conservation Region 5.

43. GREEN POND (ST. REGIS CANOE AREA)

KEY SPECIES: Brook trout.

DESCRIPTION: The northern—and runt—of the two Green Ponds in the town of Santa Clara, this 22-acre pond averages 18 feet deep and drops to a maximum depth of 30 feet; its floor is mostly sand, pebbles, and rock.

TIPS: Cast small spinners and spoons over and along the northeastern shoal.

THE FISHING: This pond boasts a thriving population of naturally reproducing brook trout. The state supplements their numbers by regularly stocking 1,500 fall fingerlings. Brookies average 8 inches, with quite a few growing larger, some up to 20 inches. Fish for them with worms or by drifting wet flies like March Browns.

DIRECTIONS: Take the 0.25-mile portage on Little Long Pond's (**site 42**) south end.

ADDITIONAL INFORMATION: There is a primitive campsite on the northwestern corner, just north of the portage to St. Regis Pond (**site 44**), and another on the south bank.

CONTACT: New York State Department of Environmental Conservation Region 5.

44. ST. REGIS POND

KEY SPECIES: Brook trout, lake trout, and splake.

DESCRIPTION: The largest of the ponds along the highly popular Seven Carries Route of the St. Regis Canoe Area, this 401-acre body of water averages 15 feet deep and has a maximum depth of 31 feet. Its wonderfully irregular shoreline is wooded, and it has several islands.

TIPS: Paddle-troll a Muddler Minnow on a sinking line.

THE FISHING: This pond is managed as a diverse coldwater fishery. The state regularly stocks a couple thousand splake averaging 10 inches. They find the pickings good and easily grow to 20 inches; 25-inchers have been reported. "Splake fishing seems to really turn on the last half of September . . . and there is no better time to be in the Adirondacks than that," advises retired fisheries biologist Rich Preall. They orient toward bottom and will take a large streamer. Brook trout occur naturally and range from 4 to 12 inches. They'll take a worm early in the season and flies in late May and June. Lake trout range from 12 to 25 inches. They take bucktail jigs or spoons jigged on bottom in deep water.

Minimum length for lake trout is 15 inches.

DIRECTIONS: Located about 0.25 mile due west of Green Pond (**site 43**) via trail.

ADDITIONAL COMMENTS: The pond has numerous beach campsites, including one on each of its two largest islands, and a lean-to on the southern point, at the entrance into the west bay.

CONTACT: New York State Department of Environmental Conservation Region 5.

45. OCHRE POND

KEY SPECIES: Brook trout and lake trout.

DESCRIPTION: This 22-acre pond is completely surrounded by wild forest, averages 18 feet deep, and has a maximum depth of 52 feet.

TIPS: Work a beadhead Woolly Bugger slowly on bottom with a sinking line.

THE FISHING: This lovely pond is managed for brook trout. The state stocks 800 every couple of years averaging 4.5 inches. Most are caught on worms by locals shortly after dropping in. Survivors are few . . . and savvy. A survey conducted earlier in the century revealed brookies average a whopping 12 inches, with a few reaching 16 inches. They will respond to a wet fly or streamer. Lake trout typically range from too small to 23 inches. Keepers are hard to come by. Most are taken after ice-out on spoons cast near shore. Come summer, a few are taken on streamers like Gray Ghosts and Black Nosed Daces tied about a foot behind a wobbler or similar attractor and trolled deep at paddling speed.

DIRECTIONS: Take the trail on the northwestern corner of St. Regis Pond's west bay (**site 44**) for about 0.4 mile.

ADDITIONAL INFORMATION: A campsite is on the east shore, several hundred feet north of the portage to St. Regis Pond.

CONTACT: New York State Department of Environmental Conservation Region 5.

46. FISH POND

KEY SPECIES: Brook trout and lake trout.

DESCRIPTION: This 116-acre pond averages 23 feet deep and has a maximum depth of 50 feet. Underwater springs keep it cool. Its outlet feeds Little Fish Pond (**site 47**).

TIPS: Use Black Nosed Dace or Black Ghost streamers after ice-out.

THE FISHING: This pond is notorious for wild lakers. Most are a little short, but enough keepers are around to claim a dedicated following of anglers who target them with streamers, spinners, and crankbaits early in the season and in autumn. In the summer, they head for deep water and respond to spoons jigged off bottom. The place used to get stocked heavily with brookies, but state surveys showed all they were doing was feeding the lakers, so the program was discontinued. Still, a lot of natural brookies averaging 8 inches are present, and anglers report catching 19-inchers with surprising regularity. They're most active close to shore in the early weeks of the season and respond to in-line spinners, small spoons, and streamers worked on sinking lines and jerked periodically to imitate the erratic behavior of panicking baitfish.

DIRECTIONS: Take the portage on Ochre Pond's (**site 45**) northwestern corner for about a mile (you'll pass tiny Mud Pond).

ADDITIONAL INFORMATION: The pond offers lean-tos on its north and south shores, and several hardened-beach campsites.

CONTACT: New York State Department of Environmental Conservation Region 5.

47. LITTLE FISH POND

KEY SPECIES: Brook trout and lake trout.

DESCRIPTION: This 24-acre pond averages 14 feet deep and has a maximum depth of 30 feet.

TIPS: Cast silver spoons after ice-out.

THE FISHING: This pond has wild brook trout averaging 9 inches. They respond most readily to worms in the spring; flies, tiny jigs, and lures the rest of the season. Lake trout, also naturally bred, are much more plentiful and reach up to 23 inches. Early in the season they can be caught near shore on spinners, crankbaits, and small tube jigs. Come summer, they go deep and take spoons and scented, soft plastic minnows jigged on bottom.

Minimum length for lake trout is only 15 inches.

DIRECTIONS: Head southwest for about 150 yards on the portage skirting Fish Pond's (**site 46**) outlet (northwestern corner).

ADDITIONAL INFORMATION: A primitive campsite is off the portage from Fish Pond, and another is in the pond's southwestern corner.

CONTACT: New York State Department of Environmental Conservation Region 5.

48. LITTLE LONG POND (WEST)

KEY SPECIES: Brook trout.

DESCRIPTION: This 40-acre pond averages 19 feet deep and has a maximum depth of 41 feet.

TIPS: Move carefully and wear camouflage.

THE FISHING: This pond's water ranks among the clearest in the Adirondacks. Living in such lucid environs makes the fish super spooky. If one spots you and panics, every trout in the drink takes cover and clams up. Indeed, during one survey, sloppy state personnel spooked the pond and only two brookies averaging 3.7 inches were netted. In a later survey, the experts were a little more careful and netted three brookies averaging 15 inches. Rich Preall says the more flattering survey is the accurate one. "This pond has produced state record brook trout in the past," says the retired fisheries biologist, "and big fish are still present. However, recent fishing pressure has been heavy (the word is out) so only the most patient and artful are finding the big ones."

The state stocks brook trout regularly (1,200 5-inchers in 2013). They grow to range anywhere from 6 to 20 inches, even bigger. The 20-something-inchers are few but they're definitely there, and will drive you crazy by rushing your dry fly, giving you a wink, and simply swimming away. According to Preall, some are taken by anglers running Woolly Buggers, on sinking lines, 100-something feet behind the canoe and trolling in a figure-eight pattern.

DIRECTIONS: South of Little Fish Pond (**site 47**), via a 150-yard portage.

ADDITIONAL INFORMATION: There is a campsite on the point poking out of the north shore.

CONTACT: New York State Department of Environmental Conservation Region 5.

49. LYDIA POND

KEY SPECIES: Brook trout.

DESCRIPTION: This 20-acre pond averages 21 feet deep and has a maximum depth of 38 feet.

TIPS: Paddle slowly and troll a cone-head Woolly Bugger.

THE FISHING: "This pond is named after the wife of famed guide and hotelier Paul Smith," says Rich Preall. The state manages it as a brook trout fishery and dumps 700 of them, averaging 4.5 inches, aerially each year. Those who hit the water swimming, and avoid becoming prey during their first few weeks of freedom, end up growing to range from 8 to 20 inches on the abundant minnow population. They take worms paddle-trolled slowly (the slower the better) behind wobblers in spring; flies, in-line spinners, and small spoons the rest of the year.

DIRECTIONS: About 200 yards west of Little Long Pond (**site 48**).

ADDITIONAL INFORMATION: There is a primitive campsite on the beach at the end of the portage from Little Long Pond.

CONTACT: New York State Department of Environmental Conservation Region 5.

50. KIT FOX POND

KEY SPECIES: Brook trout.

DESCRIPTION: Covering a little less than 10 acres, this pond averages 14 feet deep and has a maximum depth of 38 feet. This is another one of the clearest ponds in the mountains; its water is borderline acidic.

TIPS: Stay as invisible as possible by wearing colors matching the surroundings—that is, sky colors: blue and white if you're in a canoe, green and brown if you're fishing from the bank.

THE FISHING: The state stocks 500 brook trout averaging 4.5 inches aerially about every other year. The move from the hatchery fills them with a healthy fear of man. When the place was surveyed at the turn of the century, the researcher's nets failed to catch anything over 12 inches. However, state biologist Rich Preall, an expert fly fisherman, claims the pond "has been a consistent producer of brookies in the 14–16 inch range. I've seen some absolutely huge trout here, up to 20 inches." They strike wet flies and small lures.

DIRECTIONS: Head due south for a couple hundred yards on the portage at the southeastern tip of Little Long Pond (**site 48**).

ADDITIONAL INFORMATION: "Kit Fox seems to produce when fishing is off in nearby ponds," reveals Preall.

CONTACT: New York State Department of Environmental Conservation Region 5.

51. NELLIE POND

KEY SPECIES: Brook trout.

DESCRIPTION: This 13-acre pond averages 11 feet deep and has a maximum depth of 19 feet.

TIPS: Work Woolly Worms along the shore from mid-August through September.

THE FISHING: This water has been free of human intervention for years, and like all fisheries allowed to return to their natural state it doesn't make any promises. Its population of wild, Horn Lake strain brookies varies from year to year. "Sometimes there are good numbers of small fish, other years there are just a few big ones," explains retired fisheries biologist Rich Preall. Normally, they average about 6 inches, with a few going more than twice that. Not used to being treated gently by man or beast, these fish clam up at the slightest indication something isn't right, so careful presentation is essential. A tiny terrestrial dropped near a windfall in summer is always a good bet.

DIRECTIONS: Head southwest on the portage at the southwestern tip of Kit Fox Pond (**site 50**) for about 0.25 mile.

ADDITIONAL COMMENTS: There are a couple of campsites at the end of the portage from Kit Fix Pond. This pond and Bessie Pond (below) are named after the daughters of legendary Adirondack guide and developer Paul Smith, notes Preall.

CONTACT: New York State Department of Environmental Conservation Region 5.

52. BESSIE POND

KEY SPECIES: Brook trout.

DESCRIPTION: Measuring 16.5 acres, this pond averages 15 feet deep and has a maximum depth of 50 feet.

TIPS: Fish maggot patterns at a dead drift.

THE FISHING: Like its sister, Nellie Pond (**site 51**), this pond is a natural fishery, home to Horn Lake strain brook trout native to the Adirondacks. The fish range from 6 to 12 inches and will take wet flies worked at a dead drift, as well as leech-imitating streamers trolled deep on a sinking line.

DIRECTIONS: Head due south on the portage at the south end of Nellie Pond for a few hundred yards to the junction, turn left, and continue east for a few hundred feet.

ADDITIONAL COMMENTS: A primitive campsite is located on the west side, at the end of the portage from Nellie Pond.

CONTACT: New York State Department of Environmental Conservation Region 5.

53. CLAMSHELL POND

KEY SPECIES: Brook trout.

DESCRIPTION: Covering 35 acres, this pond averages 13 feet deep and has a maximum depth of 28 feet. A wetland clings to its southern tip.

TIPS: This is a local hot spot because it always produces big fish in early spring, before the weeds become a nuisance.

THE FISHING: The state manages this pond for brook trout. Springs keep it at just the right temperature year-round. The brookies average 8 inches, but 14-inchers are caught frequently. They hit worms trolled close to shore, behind wobblers in the spring, and in-line spinners in summer.

ADDITIONAL INFORMATION: Retired fisheries biologist Rich Preall warns: "Chubs and sunnies drive bait anglers crazy later in the spring."

DIRECTIONS: Head south for about 0.5 mile on the portage located at the end of the long bay on the southwestern corner of Fish Pond (**site 46**).

CONTACT: New York State Department of Environmental Conservation Region 5.

54. GRASS POND

KEY SPECIES: Brook trout.

DESCRIPTION: Spread over 22 acres, this pond averages 4.5 feet deep and has a maximum depth of 12 feet. It is bordered in equal measure by evergreens, shrubs, and wetland.

TIPS: Cast in-line spinners like Panther Martins.

THE FISHING: Although this pond is rather shallow, springs keep its temperature at ideal levels for brookies. The state airlifts over 1,000 averaging 4.5 inches every couple of years; those that hit the pond eventually end up averaging 10 inches. They have a taste for worms after ice-out; streamers and wet flies the rest of the time.

DIRECTIONS: Take the southern portage at the end of St. Regis Pond's (**site 44**) west bay for about 0.25 mile to the T. Bear right on a northwestern heading for about 0.1 mile to the next junction, turn left, and head due west for about 0.4 mile.

ADDITIONAL INFORMATION: A primitive beach campsite is at the end of the portage.

CONTACT: New York State Department of Environmental Conservation Region 5.

55. TURTLE POND

KEY SPECIES: Largemouth bass.

DESCRIPTION: This 68-acre pond averages 7 feet deep and has a maximum depth of 35 feet.

TIPS: Early in the morning, twitch a Rapala over the patch of weeds in front of the culvert.

THE FISHING: This pond's relatively warm water is loaded with bucketmouths ranging from 2 to 6 pounds. They hit soft jerkbaits ripped over the surface in and around lily pads, and Texas-rigged worms and craws tossed into windfalls and dragged along undercut banks.

DIRECTIONS: The easiest way to get here is to go through the culvert or over the tracks at the channel connecting it to the northwestern corner of Hoel Pond (**site 61**). It's also accessible via the mile-long portage at the southern end of Clamshell Pond (**site 53**).

ADDITIONAL INFORMATION: Campsites are located east and west of the culvert, on the point sticking out of the north bank, and in the northwestern corner.

CONTACT: Franklin County Tourism and New York State Department of Environmental Conservation Region 5.

56. SLANG POND

KEY SPECIES: Largemouth bass.

DESCRIPTION: Spread over 45 acres, this pond averages 10 feet deep and has a maximum depth of 19 feet.

TIPS: Cast a jig-rigged stickworm toward shore and drag it down the drop-off at the entrance to the southwestern bay for postspawn bucketmouths.

THE FISHING: This warmwater pond is loaded with largemouth bass that can range anywhere from 2 to 6 pounds, with larger fish possible. They find soft plastic jerkbaits worked through windfalls and around vegetation irresistible, especially early and late in the day.

DIRECTIONS: About 100 yards up the channel on Turtle Pond's (**site 55**) west end.

ADDITIONAL INFORMATION: Campsites are located at the northwestern tip, on the north shore point, and off the small bay tucked into the southeastern corner.

CONTACT: Franklin County Tourism and New York State Department of Environmental Conservation Region 5.

57. LONG POND

KEY SPECIES: Largemouth bass and smallmouth bass.

DESCRIPTION: Totally surrounded by forest, this remote pond sprawls over 338 acres, averages 12.5 feet deep, and has a maximum depth of 49 feet.

TIPS: Cast hard crankbaits around shoreline structure.

THE FISHING: Largemouth and smallmouth bass are about equally represented. Smallmouths ranging from 12 to 16 inches occupy rocky and muddy floors in 10 to 20 feet of water, where they'll take a worm or crayfish drifted on bottom. Largemouths up to 5 pounds claim shallower habitats near shore, especially around windfalls and emergent vegetation. There they respond to soft plastic swimbaits running in and out of the cover, and to noisy surface baits like buzzbaits and darters rumbling over it.

DIRECTIONS: From the NY 30/CR 46 intersection west of Saranac Inn, head west on Floodwood Road for roughly 4 miles and turn right at the sign. Or take the 0.25-mile portage midway down the west side of Slang Pond (**site 56**).

ADDITIONAL INFORMATION: This pond is about 0.5 mile from the parking area, down a well-beaten path. A very popular destination among wilderness travelers, it boasts several hardened campsites right on the water, mainly on points. Loons like the place, and their song fills the early evening.

CONTACT: New York State Department of Environmental Conservation Region 5.

58. MOUNTAIN POND (ST. REGIS CANOE AREA)

KEY SPECIES: Brook trout and bullhead.

DESCRIPTION: Nestled in deep woods, this 12-acre pond averages 10 feet deep and its maximum depth is 22 feet.

TIPS: Small Panther Martin spinners produce for a couple of weeks after ice-out.

THE FISHING: This pond is managed as a brook trout fishery. The state occasionally air-drops 450 or so 8-inchers. Those that survive the fall have a good chance of making it to 10 inches. Many fish up to 14 inches are present. Spinners and small plugs produce best in the spring. Recently bullheads have been appearing. As their number and size increase, the brook trout population may decrease. Still, these whiskered delicacies are here to stay for a little while, offering anglers some action when the brookies have lockjaw. They'll take worms, liver, and other bloody, smelly things fished on bottom.

DIRECTIONS: Head north for about 0.5 mile on the portage located on the east side of the point poking into the north end of Long Pond's (**site 57**) western arm.

ADDITIONAL INFORMATION: A campsite is located on the northwestern corner. A path runs along most of the pond, making shore fishing relatively easy.

CONTACT: New York State Department of Environmental Conservation Region 5.

59. PINK POND

KEY SPECIES: Largemouth bass.

DESCRIPTION: Covering 13 acres, this pond averages 6 feet deep and has a maximum depth of 14 feet.

TIPS: Use buzzbaits on still days.

THE FISHING: Largemouth bass run from 8 to 14 inches. Some get bigger. They hit crankbaits and bass bugs; wacky-rigged 4- to 7-inch worms ripped rapidly over the surface, or dragged on bottom on Texas rigs; and all the other usual suspects.

DIRECTIONS: About 0.25 mile due north via the channel coming into the north shore of Long Pond's (**site 57**) southwestern arm.

ADDITIONAL INFORMATION: The area's beavers are industrious, so be prepared to carry your canoe over dams.

CONTACT: New York State Department of Environmental Conservation Region 5.

OUTSIDE THE ST. REGIS CANOE AREA

60. RAT POND

KEY SPECIES: Brown trout.

DESCRIPTION: This 29-acre pond averages 12 feet deep and has a maximum depth of 29 feet. The Remsen–Lake Placid Railroad runs along its north shore.

TIPS: Apply herring oil or a similar masking scent to crankbaits.

THE FISHING: This pond is annually stocked with about 500 8-inch brown trout. Most are taken on dry flies by mid-June. The survivors become the smallest members of a trout population ranging from 10 to 18 inches. They take worms after a rain, silver spoons and crankbaits like Challenger Minnows the rest of the time.

The use or possession of baitfish is prohibited.

DIRECTIONS: The pond is located about 0.5 mile due north of Saranac Inn. Take the first dirt road on the north side of NY 30, just east of the eastern terminus of CR 46, and travel north about 0.25 mile.

ADDITIONAL INFORMATION: There are several primitive campsites on the west and east banks.

CONTACT: New York State Department of Environmental Conservation Region 5 and Franklin County Tourism.

61. HOEL POND

KEY SPECIES: Lake trout, landlocked Atlantic salmon, smallmouth bass, largemouth bass, and yellow perch.

DESCRIPTION: Located off one of the greens of the Saranac Inn Golf Course, 25 percent of this 455-acre pond's shoreline, mainly on the west bank, is developed with private homes. Averaging 30 feet deep, its maximum depth is 80 feet and it has good levels of dissolved oxygen throughout the water column.

TIPS: In the spring, flatline Sutton spoons.

THE FISHING: Lake trout are the primary predator and range from 2 to 10 pounds. They can be caught in the spring by flatlining crankbaits and spoons, and in summer by running these baits deep on Seth Green rigs. Atlantic salmon have been stocked periodically since 1996 (500 6.5-inchers in 2013) and anecdotal evidence indicates they do well, easily reaching 15 to 21 inches in length; a few 8-pounders have been caught over the years. In spring and fall they respond to tandem streamers and small Rapalas flatlined at a relatively fast clip. Smallmouth bass outnumber largemouths in the main lake and take worms, crayfish, and bucktail jigs tipped with scented baits like curly-tailed grubs. Largemouths claim the shallows along the shoreline and the northeastern bay, where they like floating crankbaits twitched on the surface. Perch range a decent 7 to 10 inches and hit worms and small lures.

DIRECTIONS: From the NY30/CR 46 intersection at Saranac Inn, head west on Floodwood Road for 0.4 mile and bear right on Hoel Road. Turn left onto the dirt road that parallels the golf course fairway 0.2 mile later and follow it to the cartop launch.

ADDITIONAL INFORMATION: Primitive camping is allowed on the public land bordering the north, south, and west sides; and there are hardened sites near the launch site and on the point on the north bank.

CONTACT: Franklin County Tourism and New York State Department of Environmental Conservation Region 5.

62. EAST PINE POND

KEY SPECIES: Largemouth bass and panfish.

DESCRIPTION: Nestled in deep forest, this 60.5-acre pond averages about 15 feet deep and has a maximum depth of 33 feet. Levels of dissolved oxygen are low below 20 feet.

TIPS: Work a weightless worm or soft jerkbait through windfalls and over vegetation.

THE FISHING: This pond has a good population of bucketmouths averaging 14 inches, a feisty size that spends almost as much time in the air as in the water when struggling to shake a hook. The shallow, northern bay contains the bulk of the pond's aquatic vegetation and is a great spot for working poppers and other topwater baits. State surveys indicate good populations of keeper panfish. Crappies reach over 12 inches long, bullheads can go 14 inches, yellow perch run 4 to 10 inches, and pumpkinseeds average 6 inches, with some stretching the tape to over 8 inches. All but the crappies like worms, and all but the bullheads will take streamers and wet flies.

DIRECTIONS: On Floodwood Road, 0.5 mile west of Floodwood Pond (**site 67**).

ADDITIONAL INFORMATION: Several primitive campsites are located at the cartop boat launch off Floodwood Road.

CONTACT: New York State Department of Environmental Conservation Region 5.

63. WEST PINE POND

KEY SPECIES: Brook trout, lake trout, and kokanee salmon.

DESCRIPTION: Primarily spring-fed, this 62.5-acre pond averages 18 feet deep and has a maximum depth of 38 feet.

TIPS: Drift near shore with a free-floating worm.

THE FISHING: Retired state fisheries biologist Rich Preall claims: "Reclamation plans for West Pine Pond remain on hold because the trout fishery is so good." This pond is best known for wild brookies ranging 6 to 10 inches long. They'll take small in-line spinners and jigs. Lake trout and kokanee salmon were stocked by mistake early in the century. Both took to the habitat very well and maintain their presence through natural reproduction. It's not uncommon to have "lakers up to 8 pounds test light tackle," says Preall. They'll take spoons jigged on bottom. "Kokanee may still be present," Preall adds, "but those soft-mouthed fish usually get off the line before they get in the boat." Ranging from 6 to 12 inches, they're known to take small worms trolled slowly behind attractors.

DIRECTIONS: From the NY 30/CR 46 intersection west of the hamlet of Saranac Inn, head west on Floodwood Road for about 4.8 miles to the dirt road on the left. Park and hike down the trail for about 0.5 mile. The trail ends at a canoe launch and beach campsite.

ADDITIONAL INFORMATION: You can also get there from East Pine Pond (**site 62**), via the portage on the southwest corner; you'll have to climb a steep esker.

CONTACT: New York State Department of Environmental Conservation Region 5.

64. GREEN POND

KEY SPECIES: Landlocked Atlantic salmon, splake, brown trout, and brook trout.

DESCRIPTION: Located across the street from a golf course, this pond's shoreline is partially developed with summer cottages. Spread over 63 acres, it averages about 40 feet deep and has a maximum depth of 69 feet.

TIPS: Work the edges of the shoal in the middle.

THE FISHING: Retired fisheries biologist Rich Preall says, "Most years the DEC puts 25–50 broodstock Atlantic salmon in Green Pond in early November. They chow down on the abundant alewife population," luring swarms of locals in the spring who try catching them with worms and silver minnowbaits. About 300 splake averaging 7.5 inches are stocked regularly. Many make it to 3 pounds, and some reach 8. The technique favored by locals is to drag a worm behind a Lake Clear Wabbler off bottom, in deep water, just fast enough to give it some action. Recently, the state has also been stocking several hundred yearling brown trout. Although they're dumb upon release, it only takes one brush with a hook to enlighten them in the ways of the world—they clam up quick. Many are reaching 5-pounds-plus and are often seduced by crankbaits like Storm's Jr. ThunderSticks. Fingerling brook trout are planted to the tune of 1,400 annually. They grow to 16 inches, some better, and take worms in the spring and fall, spinners and spoons in summer.

Use or possession of baitfish is prohibited.

DIRECTIONS: NY 30 brushes the pond's east side about a mile south of the hamlet of Saranac Inn.

ADDITIONAL INFORMATION: A fishing access site with a beach launch and parking for about 10 cars is on NY 30, a few hundred yards from its intersection with CR 46. Paddlers can get there by taking the 0.25-mile portage on the northern tip of Follensby Clear Pond (**site 68**).

CONTACT: New York State Department of Environmental Conservation Region 5.

65. POLLIWOG POND

KEY SPECIES: Lake trout, brown trout, and smallmouth bass.

DESCRIPTION: This 185-acre pond comes about as close to wilderness as you can get alongside an improved dirt road. Pristine and cool, it averages 33 feet deep and drops to a maximum depth of 72 feet.

TIPS: In summer, work a bucktail jig over deep rock fields.

THE FISHING: The state "started stocking lake trout in 2006 and a 2013 survey netted some up to 26 inches," says retired fisheries biologist Preall. They'll hit worm–Wabbler rigs, bucktail jigs, and minnows. The state annually stocks about 1,800 brown trout averaging 8 inches, with a couple hundred 14-inchers thrown in occasionally to keep things interesting. The small ones will take a dry fly on a warm, sunny afternoon in late spring or early summer. Bigger ones, up to 5 pounds, are a little smarter and hit worms after a rain, streamers and crankbaits during periods of low light. Lunker browns are smart so be patient and persistent. "Smallmouth bass appeared about 12 years ago and are now abundant inshore and range 10 to 18 inches," reveals Preall. They like crayfish, minnows, and Carolina-rigged finesse worms dragged on bottom in anywhere from 10 to 15 feet of water in spring and fall; twice that depth in summer.

DIRECTIONS: Take Floodwood Road for 1.1 miles from its intersection with CR 46/NY 30, west of Saranac Inn.

ADDITIONAL INFORMATION: There are several campsites (usually occupied) and two cartop boat launches off Floodwood Road. Use or possession of minnows is prohibited.

CONTACT: Franklin County Tourism and New York State Department of Environmental Conservation Region 5.

66. MIDDLE POND

KEY SPECIES: Bullheads, largemouth bass, northern pike, yellow perch, and panfish.

DESCRIPTION: This 60-acre pond averages 5 feet deep and has a maximum depth of 11 feet. Circled by lily pads and carpeted with weeds, it is ideal warmwater habitat.

TIPS: Still-fish worms on bottom for monster brown bullheads.

THE FISHING: Gallon for gallon, this pond harbors more bullheads stretching beyond 12 inches than most lakes twice its size. Ranging from 11 to 14 inches, these tasty bottom dwellers are often sought in the spring by local family groups teaching kids the pleasures of bank fishing. Fly fishermen find exciting action at the edges of lily pads with bass bugs. Cast into the middle of the bed and hop the offering from pad to pad to the last one at the edge of open water, then stop. Oftentimes this draws bass out of their cover to see what's bouncing on the roof. They sit impatiently, on the edge, waiting, sometimes even nosing up to the pad and tipping it, hoping to slide the critter off. Twitching the rod gently to send the bug into the drink often drives the bucketmouth to erupt through the surface in an exciting spray of foam and water to grab it. Northerns ranging from 18 to 22 inches are plentiful. They like buzzbaits and spinnerbaits. Perch from 6 to 8 inches and pumpkinseeds from 5 to 7 inches are also abundant and take worms suspended below tiny, marble-sized bobbers. Avoid using bobbers the size of softballs—they're too big for panfish to pull down.

DIRECTIONS: On Floodwood Road, about a mile west of Polliwog Pond (**site 65**).

ADDITIONAL INFORMATION: A beach launch for canoes with parking for about five cars, along with several primitive camping sites (they fill up fast), are off the shoulder of Floodwood Road.

CONTACT: New York State Department of Environmental Conservation Region 5.

67. FLOODWOOD POND

KEY SPECIES: Northern pike, largemouth bass, smallmouth bass, and panfish.

DESCRIPTION: This 222-acre pond has several private dwellings along its shore. Easy access makes it one of the most popular canoeing ponds in the Saranac Lakes Wild Forest. Averaging 17 feet deep, it has a maximum depth of 36 feet.

TIPS: Work lipless, rattling crankbaits parallel to drop-offs.

THE FISHING: This pond is dynamite warmwater habitat. Northern pike range between 4 and 10 pounds and seem particularly disposed to violently attacking any rattling crankbait violating the pond's silence. Largemouth bass ranging from 1 to 4 pounds are equally prejudiced against Rat-L-Traps but seem to have an identical aversion for surface baits that rattle. Smallmouth bass typically go from 0.75 to 2 pounds and like countdown crankbaits worked in open water, and spinnerbaits cast into structure like windfalls. Yellow perch up to 12 inches and pumpkinseeds exceeding 6 inches are plentiful. They'll hit tiny jigs and poppers, respectively. John Fieroh, a state fisheries biologist familiar with the beat, says this is a great pond for bullheads. They like worms still-fished on bottom. "Repeated rumors of black crappies, likely immigrants from East Pine Pond, have not been verified by the state," claims retired fisheries biologist Rich Preall.

DIRECTIONS: On Floodwood Road, 0.75 mile west of Middle Pond (**site 66**).

ADDITIONAL INFORMATION: There are several numbered campsites on the pond's shore and its largest island; beach camping permitted in designated sites only. A canoe launch on the shoulder of Floodwood Road has parking for about 10 cars.

CONTACT: New York State Department of Environmental Conservation Region 5.

68. FOLLENSBY CLEAR POND

KEY SPECIES: Northern pike, largemouth bass, smallmouth bass, landlocked Atlantic salmon, rainbow smelt, and panfish.

DESCRIPTION: Covering 491 acres, totally surrounded by state forest, this pond has several islands along with numerous shoals, points, and bays. It averages about 21 feet deep and has a maximum depth of 60 feet. The shoreline is totally undeveloped except for hardened campsites.

TIPS: Work the weeds on the southeastern end of the pond for bucketmouths.

THE FISHING: While their numbers have been down lately, there are still enough northern pike in the 22- to 36-inch range to make going after them worthwhile. The large numbers of big fish send small northerns into deep cover, so you hardly ever catch a "pin pike." Pikeasauruses are notorious for reacting with extreme prejudice to spinnerbaits and rattling crankbaits entering their space. Largemouth bass go from 12 to 18 inches and hit the same baits, but also have a taste for soft plastics like 7-inch worms and 3-inch scented minnows. Smallmouths range 1 to 3 pounds and like deeper habitat. They hang out in the channels between the islands and hit jigs tipped with minnows or crayfish. Landlocked salmon from 15 to 21 inches can be taken on tandem streamers and minnowbaits like Rapalas worked over the deep water due west of the northern access site. Smelt averaging 8 inches are popularly targeted in this same deep area by ice fisherman jigging smelt bellies. Yellow perch up to 10 inches, pumpkinseeds up to 8 inches, and brown bullheads up to 12 inches are plentiful and respond to worms.

DIRECTIONS: From the hamlet of Saranac Inn, head south on NY 30 for a little over 2 miles to the fishing access site; a shoulder access site is located about a mile farther south on NY 30, at the pond's southern tip. Canoeists can access the pond from the west bank of Upper Saranac Lake (**site 75**) by paddling up Fish Creek Bay, hugging the east shore of Fish Creek Pond, and taking the Spider Creek Passage.

ADDITIONAL INFORMATION: The north access site has a beach launch suitable for small trailered craft, and parking for about seven rigs. Several campsites punctuate the shoreline and islands.

CONTACT: New York State Department of Environmental Conservation Region 5.

69. HORSESHOE POND

KEY SPECIES: Brook trout, rainbow trout, and brown trout.

DESCRIPTION: Set entirely on forested state land, this 82-acre V-shaped pond averages 14 feet deep and has a maximum depth of 26 feet.

TIPS: Work a small spoon slowly with one rod and still-fish on bottom with worms on another right after ice-out.

THE FISHING: State aquatic biologist Rich Preall says this pond was reclaimed several times in the past century by killing all the fish with rotenone. It is managed as a brook trout fishery and boasts a naturally reproducing population. Still, the state stocks about 4,000 averaging 4 inches every other year or so. Brookies range from 8 to 15 inches; 20-inch trophies are possible. Roughly 1,000 rainbows averaging 9 inches are also stocked regularly, and many reach 12 to 16 inches. Brown trout were introduced accidentally a few years ago and the residual population, though not large, seems to be doing well on its own, with browns over 16 inches caught each year. Each species hits worms, flies, in-line spinners like Panther Martins, and minnowbaits.

Use or possession of baitfish is prohibited.

DIRECTIONS: Located a few hundred yards west of Follensby Clear Pond (**site 68**), via the portage at the end of the bay, midway down the lake; or by hiking 0.75 mile on the groomed trail from Fish Creek Ponds Public Campground (**site 70**).

ADDITIONAL INFORMATION: The pond has several campsites on its east bank. The possession or use of baitfish is prohibited.

CONTACT: New York State Department of Environmental Conservation Region 5.

70. FISH CREEK PONDS

KEY SPECIES: Northern pike, smallmouth bass, largemouth bass, panfish, landlocked salmon, and lake trout.

DESCRIPTION: This system consists of three ponds (four if you split the long one west of NY 30 into First and South Ponds) covering a combined total of 355 acres. The pond on the east side of the road and the long one on the west side are Fish Creek Ponds; the westernmost is Square Pond. The Fish Creek Ponds average 12 feet deep and drop to a maximum of 20 feet, while Square Pond averages 30 feet deep and has a maximum depth of 55 feet.

TIPS: Work 3-inch scented minnows, on dropshot rigs, along drop-offs.

THE FISHING: Relatively shallow, these ponds are ideal warmwater habitat. Northern pike range from 20 to 30 inches and largemouth bass from 12 to 16 inches. Both can be found virtually anywhere and provide consistent action to anglers throwing rattling crankbaits and jerkbaits. Bronzebacks from 10 to 14 inches are also present; the majority seems to migrate to Square Pond's drop-offs as the weather warms up. Vertically jig bladebaits like Heddon Sonars. Yellow perch up to 12 inches and pumpkinseeds up to 7 inches are plentiful and hit worms.

DEC stocked landlocked Atlantic salmon into Square Pond for five years at the beginning of the century; the program was discontinued in 2006. "Anglers may still catch a stray salmon or lake trout coming from Saranac

Lake or other ponds in the watershed," says retired fisheries biologist Rich Preall. Both like deep water—the salmon suspend and the lakers hug bottom. The Atlantics like flatlined tandem streamers and minnowbaits, while the lakers prefer spoons trolled near bottom or jigged in deep water.

DIRECTIONS: Take NY 3 south for about 13 miles from the village of Saranac Lake, then head north on NY 30 for about 4 miles to Fish Creek Ponds Public Campground.

ADDITIONAL INFORMATION: Fish Creek Public Campground skirts the entire system's shoreline west of NY 30. This fee area offers 355 no-frill sites, many on the beach, along with canoe and boat rentals, coin-operated showers, potable water, a dumping station, picnic areas, a basketball court, playing fields, a swimming beach, and a wood truck that comes around in the evening. A day-use fee is charged when the campground is open, mid-April through mid-November.

CONTACT: New York State Department of Environmental Conservation Region 5.

71. LITTLE SQUARE POND

KEY SPECIES: Smallmouth bass, largemouth bass, and northern pike.

DESCRIPTION: This 117-acre pond averages 10 feet deep and has a maximum depth of 29 feet.

TIPS: Cast buzzbaits along shore on quiet evenings.

THE FISHING: This warmwater fishery has good populations of smallmouth and largemouth bass ranging from 10 to 16 inches. As in many Adirondack ponds, largemouths are becoming far more numerous, causing some to speculate this is a sign of global warming. Both species can be taken on swimbaits, and on Texas- and Carolina-rigged worms. Northerns in the 22- to 32-inch range are also present. They hit spinnerbits and jerkbaits.

DIRECTIONS: Paddle up Fish Creek, or hike the trail skirting it, from the northern tip of Fish Creek Pond (west).

CONTACT: New York State Department of Environmental Conservation Region 5.

72. ROLLINS POND

KEY SPECIES: Lake trout, landlocked salmon, northern pike, smallmouth bass, brown bullheads, and pumpkinseeds.

DESCRIPTION: Covering approximately 442 acres, this pond averages 30 feet deep and has a maximum depth of 77 feet. Its west bank is completely forested.

TIPS: Pitch stickworms into snags.

THE FISHING: Lake trout averaging about 3 pounds are relatively abundant. The state supports their numbers by stocking them regularly, 720 7-inchers in

2013. They respond to minnows and spoons jigged on bottom in up to 55 feet of water—oxygen levels are too low below that. The state stocks several hundred landlocked Atlantic salmon regularly, as well. They end up averaging 15 inches and respond to small minnowbaits like Jr. ThunderSticks and silver spoons. This pond is notorious for northern pike ranging from 30 to 40 inches. They'll hit minnows, spinnerbaits, and spoons worked along the shoreline in 5 to 15 feet of water. Smallmouths in the 1- to 2-pound range are abundant and take deep-diving crankbaits, bucktail jigs, crayfish, and minnows. Brown bullheads run up to 14 inches and pumpkinseeds go from 5 to 7 inches. Both take worms.

Motorboats over 25 horsepower are prohibited.

DIRECTIONS: Head south on NY 3 out of Saranac Lake village for about 13 miles, then north on NY 30 for about 4 miles to the first entrance to Fish Creek Ponds Public Campground (**site 70**). Follow its road for about a mile, turn left on Rollins Pond Road, and travel for about a mile.

ADDITIONAL INFORMATION: Rollins Pond Public Campground skirts the entire east shore. This fee area offers 287 campsites suitable for everything from pup tents to RVs 40 feet long, coin-operated showers, a pumping station, canoe and rowboat rentals, and a paved ramp with parking for 10 rigs. A day-use fee is charged when the campground is open, mid-May through Labor Day.

Rollins Pond and Fish Creek Public Campgrounds honor each other's day use tickets. However, Fish Creek charges a slightly higher fee because it has a swimming beach. If all you want to do is fish, tell the attendant at the Fish Creek Campground gate you're heading to Rollins Pond; you'll be allowed to go through to pay the cheaper rate up ahead.

CONTACT: New York State Department of Environmental Conservation Region 5.

73. WHEY POND

KEY SPECIES: Brown trout and rainbow trout.

DESCRIPTION: This pond covers 108 acres, averages about 12 feet deep, and has a maximum depth of 20 feet. Its shoreline is completely undeveloped.

TIPS: Cast terrestrial patterns near shore at dusk.

THE FISHING: Easy access and a naturally reproducing population of Windfall strain brook trout made this pond one of the most popular fishing destinations in the Adirondacks up until this century. Indeed, it was so productive, it used to be one of the state's sources for brood-stock brook trout. "Recently, the fishery has fallen on hard times," laments former state fisheries biologist Rich Preall. "Brown bullheads have become superabundant, and it is now nearly impossible to catch a trout . . . I stopped stocking

Windfall [brookies] in 2013 and have now started stocking brown trout instead. Hopefully, the browns will enjoy eating baby bullheads and trim the population down. It will take 2–5 years to see if the browns can tame the bullheads. Rainbow trout stocking is being continued."This pond is restricted to artificial lures only.

DIRECTIONS: Nestled in the southeastern corner of Rollins Pond Public Campground (**site 74**), a 100-foot-long access trail, directly across the street from the campground's boat launch, leads to the pond.

ADDITIONAL INFORMATION: From Memorial Day to Labor Day, a day-use fee is charged noncampers because you have to take the Fish Creek Ponds Campground Road to Rollins Pond Road to get here. However, the cost is cheaper at Rollins Pond Campground because there's no swimming beach. Just tell the attendant at the Fish Creek Ponds gate you'll pay at Rollins Pond Campground; you'll be allowed to go through to get the lower rate.

CONTACT: New York State Department of Environmental Conservation Region 5.

74. BLACK POND

KEY SPECIES: Brook trout and rainbow trout.

DESCRIPTION: Completely surrounded by wild forest punctuated by a tiny wetland, this 20-acre pond averages 20 feet deep and has a maximum depth of 44 feet.

TIPS: Suspend worms below bubble bobbers.

THE FISHING: This small pond is stocked most years with about 300 brook trout fingerlings—recently reduced from 800. They do all right, growing to average 10 inches, and respond to worms and flies. Retired fisheries biologist Rich Preall says, "Black Pond rather than its neighbor Whey Pond is now the place Fish Creek Campers should pursue trout." The state also stocks anywhere from 100 to 400 rainbows averaging 9 inches annually. "This was done to improve growth rates . . . my angler contacts report that 14- to 16- inch rainbows are now showing up and the brookies seem bigger, too," says Preall. The rainbows hit spinners and silver or perch-colored spoons.

Use or possession of baitfish is prohibited.

DIRECTIONS: Located about 0.5 mile southeast of Whey Pond (**site 73**). Two footpaths lead there from the Rollins Pond Road, striking off into the bush a few hundred feet north of the shower building just beyond the intersection on the west side of Square Pond.

ADDITIONAL INFORMATION: This pond is very susceptible to acid rain and is limed regularly.

CONTACT: New York State Department of Environmental Conservation Region 5.

SARANAC LAKES CHAIN

Popular with canoeists and anglers alike, this web of waterways contains the Saranac River, Upper Saranac Lake, Middle Saranac Lake, Lower Saranac Lake, Weller Pond, Oseetah Lake, Kiwassa Lake, Lake Flower, Lake Colby, and several smaller ponds and feeder streams. All but Upper Saranac Lake and Lake Colby are connected by navigable stretches of the Saranac River.

75. UPPER SARANAC LAKE

KEY SPECIES: Lake trout, brown trout, rainbow trout, northern pike, smallmouth bass, largemouth bass, rainbow smelt, and yellow perch.

DESCRIPTION: This 4,776-acre lake averages 33 feet deep and has a maximum depth of 103 feet. Although only about 7 miles long, its shoreline is highly irregular; if you stretched it out, it would measure over 20 miles. Kick in the lake's islands and you get a couple more miles of beach.

TIPS: Cast small streamers near shore in spring for trout and yellow perch.

THE FISHING: Ever since the state stopped stocking Atlantic salmon, rainbow trout, and brown trout in 2004, lake trout averaging 10 pounds have been the bread-and-butter salmonid. They are normally targeted with spoons trolled deep on Seth Green and Christmas tree rigs. Recently DEC resumed stocking Atlantic salmon (3,300 7-inchers in 2013). They did well in the past (a survey conducted in 2006, two years after stocking ceased, resulted in more salmon than lakers), and there's no reason they shouldn't do well in the future. They like to hang out higher in the water column than lakers and respond to tandem streamers and small spoons flatlined at a pretty rapid clip, 1.7 mph or better. "The smelt in Upper Saranac Lake are large, ranging from 6 to 8 inches, so anglers need to think big baits to entice the lakers," suggests retired fisheries biologist Rich Preall, adding "Ice-fishing for smelt has been quite popular in recent years." Locals take the smelt by jigging strips of smelt belly through the ice. Several islands and the irregular shoreline's bays and shallow flats conspire to make this lake northern-pike- and smallmouth-bass-friendly. Pike range from 22 to 30 inches and respond best to large minnows, Dardevles, and chartreuse spinnerbaits. Bronzebacks average about 1.5 pounds and take live bait, curly-tailed grubs, Carolina-rigged 4-inch finesse worms, and spinnerbaits. Largemouth bass somehow found their way into the system and are becoming increasingly common. They range from 2 to 4 pounds and take surface poppers and darters.

Minimum length for lake trout is 23 inches. Ice fishing is permitted but tip-ups are prohibited.

DIRECTIONS: Take NY 3/30 east out of the hamlet of Tupper Lake for about 6 miles. When the highways separate, NY 30 heads north and parallels the lake's west bank.

ADDITIONAL INFORMATION: A dam midway down its outlet (the Saranac River) blocks boats from accessing this lake from Middle Saranac Lake. A state boat launch with a double-wide paved ramp and parking for 50 rigs is on CR 46, in the north-shore hamlet of Saranac Inn. Bank fishing is prohibited at the launch site.

CONTACT: Saranac Lake Area Chamber of Commerce and the New York State Department of Environmental Conservation Region 5.

75A. Indian Carry Fishing Access Site

DESCRIPTION: This site has a beach launch for cartop craft and parking for 15 cars.

DIRECTIONS: Head west on NY 3 from Saranac Lake Village for about 10 miles to the sign on Old Dock Road.

76. SARANAC RIVER

KEY SPECIES: Northern pike, smallmouth bass, largemouth bass, walleyes, brown trout, rainbow trout, landlocked salmon, yellow perch, and panfish.

DESCRIPTION: Spawned as the outlet of Upper Saranac Lake, this river flows northeast for about 60 miles to its mouth in Lake Champlain at Plattsburgh. Along the way, it feeds and drains several lakes and ponds and picks up its North Branch in Clayburg, New York.

TIPS: Jig salted tubes in rapids and deep holes, and along outcrops, deadfalls, and undercut banks, for smallmouths, walleyes, and northern pike.

Blue heron fishing on the Saranac River.

THE FISHING: This river's greatest predator is the northern pike. Ranging from 22 all the way to 40-something inches, the species is true to its nature, hitting anything bite-sized that moves. Locals target them with tandem streamers in fast water, big minnows, large bucktail spinners, and jigs in pools and slow runs. Smallmouth bass between 10 and 16 inches reign in deep channels, large pockets, and the rapids at the heads and tails of pools, where they can be taken on live bait and soft plastic tubes, grubs, and jerkbaits. Probe lily pads, slop lines where wetlands brush the stream, and the weed edges at drop-offs, with jig-n-pigs and jig-n-craws for bucketmouths ranging from 1 to 3 pounds. Walleyes running from 15 to 18 inches hang out in deep channels, especially downstream of the Franklin Falls dam, and relish bucktail jigs fished plain or tipped with a Berkley Honey Worm or half a night crawler. Yellow perch up to 12 inches, rock bass up to 8 inches, pumpkinseeds between 5 and 8 inches, and bullheads running 8 to 14 inches thrive in slow sections of the river. The perch and rockies take small minnows and lures; the sunnies hit flies and poppers; and they all love worms.

Each year, the state stocks about 10,500 brown trout ranging from 8 to 15 inches and 4,600 rainbow trout averaging 8.5 inches. Many overwinter, and numerous others enter the river from tributaries. Also, a lot of Lake Champlain browns ranging from 16 to 20 inches run the lower river near the mouth in fall and spring. They're targeted by purists casting salmon flies and meat anglers using live bait. In addition, tens of thousands of Atlantic salmon fry are stocked annually into the river near Plattsburgh. Spending most of their lives in Lake Champlain, landlocks stage two major runs each year. The largest numbers appear April through mid-May and average 18 inches. Autumn sees fewer fish—but they're bigger, up to 8 pounds. They seem hungriest in the spring, but hit worms, lures, and streamers during both runs. Some lake-run rainbows in the 1- to 3-pound class are present from autumn through spring, and take worms, egg sacs, small spinners, and plugs.

DIRECTIONS: NY 3 parallels much of the river, and many informal pull-offs exist along the shoulder.

ADDITIONAL INFORMATION: The lower river up to the first dam impassable by fish is governed by special regulations, including restrictions on terminal tackle and fishing hours, all of which are listed in the special Lake Champlain Regulations section of the New York State Department of Environmental Conservation *Fishing Regulations Guide*. Many stretches of this river have special regulations, including catch-and-release-only sections. Check the Essex and Clinton County sections in Region 5's "exceptions to the statewide angling regulations" in the *NY Fresh Water Official Regulations Guide* for details.

CONTACT: Saranac Lake Area of Commerce, Plattsburgh–North Country Chamber of Commerce, and New York State Department of Environmental Conservation Region 5.

Fishing the Saranac River.

76A. Second Pond Fishing Access

DESCRIPTION: Located on a bulge in the river, this state site boasts parking for 100 rigs and two paved ramps. It's a popular alternative to launching on Lake Flower (**site 82**) because it shaves off an hour and a lock-through from the trip to Lower Saranac Lake.

DIRECTIONS: From its intersection with NY 86 in the heart of Saranac Lake village, head west on NY 3 for 3.2 miles.

ADDITIONAL INFORMATION: The registration kiosk for camping on the Saranac Lake Islands Campground is located on-site.

76B. Fishing Access

DESCRIPTION: This village site, straddled by three-car parking lots, offers access to a long stretch of flat water below some fishy rapids.

DIRECTIONS: At the Pine Street bridge in the village of Saranac Lake.

ADDITIONAL INFORMATION: This spot offers good trout fishing early in the season and has been known to surrender huge northern pike in the fall.

76C. Canoe-Fishing Route

DESCRIPTION: Retired fisheries biologist Rich Preall claims this stretch of river is a great float trip for smallmouth bass and northern pike, punctuated by countless fallfish, some over a foot long, and rock bass. "Only about 4 miles long by road, the river's twists and turns and its numerous pools and deep runs will take you all day to fish," he says.

DIRECTIONS: Launch at the sewage treatment plant on NY 3, north of Saranac Lake village (park across the road), and take out at the next bridge downstream.

76D. Fishing Access

DESCRIPTION: Located a little below the foot of the 1.8-mile stretch of Class II and III white water locals call the Permanent Rapids, this scenic pool is easy to reach from the road by a 100-something-yard hike and an environmentally friendly stone staircase.

DIRECTIONS: Take NY 3 east out of Saranac Lake village for about 6 miles to Bloomingdale, hook a right onto River Road (CR 18) after crossing the bridge over Sumner Creek, and travel 4.1 miles to the parking area (nothing but a notch in the road big enough for three cars) about 100 feet past the end of the guardrail.

ADDITIONAL INFORMATION: A hardened campsite is just off the parking lot.

Pool below the Permanent Rapids (site 76D), Saranac River.

76E. Fishing Access

DESCRIPTION: This site has parking for five cars.

DIRECTIONS: Head east out of Saranac Lake village on NY 3 for 24 miles to Clayburg. Turn south on CR 1 (Silver Lake Road).

ADDITIONAL INFORMATION: The North Branch of the Saranac River enters the main stem at Clayburg.

76F. Fishing Access

DESCRIPTION: This site has parking for five cars.

DIRECTIONS: About 1 mile south of **site 76E.**

76G. Fishing Access

DESCRIPTION: This site has parking for five cars.

DIRECTIONS: About 1 mile south of **site 76F.**

76H. Fishing Access

DESCRIPTION: This site has parking for five cars.

DIRECTIONS: Head east out of Clayburg on NY 3 for about 2.5 miles to Redford and turn south on Cane Road.

76I. Parking

DESCRIPTION: The State University of New York field house parking lot is huge and close to some of the best seasonal salmon and trout action on the river.

DIRECTIONS: Off Ruger Street, Plattsburgh.

76J. Fishing Access

DESCRIPTION: This site has a handicapped fishing platform and shoulder parking for about five cars.

DIRECTIONS: At the Macdonough Monument, off City Hall Place, Plattsburgh.

76K. Fishing Access

DESCRIPTION: This site, located at the mouth of the river, has a hard-surface ramp and parking for 20 cars, It's popular with surf anglers.

DIRECTIONS: On Green Street (off US 9/Bridge Street), Plattsburgh.

77. MIDDLE SARANAC LAKE

KEY SPECIES: Northern pike, smallmouth bass, and yellow perch.

DESCRIPTION: Spread over 1,393 acres, this lake averages 9 feet deep and its maximum depth is 21 feet. The shoreline is virtually undeveloped.

TIPS: Drag Carolina-rigged finesse worms off points and around boulder fields for smallmouth bass.

THE FISHING: This warmwater fishery is loaded with northern pike ranging from 2 to 6 pounds. While they take minnows, they can't seem to keep their mouths shut around spinnerbaits. Smallmouth bass average 1.5 pounds and hit crankbaits like Bomber Long A's. Perch average 7 inches and hit worms and small crayfish.

DIRECTIONS: Nestled in the Adirondack high peaks, off NY 3, midway between the hamlets of Saranac Lake and Tupper Lake.

ADDITIONAL INFORMATION: Most folks get to this lake by launching on the Saranac River at the State Bridge (Second Pond) Fishing Access Site (paved ramp, parking for 75 rigs, toilets), 6 miles west of Saranac Lake village on NY 3. Head upstream, turn left, and head southwest on Lower Saranac Lake for about 4 miles to the mouth of the Saranac River. Middle Saranac Lake is about 2.75 miles upstream. You'll have to go through a small no-fee lock to get around a set of rapids. A lock tender is usually present on weekends but if he's not, instructions on site show how to operate the thing.

This lake has several islands, and the larger ones have primitive campsites. Permits are needed to camp. They are available at the State Bridge Boat Launch Site.

CONTACT: Saranac Lake Area Chamber of Commerce or New York State Department of Environmental Conservation Region 5.

Fighting one that got away on the Saranac River.

77A. South Creek Fishing Access Site

DESCRIPTION: Beach launch for cartop craft and parking for 20 cars.
DIRECTIONS: Head southwest out of Saranac Lake village on NY 3 for about 10 miles.

78. WELLER POND (FRANKLIN COUNTY)

KEY SPECIES: Northern pike, largemouth bass, smallmouth bass and panfish.
DESCRIPTION: This 180-acre wilderness pond averages 10 feet deep and has a maximum depth of 22 feet.
TIPS: Ricochet a rattling crankbait off timber poking through the surface, and brace yourself for a violent strike when it hits the water.
THE FISHING: This small pond has good numbers of northern pike between 18 and 24 inches. What these guys lack in size they more than make up for in vicious strikes. They like noisy baits like Rat-L-Traps. Largemouth bass range from 1 to 2.5 pounds. They react violently to stickworms dropped along the edges of vegetation and into weed openings, and jerkbaits worked in timber. Smallmouth bass also claim the shallows, especially during morning and evening calms, but they're more likely to suspend over drop-offs and rock beds in deep water. They'll take the same baits bucketmouths do, but also respond enthusiastically to Carolina- and Texas-rigged worms and craws dragged on the floor. Yellow perch up to 10 inches, pumpkin-seeds in the 5- to 7-inch range, and bullheads averaging 10 inches are plentiful and hit worms.
DIRECTIONS: There are no roads to the pond. Boats can get there from Middle Saranac Lake by heading up the slow-moving channel at the northeastern corner of Hungry Bay, the big bay in the middle of the lake's north shore.
ADDITIONAL INFORMATION: There's a lean-to in the northwestern corner, as well as several hardened campsites along the shore and on Tick Island, just off the large point on the west bank.
CONTACT: Saranac Lake Area Chamber of Commerce and New York State Department of Environmental Conservation Region 5.

79. LOWER SARANAC LAKE

KEY SPECIES: Northern pike, smallmouth bass, largemouth bass, walleyes, yellow perch, and pumpkinseeds.
DESCRIPTION: This 2,214-acre lake averages 28 feet deep and has a maximum depth of 65 feet. Its shoreline is lightly developed with summer cottages and commercial establishments, including an apartment complex and a marina.
TIPS: Work 3-inch scented worms on dropshot rigs below island cliffs and along the shoals poking out of the waves in various parts of the lake.

THE FISHING: This lake's northern pike range from 4 to 10 pounds, but some monsters twice that size are caught through the ice on big minnows each year. Smallmouths range from 8 to 22 inches and hit fat-bodied crankbaits, tube jigs, and 4-inch worms on Carolina rigs. Bucketmouths typically run from 1.5 to 4 pounds, but 6-pounders are reported regularly. They hang out in shoreline vegetation and windfalls and respond to buzzbaits, spinnerbaits, and Texas-rigged or free-floating plastic worms tossed into cover and structure. The state stocked about 40,000 advanced walleye fingerlings annually for several years starting in 1999, but discontinued the program after "surveys in 2005 and 2006 only caught three walleyes total (versus hundreds of smallmouths)," explains retired fisheries biologist Rich Preall. Some "oops" walleyes are still caught every now and then on jigs and crankbaits targeting bronzebacks. Yellow perch range from 6 inches to a whopping 14 inches and love 2-inch scented grubs and small minnows. Pumpkinseeds grow to a respectable 8 to 10 inches and hit worms. Both yellow perch and sunfish are popular with ice fishermen, who catch them on ice jigs tipped with grubs.

DIRECTIONS: Off NY 3 on the west side of the village of Saranac Lake.

ADDITIONAL INFORMATION: The State Bridge fishing access site on NY 3, 6 miles west of Saranac Lake village, offers hard-surface ramps, parking for 75 rigs, and toilets. Lower Saranac Lake is peppered with undeveloped islands; the bigger ones make up the Saranac Lake Islands Public Campground. A permit is needed to camp at the hardened sites and can be obtained at the ranger shack at the State Bridge fishing access site.

CONTACT: Saranac Lake Area Chamber of Commerce and New York State Department of Environmental Conservation Region 5.

79A. Ampersand Bay Public Launch

DESCRIPTION: This is the site DEC uses when working on the Saranac Lakes Chain. It offers a hard-surface ramp and parking for about five cars in the lot directly above the launch turnaround. No trailers are allowed in the parking lot. The curfew is strictly enforced and the gate is closed at the posted time, normally 8 p.m.

THE FISHING: One of the lake's most productive spawning grounds for warmwater species, Ampersand Bay is a massive fish nursery, a favorite haunt of predators ranging from largemouth bass and northern pike to panfish.

DIRECTIONS: Take NY 3 south out of the heart of Saranac Lake village for about 2 miles, turn right on Edgewood Road, then head left a few hundred yards later.

Ampersand Bay public access site, west side of Saranac Lake village.

80. OSEETAH LAKE

KEY SPECIES: Largemouth bass, smallmouth bass, northern pike, and panfish.

DESCRIPTION: This 826-acre body of water only averages 3 feet deep and has a maximum depth of 7 feet. Its flats are punctuated with ancient stumps and submerged snags. The shoreline is largely undeveloped, and a scenic ring of high peaks, including McKenzie and Scarface Mountains, towers over it.

TIPS: Keep an eye out for snags when running your motor outside the buoys marking the channel.

THE FISHING: Largemouth bass grow big in this fertile habitat. They average 1.5 pounds, and 5-pounders are common. Darters, propbaits, and weightless worms worked around stumps generally produce explosive strikes. Smallmouths up to 16 inches hang out along the ancient riverbed and the fast water in the channels leading to neighboring lakes. They respond to spinnerbaits, tubes, and curly-tailed grubs. Northern pike ranging from 3 to 10 pounds are so plentiful, locals expect to catch 20 or more every time they go out. They're partial to spinnerbaits and jerkbaits worked over weed beds and other cover, especially around the islands. Yellow perch easily reach 10 inches, pumpkinseeds average 7 inches, and bullheads get up to 12 inches. The perch and sunnies hang out in any cover they can find and take worms, tiny jigs, and flies; the bullheads like the muddy flats and respond to worms still-fished on bottom after dark, and on overcast days, particularly after a rain.

DIRECTIONS: Connected to the southern end of Lake Flower (**site 82**) by a navigable channel.

ADDITIONAL INFORMATION: The easiest way to get here is to launch at the Lake Flower state ramp on NY 86, in the heart of the village of Saranac Lake, and head due south.

CONTACT: Saranac Lake Area Chamber of Commerce and New York State Department of Environmental Conservation Region 5.

81. KIWASSA LAKE

KEY SPECIES: Largemouth bass, smallmouth bass, northern pike, walleyes, and panfish.

DESCRIPTION: This 282-acre lake has an average depth of 21 feet and a maximum depth of 45 feet. Roughly 50 percent of its shoreline is developed with summer homes.

TIPS: If you launch from the beach at the end of Kiwassa Lake Road, don't block private driveways when you park.

THE FISHING: This lake is a local favorite because the fish always seem to cooperate.

Largemouth bass averaging 2 pounds occupy the northern and southwestern bays, and love spinnerbaits and poppers. Smallmouth bass ranging from 1.5 to 3 pounds hang out on drop-offs and the humps in the southwestern corner, hitting everything from spinner-rigged curly-tailed grubs and 3-inch artificial minnows on dropshot rigs to jerkbaits and fat-bodied crankbaits. Northerns average about 4 pounds, but fish up to 10 pounds are taken regularly. They're partial to live minnows but also like spinnerbaits, flatfish, and minnow-imitating crankbaits. Retired fisheries biologist Rich Preall says a 2006 survey convinced him to stock walleyes. "We caught three averaging 20 inches, plus plenty of yellow perch forage. The new policy started in 2014 and will go for 5 years." Yellow perch range from 6 to 12 inches, pumpkinseeds 6 to 10 inches, and rock bass 5 to 8 inches. They like a worm suspended a couple of feet below a tiny bobber and cast into windfalls, or fished on bottom near shore.

DIRECTIONS: At the end of the 0.5-mile-long channel entering the north end of Oseetah Lake's (**site 80**) western bay.

ADDITIONAL INFORMATION: A beach launch is at the end of Kiwassa Lake Road, 2.2 miles from its intersection with NY 3 in the village of Saranac Lake. Parking for about five cars and shoulder parking for about three rigs.

CONTACT: Saranac Lake Area Chamber of Commerce and New York State Department of Environmental Conservation Region 5.

82. LAKE FLOWER

KEY SPECIES: Northern pike, largemouth bass, smallmouth bass, and panfish.

DESCRIPTION: This 166-acre lake's average depth is 5 feet and its maximum depth is 12 feet. Created by a dam built on the Saranac River to power sawmills, the area was quickly settled and Saranac Lake village sprang up on its north shore.

TIPS: Flatline Mepps bucktail spinners for northern pike.

THE FISHING: Northern pike range from 4 to 7 pounds, but 10-pounders are common and 15-pounders are possible. They take minnows drifted or suspended below bobbers, and spoons like Dardevles trolled along the channel drop or cast at right angles to shore. This lake is loaded with bucketmouths weighing between 2 and 4 pounds. They hit buzzbaits worked around lily pads or Texas-rigged worms pitched under docks. Though not as common as their bigmouthed cousins, smallmouths in the 1- to 2-pound range are plentiful enough to make targeting them worthwhile. Jigging or dragging salted tubes on bottom is a productive technique for these scrappy fighters. Perch averaging 8 inches are plentiful and mouth every small minnow and 2-inch curly-tailed grub they can find. Rock bass and pumpkinseeds averaging 7 inches and brown bullheads up to 14 inches are delicious local favorites. The sunfish and rockies respond to wet and dry flies and poppers. The bullheads like worms still-fished on bottom. "A popular local shore-fishing spot for bullheads is near the tennis courts on the east side of the lake," reveals retired fisheries biologist Rich Preall.

ADDITIONAL INFORMATION: A two-lane, paved boat launch is on NY 86, in the heart of the village of Saranac Lake. The parking lot has 6 spots for cars and 15 for rigs.

CONTACT: Saranac Lake Area Chamber of Commerce and the New York State Department of Environmental Conservation Region 5.

83. FRANKLIN FALLS POND

KEY SPECIES: Northern pike, smallmouth bass, walleyes, yellow perch, and brown bullheads.

DESCRIPTION: This 455-acre impoundment on the Saranac River measures 2.5 miles long by 0.75 mile wide, averages 10 feet deep, and has a maximum depth of 30 feet. Mostly forested, its banks are punctuated with several camps.

TIPS: Work the eddies around the river's mouth and along channel drops with jigs.

THE FISHING: The NYSDEC website claims: "Walleye is king here . . ." The state started a five-year walleye stocking program in 1998, releasing 9,000 4-inchers annually. Rich Preall, a retired aquatic biologist assigned to the beat at the time, says: "There was great survival and a huge increase in fishing pressure." When the stocking stopped, the fishing pressure abated. Natural reproduction sustains the fishery, and the last survey showed walleyes range from 16 to 25 inches. Troll for them with crankbaits or drift with worms on spinner harnesses. Northern pike typically range from 18 to 22 inches and hit any spinnerbait or crankbait they can fit in their mouths. Smallmouths average 13 inches and like minnows and crayfish drifted along the old river channel. Yellow perch averaging 7 inches and brown bullheads up to 14 inches are plentiful. Both hit worms; the perch also like minnows and tiny jigs.

Walleyes are plagued with high concentrations of chemicals. The state advises against eating them.

DIRECTIONS: Take NY 3 north out of the village of Saranac Lake for about 6 miles to Bloomingdale, turn right on River Road (CR 18), and travel for 4.9 miles.

ADDITIONAL INFORMATION: The state fishing access site on CR18 offers a beach launch for cartop craft, parking for eight cars, and shore-fishing access. Additional access sites dot the shoulder of CR 18, including a large landing just above the dam. Several hardened-beach campsites are available on the south end off CR 18 and on the big islands; first come, first served. Camping is prohibited on the smaller islands.

CONTACT: New York State Department of Environmental Conservation Region 5.

84. UNION FALLS POND (FLOW)

KEY SPECIES: Northern pike, smallmouth bass, walleye, yellow perch, and brown bullheads.

DESCRIPTION: This 1,672-acre Saranac River impoundment averages 10 feet deep and has a maximum depth of 22 feet. Rocky and shallow around the edges, filled with water stained dark brown, this impoundment is tricky to navigate with a motor.

TIPS: Be on the lookout for eagles begging for fish.

THE FISHING: "Union Falls has one of the best balanced fish communities in the Adirondacks," reports retired fisheries biologist Rich Preall. Northerns grow to a respectable 30 inches and strike minnows and their imitations worked near cover. Smallmouth bass range from 12 to 15 inches and also like minnows but quite a few are taken on spinnerbaits with tandem blades. This was one of only two lakes in the Adirondacks in which the authorities stocked 228,000 walleye fry annually for several years early in the century. The program was discontinued in 2006 when it was determined the walleyes were able to sustain their population through natural reproduction. Typically running from 1 to 3 pounds, they like worms, bladebaits, and jigs worked on bottom. "Walleye anglers do best by fishing the sloping sides of the old river channel as it winds around in the impoundment," advises Preall. Yellow perch averaging 11 inches and brown bullheads up to 14 inches are plentiful and take worms or crayfish fished on bottom.

DIRECTIONS: Head north from **site 83** on CR 18 (it turns to CR 48 when you cross the county line) for less than a mile.

ADDITIONAL INFORMATION: While there is no formal fishing access site, locals fish from shore—and launch cartop craft—from the shoulder of CR 48, on the east side of the Saranac River, just below the Franklin Falls Pond dam. You'll have to float a few hundred feet to the lake. This area is a well-established bald eagle nesting site, and anglers are advised to stay out of the bay cordoned off by buoys on the east shore. These big raptors are notorious mooches, and locals call them the begging eagles. Another curious thing about this place is that even though it is directly below Franklin Falls, eating the fish falls under the state's regular health advisory.

CONTACT: New York State Department of Environmental Conservation Region 5.

85. WEST BRANCH AUSABLE RIVER

KEY SPECIES: Brook trout, brown trout, and rainbow trout.

DESCRIPTION: Spawned in the shadow of Mount Marcy, the highest peak in the Adirondack Mountains, this splendid river runs independently for about 30 miles before linking up with the East Branch at Ausable Forks. Along the way, it undergoes many changes in character, everything from quiet and gentle flows through fertile mountain meadows to raging white water squeezed between austere mountain cliffs. Every trout habitat imaginable can be found in its path, earning the West Branch a reputation as one of the greatest trout streams in the Northeast.

TIPS: In the opening weeks of the season, fish worms and minnows slowly on bottom in pools and deep runs.

THE FISHING: Brook trout up to 10 inches occupy the wilderness portion of the river a few miles south of the village of Lake Placid. In addition, a few lunker speckled trout, refugees from the numerous tiny feeders, are caught each year in other sections of the river. They are mostly taken with worms and small spoons like Dardevles. One of the most heavily stocked streams in the state (24,270 browns averaging 8.5 inches and 1,600 two-year-olds in 2014; 1,625 rainbows averaging 13.5 inches and 750 18-inchers in 2013; and 1,550 8-inch brook trout in 2013), the West Branch is loaded with salmonids from the Olympic ski jumps towering over the south side of Lake Placid village all the way to Ausable Forks. A combination of plentiful cover (boulder fields, windfalls, and heavily wooded undercut banks), cool water temperatures (maintained by cold mountain springs, shady banks, and sun-blocking cliffs), and a good food supply (abundant populations of aquatic and terrestrial insects, crayfish, and minnows) conspire to make the river ideal trout habitat. Fish between 12 and 16 inches are common, and browns and rainbows tipping the scale at 8-something-pounds are caught every year. The fish can be taken on everything from minnows and worms to spoons, in-line spinners, streamers, and flies.

The West Branch offers a couple of catch-and-release, artificial-lures-only sections that are open to year-round angling. One stretches from the mouth of Holcomb Pond Outlet, off River Road (CR 21), to the marked boundary 2.2 miles downstream of Monument Falls; the other runs from the Whiteface Ski Center bridge downstream to the NY 86 bridge.

DIRECTIONS: NY 86 parallels the river from the bridge just north of the village of Lake Placid all the way to Wilmington, offering numerous pull-offs and parking areas.

ADDITIONAL INFORMATION: When this book was being written in 2015, retired fisheries biologist Rich Preall noted: "The most recent DEC angler survey found that the West Branch was voted the most popular fishing site in all of New York State." Located a little west of the stream's headwaters, Lake Placid Village, site of the 1936 and 1980 Olympic Games, offers food and lodging spanning the price spectrum. Primitive camping is allowed on forest preserve lands skirting the stream.

CONTACT: New York State Department of Environmental Conservation Region 5.

85A. Wilmington Notch Public Campground

DESCRIPTION: A fee area on the east edge of the Wilmington Notch, a deep canyon carved out of the granite mountain by the river, this scenic campground offers 54 sites, showers, toilets, and a trailer dumping station. Open from April through October.

DIRECTIONS: Head north on NY 86 out of Lake Placid village for 8 miles.

ADDITIONAL INFORMATION: The campground's west side sits 300 feet above the river; a steep, difficult trail leads down. The entrance to Whiteface Mountain Ski Area, site of the 1980 Winter Olympic Games, is s short distance north of the campgrounds.

86. EAST BRANCH AUSABLE RIVER

KEY SPECIES: Brown trout and rainbow trout.

DESCRIPTION: Starting out as the outlet of Lower Ausable Lake, this river snakes north for about 25 miles to join the West Branch at Ausable Forks. Relatively mild-mannered compared with its sibling, the East Branch is far safer and easier to wade.

TIPS: Fish the runs and pools around tributary mouths.

THE FISHING: While not as generously stocked as its western sibling, the East Branch Ausable still gets loads of public assistance: The state released 8,700 browns, 2,370 rainbows, and 2,400 brookies averaging 8.5 inches in 2014. From mid-May through early June, when water temperatures are rising and the river is downsizing from spring runoff to summer levels, it becomes wonderful dry-fly fishing territory through most of its length, and large patterns like the Irresistible and Ausable Wulff are productive. Come July and August, the pickings turn slim as trout hole up in the river's few widely scattered pools and runs or migrate into small feeders. According to retired state fisheries biologist Rich Preall: "Hurricane Irene [1999] and Tropical Storm Sandy [2012] benefited the East Branch by scouring new holes and blowing out finer silts. A Trout Unlimited stream improvement project just west of Keene Valley has benefited about a third of a mile of formerly heavily eroded streambank, creating new pools, riffles, and runs with vegetated banks."

DIRECTIONS: NY 73 parallels the river through the Keene Valley, and NY 9N follows it from the hamlet of Keene to Ausable Forks.

ADDITIONAL INFORMATION: Most of the East Branch flows through private property. However, the state has acquired public fishing rights to roughly 80 percent of it, mostly skirted by and within easy walking distance of NY 9N. The 2-mile stretch of west bank just south of the hamlet of Upper Jay is in the Sentinel Range Wilderness Area, and primitive camping is allowed. The covered bridge on CR 22 in the hamlet of Jay is a popular tourist attraction.

CONTACT: New York State Department of Environmental Conservation Region 5.

87. MAIN STEM AUSABLE RIVER

KEY SPECIES: Brown trout, rainbow trout, landlocked Atlantic salmon, and smallmouth bass.

DESCRIPTION: Formed by the union of the East and West Branches in Ausable Forks, this stream runs northeast for about 16 miles to feed Lake Champlain.

TIPS: Fish around the US 9 bridge in spring and autumn.

THE FISHING: Running wide and shallow, the main stem's upper reaches support brown trout in the 12- to 18-inch range. They are mostly caught on live bait and flies by locals who know the locations of spring pools. However, the fishing peters out as July and August heat the water to temperatures trout find all but unbearable. Add to that the fact that most of the stream flows through private property and you come up with a less-than-perfect fishery.

The stretch of river from the mouth upstream to the falls at Ausable Chasm is a different story. The state regularly stocks around 40,000 landlocked Atlantic salmon running from 1 to 7.5 inches. Additionally, the authorities periodically throw in some large rainbows (1,500 13-inchers and 100 18-inchers in 2013) and browns (400 13-inchers). The fish return in spring and fall. Ice-out sees runs of landlocked Atlantic salmon and steelhead in the 15- to 21-inch range. They return in the fall, only this time they average a couple of inches longer and their numbers include spawn heavy brown trout. Each species likes worms after a rain. Mainstream anglers fill their creels working spoons like green/silver Dardevles and Little Cleos, and in-line spinners like Rooster Tails, through pools and rapids. Fair-weather fly fishermen do well casting emerald shiner patterns like chartreuse flatwing streamers and Woolly Buggers. In late spring, great quantities of smallmouth bass run the lower river up to the US 9 bridge and respond to all the above.

From its mouth upstream to the falls at Ausable Chasm, the river is governed by Lake Champlain Regulations.

DIRECTIONS: NY 9N and US 9 parallel the river.

ADDITIONAL INFORMATION: A fishing access site, complete with a cartop launch, is located at Ausable Point Public Campground, on the mouth of the river. This state-run fee area has 123 campsites (43 with electrical hookups), hot showers, a 0.25-mile sandy swimming beach, a bathhouse, playgrounds, and a basketball court. Open from mid-May through mid-October. A day-use fee is charged noncampers during summer. This area is popular with windsurfers.

CONTACT: New York State Department of Environmental Conservation Region 5.

88. LAKE COLBY

KEY SPECIES: Rainbow trout, brown trout, landlocked salmon, largemouth bass, smallmouth bass, yellow perch, and brown bullheads.

DESCRIPTION: Easy access off a major highway makes this 286-acre lake one of the most popular fisheries in the Saranac Lake Region. It averages 20 feet deep and has a maximum depth of 46 feet. A railroad causeway runs across the south bay, creating Little Colby Pond. Though too shallow and narrow for most motorboats, the channel is deep enough for the fish to go back and forth.

TIPS: Suspend minnows a couple of feet below tip-ups for brood-stock salmon the state releases into the lake each fall.

THE FISHING: After stripping them of eggs in autumn, the state stocks roughly 100 landlocked Atlantic salmon averaging 23.5 inches. Anglers target them immediately by wading out from the fishing access site on NY 86 and casting spoons and minnowbaits. Come winter, they're targeted with minnows suspended a couple of feet below the ice with tip-ups. In spring, anglers put their boots on again and wade out to cast spoons and crankbaits. The state stocks 2,800 brown trout and 3,200 rainbow trout averaging 8 inches; and 750 14-inch brown trout. The rainbows hit dry flies at dawn and dusk, and streamers like Black Nose Dace and Gray Ghosts trolled 30 feet down behind lead-core line during summer. The browns like it all: minnows, worms, flies, and crankbaits. The place used to be loaded with smallmouth and largemouth bass ranging from 10 to 14 inches. Indeed, largemouth bass were first observed in research nets during a 1987 survey, and by 1993 their numbers had increased to the point that the state netted them for resettlement in local, bass-challenged waters. The state introduced a no-size limit on the species, bringing the numbers into balance. Now the largemouths run up to 4 pounds and smallies range between 1.5 and 2.5 pounds. They eagerly hit crayfish, crankbaits, and spinnerbaits. Yellow perch can go 12 inches and respond to small lures, worms, and minnows. Brown bullheads run from 8 to 14 inches and are popular with bank anglers bottom-fishing with worms from the railroad causeway at the south end.

Trout and salmon season is year-round, resulting in a colorful ice-shanty village sprouting on the surface each winter. Motors exceeding 10 horsepower are prohibited.

DIRECTIONS: A half mile north of the village of Saranac Lake on NY 86.

ADDITIONAL INFORMATION: The fishing access site offers a single-lane gravel launch, parking for 25 rigs, and a toilet. Heavy use of the soft-surface ramp has left it rutted it terribly, making it very challenging to launch anything larger than a 14-foot craft.

CONTACT: Saranac Lake Area Chamber of Commerce and New York State Department of Environmental Conservation Region 5.

89. LITTLE COLBY POND

KEY SPECIES: Largemouth bass and brown bullheads.

DESCRIPTION: Separated from Lake Colby by the Remsen–Lake Placid Railroad culvert, this 35.5-acre pond averages 5 feet deep and has a maximum depth of 15 feet. It is framed in bog mats and has massive weed beds.

TIPS: Toss a Texas-rigged 4-inch tube on the edges of cattail and bog mats and shake it into the water.

THE FISHING: Although salmon and trout mill around the culvert in spring and fall, attracting anglers who cast for them, largemouth bass ranging from 2 to 4 pounds are the preferred game. The pond's vegetation makes it a spot fishery where you throw surface baits and soft plastics into openings, channels, and holes. Brown bullheads up to 14 inches are popular with locals, who bottom-fish for them with worms and crayfish, especially in late spring.

DIRECTIONS: Take Ampersand Avenue from the west side of Saranac Lake village to CR 18 (Forest Home Road) and travel about 0.5 mile.

ADDITIONAL INFORMATION: The railroad culvert is only tall enough for a canoe to pass under, provided its occupants slouch over. An informal, small craft launch is on Forest Home Road.

CONTACT: Saranac Lake Area Chamber of Commerce and New York State Department of Environmental Conservation Region 5.

90. LEWEY LAKE

KEY SPECIES: Lake trout, landlocked Atlantic salmon, northern pike, smallmouth bass, and panfish.

DESCRIPTION: This 361-acre lake's relatively symmetrical floor gently slides from the shoreline to a 50-foot-deep hole out in the middle. Averaging 25 feet deep, with a maximum depth of 55 feet, its banks are mostly surrounded by wild forest. A navigable channel connects it to Indian Lake.

TIPS: Work jigs tipped with minnows along the weed beds around the mouth of the Miami River, the major tributary on the south end, for northerns in spring and autumn.

THE FISHING: Lake trout are this site's most prevalent coldwater species. Most are targeted through the ice with minnows fished on bottom off tip-ups. A few landlocked salmon are caught incidentally each winter by lake trout anglers fishing near the mouth of the Miami River. Most think these fish were originally stocked into Indian Lake but found the pickings and spawning in Lewey Lake and its tributaries more to their liking. Indeed, many believe the species is naturally reproducing in the Miami River. Northern pike in the 3- to 8-pound range are plentiful on the shelf drops and in shallow cover. They bite best on minnows but are more exciting to catch on buzzbaits and spinnerbaits. Smallmouth bass average 13 inches and strike crankbaits and jigs. Yellow perch up to 12 inches, sunfish between 4 and 7 inches, and 10-inch bullheads are plentiful. Each likes worms, and the perch and sunnies also take flies.

DIRECTIONS: From the village of Speculator, head north on NY 30 for about 10 miles.

ADDITIONAL INFORMATION: Lewey Lake Public Campground is a fee area offering 209 campsites, a hard-surface boat launch, parking for 15 rigs, hot showers, a sand beach, and a trailer dumping station. A day-use fee is charged when the campground is open, mid-May through mid-November. Day use is free off-season.

CONTACT: New York State Department of Environmental Conservation Region 5 and Hamilton County Tourism.

91. INDIAN LAKE

KEY SPECIES: Landlocked Atlantic salmon, brown trout, lake trout, brook trout, smallmouth bass, northern pike, yellow perch, and pumpkinseeds.

DESCRIPTION: Only developed on its north end, this largely forested, 4,255-acre impoundment averages 39 feet deep and has a maximum depth of 85 feet.

TIPS: Autumn drawdown lowers the lake by up to 10 feet, leaving much of the south end high and dry.

THE FISHING: A healthy smelt population keeps predators well fed. The state used to stock several thousand Atlantic salmon regularly (3,920 7-inchers in 2013) into the lake's major tributary, the Jessup River. Eventually making it to the lake, they grow to range from 15 to 18 inches, making them popular targets for anglers trolling tandem streamers and Jr. ThunderSticks. The state also releases about 7,000 brown trout annually, averaging 8 inches. Most are caught on worms, flies, and small lures by the time they reach 12 inches. However, a lot make it to truly lunker size, and each winter anglers take browns ranging from 5 to 8 pounds through the ice on live smelt. Several thousand lake trout are stocked every couple of years or so, too (4,620 7-inchers in 2013). They fare better than the browns, prospering in the lake's deep northern end, typically growing from 1.5 to 4 pounds, with many making it to 10 pounds or better. Fish for them with flutter spoons dragged on Seth Green rigs. According to the NYSDEC, "This lake receives periodic infusions of brook trout" (3,700 4-inchers in 2013). They'll take small jigs and spinners cast near shore, especially around tributary mouths, in spring and fall, and worms and wet flies trolled deep behind wobblers in summer. Smallmouth bass find the lake's rocky areas to their liking. Ranging from 12 to 16 inches, they respond to finesse worms on dropshot and Carolina rigs. Northern pike aren't very numerous, but when you get one it is generally 8 pounds or better; 20-pounders are taken each year, primarily by ice fishermen. Use spinnerbaits in soft water and large minnows through the ice. Pumpkinseeds find this place exceptionally agreeable. Indeed, the state record, a 1-pound, 9-ounce monster, was caught here. They average an incredible 8 inches and, along with the perch—which average 9 inches (12-inchers are relatively abundant)—provide great sport on wet flies and worms.

DIRECTIONS: NY 30 parallels the west bank, south of the village of Indian Lake.

ADDITIONAL INFORMATION: The state boat launch on NY 30, on the lake's south end, at the Indian Lake Islands Public Campground, offers a hard-surface launch ramp and parking for 50 rigs. The campground has 55 campsites scattered around the lake and its islands. Access is by boat only. Open Mid-May through Labor Day.

CONTACT: New York State Department of Environmental Conservation Region 5 and Hamilton County Tourism.

92. LAKE ABANAKEE

KEY SPECIES: Lake trout, brown trout, northern pike, largemouth bass, smallmouth bass, and pumpkinseeds.

DESCRIPTION: Formed by a dam on the Indian River, this 361-acre impoundment is broken into three small lakes separated by bridges, averages 8 feet deep, and drops to a maximum depth of 21 feet.

TIPS: In spring, cast spoons and crankbaits into the plunge pool, 0.8 mile upstream of Big Brook Road, for large lake trout and brown trout.

THE FISHING: A warmwater fishery by any standard, this lake offers a unique opportunity for large salmonids. When Indian Lake is drawn down each fall, some of its large lake trout invariably go down the tubes. As the water starts warming up in the spring, they congregate in the deep water at the head of Abanakee and strike anything that resembles a smelt. Unfortunately, this body of water is "suffering from the impacts of drawdowns done four times a week in spring and summer to create a rafting bubble on the Indian and Hudson Rivers. The abundance and size of largemouth, smallmouth, and northern pike was significantly reduced," says retired fisheries biologist Rich Preall. However, he adds, "Some mighty big bass are still available." Smallmouths run from 12 to 20 inches and love crayfish and minnows. Bucketmouths up to 6 pounds hang in the shallows and can be coaxed out of cover with jig-n-pigs and floating worms. Northern pike range from 18 to 25 inches and provide exciting moments to anglers casting spinner-rigged 3-inch curly-tailed grubs and tubes tipped with minnows. Pumpkinseeds up to 8-something inches can't seem to resist a juicy worm floated in weed openings below a bobber.

There is no closed season or size limit for lake trout, but the state-wide bag limit applies.

DIRECTIONS: About a mile east of the village of Indian Lake on NY 28.

CONTACT: New York State Department of Environmental Conservation Region 5 and Hamilton County Tourism.

92A. Public Access

DESCRIPTION: This site is a picnic area but anglers use it as an informal cartop launch. Parking for four cars.

DIRECTIONS: Head south on NY 30 from the village of Indian Lake for just under a mile and turn left on Big Brook Road. Travel about 0.5 mile to the bridge.

92B. Public Access

DESCRIPTION: This informal hard-surface launch is on town property, offering parking for about five rigs and additional parking on the shoulder.

DIRECTIONS: Head east out of Indian Lake village on NY 28. Turn north, a little over a mile later, just before the bridge, onto Chain Lakes Road and travel for 0.75 mile.

93. INDIAN RIVER (HAMILTON AND ESSEX COUNTIES)

KEY SPECIES: Brown trout and rainbow trout.

DESCRIPTION: The two-something-mile stretch from the Abanakee Lake dam to the Indian River's confluence with the Hudson River is a jumble of wild and scenic pocket water punctuated with chutes and ledges littered with blowdowns.

TIPS: Work Muddler Minnows through the pockets.

THE FISHING: The state stocks about 1,200 brown trout and 1,500 rainbow trout averaging 8.5 inches, and 500 brown trout ranging between 12 and 15 inches annually. They join holdovers from previous years to offer anglers one of the most exciting fast-water fisheries in the mountains. Both species hit worms, minnows, Woolly Buggers, and stonefly nymphs by day, along with dry flies matching the hatch at dawn and dusk.

Trout season runs year-round.

DIRECTIONS: Head east out of Indian Lake Village on NY 28. Turn north about a mile later, just before the bridge, onto Chain Lakes Road and follow it for a little under a mile.

ADDITIONAL INFORMATION: Fishing is best when water is released for rafting purposes—generally between 9 and 10 a.m., on Tuesday, Thursday, Saturday, and Sunday. Numerous hardened campsites, some within view of the river, are just off Chain Lakes Road. Camping is allowed in designated sites only.

CONTACT: New York State Department of Environmental Conservation and Hamilton County Tourism.

94. UPPER HUDSON RIVER

KEY SPECIES: Brown trout, rainbow trout, northern pike, smallmouth bass, and largemouth bass.

DESCRIPTION: This section of New York's largest river runs from its source for about 110 miles to Hudson Falls. Only about the size of a big creek around Newcomb, it gets nourished by numerous tributaries, becoming a decent-sized river by the time it winds out of the Adirondacks west of Glens Falls. On the way, it slices through a magnificent gorge. During the spring thaw, this stretch's rapids and scenery make it one of the country's top 10 adventure-class white-water venues.

TIPS: Use beadhead nymphs just about anytime.

THE FISHING: The state airlifts roughly 4,270 brown trout averaging 7.5 inches and 7,400 rainbow trout averaging 8.5 inches annually into the remote stretch between Newcomb and North River. Pushed out of the plane without parachutes, those that hit the water without breaking their fins find the pickings good, growing anywhere from 10 to 16 inches. They respond to streamers, large nymphs, worms, and spinners. From Newcomb downstream for about 5 miles, the river is punctuated with large, slow-moving pools that are home to northerns, walleyes, and smallmouth bass. They all hit minnowbaits and in-line spinners, and the northerns and bass take streamers.

Downstream of North Creek, the river is wide, shallow, and, according to state aquatic biologist Rich Preall, "loaded with black rocks that draw the sun like a magnet, heating the water to levels trout can't tolerate." Below Warrensburg, the river narrows again and gets deeper. Although some trout are available, the habitat is most suitable for warmwater species. Smallmouth bass ranging from 12 to 15 inches and northern pike from 18 to 24 inches are common and respond well to streamers, spoons, and minnows. From Corinth to Fort Edward, the river and fish get bigger. Smallmouths go 12 to 20 inches, northern pike reach 15 pounds, and largemouth bass ranging from 1 to 4 pounds begin appearing. They all take spinnerbaits, large minnows, and their imitations.

There is no closed season for trout in the river flowing through Essex, Warren, and Hamilton Counties. Black bass can be taken year-round in any size and number in the Hamilton County stretch of the river.

DIRECTIONS: NY 28 parallels the river from North River to a few miles north of Warrensburg. The river forms part of the boundary between Essex and Hamilton Counties and Warren and Saratoga Counties.

ADDITIONAL INFORMATION: The vast majority of the river flows through private property, and there are no public campgrounds. However, primitive camping is allowed in the small patches of state land it runs through. The biggest swath of public property is around the mouth of the Indian River.

CONTACT: New York State Department of Environmental Conservation, Hamilton County Tourism, and Warren County Tourism.

94A. Blue Ledges

DESCRIPTION: Gateway to the Hudson River Gorge, this spectacularly scenic spot is named after towering limestone cliffs.

THE FISHING: The largest pool on the Upper Hudson is located here. The pocket water flowing in and out of it is highly oxygenated, making the whole area ideal year-round trout habitat. This spot is favored by purists who enjoy hiking into a wildly remote area for quality fly fishing.

DIRECTIONS: Take NY 28N north out of North Creek for about 8 miles to Minerva. Continue north for about 1.5 miles beyond the village and turn left (west), at the curve, onto North Woods Club Road. After about a mile, the pavement ends. Continue on the hard-surface road for about 4 more miles to the parking area on the east side of Huntley Pond (**site 95**). Follow the well-worn footpath south for about 2.1 miles to the river.

ADDITIONAL INFORMATION: The river is located deep in the gorge, down a moderately difficult trail; there isn't any level ground close to it for campsites. However, there are three large campsites at Huntley Pond.

94B. Off-Road Parking

DESCRIPTION: This site has parking for five cars.
DIRECTIONS: Across from 13th Lake Road's terminus at NY 28, about 0.25 miles north of the hamlet of North River.

94C. Off-Road Parking

DESCRIPTION: This site has a beach launch for cartop craft and parking for four cars.
DIRECTIONS: On NY 28, about 0.5 mile south of the hamlet of North River.

95. HUNTLEY POND

KEY SPECIES: Brook trout.
DESCRIPTION: This 40-acre pond is largely wooded with some wetland on the west end. It averages about 20 feet deep and has a maximum depth of 40 feet.
TIPS: Best fished from a rubber raft or canoe.
THE FISHING: The state stocks this pond periodically with brookies (2,000 4-inchers in 2013). They end up averaging 10.5 inches, with some monsters going 16 inches, even better. They respond to in-line spinners, flashy dry flies like Royal Coachmans, and streamers.
DIRECTIONS: Head north on NY 28N out of Minerva for about 1.5 miles, turn west on North Woods Club Road, and continue for about 5 miles.
ADDITIONAL INFORMATION: The western tip is owned by the North Woods Club. They don't mind folks fishing but frown on trespassers walking the property. Obey posted signs. Camping is permitted in the large clearings off the parking area.
CONTACT: New York State Department of Environmental Conservation Region 5.

96. BOREAS RIVER

KEY SPECIES: Brook trout and brown trout.
DESCRIPTION: Spawned by Boreas Ponds, this stream winds south for about 18 miles to feed the Hudson River on the east end of the Hudson Gorge.
TIPS: Use Woolly Worms in late summer.
THE FISHING: The headwaters are native brook trout habitat. The fish range from 4 to 8 inches and take worms and flies. Closer to its mouth, the state stocks a couple thousand brown trout averaging 8 inches annually. They find the

highly oxygenated pocket water to their liking and thrive, growing to average 10 inches. They like worms and nymphs.

Occasionally, the authorities release surplus brood stock—most recently in 2013 when they dumped 1,000 13-inch browns, 800 rainbows ranging from 13 to 18 inches, and 500 brookies averaging 8 inches.

DIRECTIONS: Flowing mostly through wild forest, the stream is most easily accessible at two bridges: the North Country Club Road bridge (take NY 28N north out of Minerva for 1.5 miles, turn west on North Country Club Road, and continue for about 3 miles) and the NY 28N bridge, about 8 miles north of Minerva.

ADDITIONAL INFORMATION: Squeaky-clean water and its relative remoteness make this river's fish super skittish, so wear camo and walk gently.

CONTACT: New York State Department of Environmental Conservation Region 5.

97. PISECO LAKE

KEY SPECIES: Lake trout, landlocked Atlantic salmon, smallmouth bass, and chain pickerel.

DESCRIPTION: Surrounded by wild forest and wilderness areas, this 2,842-acre lake averages 58 feet deep and has a maximum depth of 125 feet. Its cottages and lakeshore businesses offer the only civilization for miles around.

TIPS: Using a very light line, ice fish with minnows suspended about 2 feet below the ice on tip-ups for Atlantic salmon.

THE FISHING: Lake trout are the dominant predators. The state stocks about 3,500 averaging 7.5 inches regularly. They end up ranging from 18 to 26 inches and are mainly targeted by ice fishermen jigging with minnows. About 2,000 landlocked Atlantic salmon are also stocked annually. They do very well, typically reaching between 18 and 20 inches. While some are caught in summer by trolling streamers and minnowbaits, most are targeted in winter by suspending live smelt a couple of feet below the ice with tip-ups. Smallmouth bass up to 16 inches rule the rocky drops and have an appetite for minnows and crayfish. Pickerel are showing up with increasing regularity. They'll take worms retrieved at a steady clip on spinner harnesses, and anything that resembles a live minnow.

Lake trout and salmon can be taken year-round. Minimum length for lakers is 21 inches, and the daily limit is two. Minimum length for salmon is 18 inches, with a daily limit of two.

DIRECTIONS: Head east out of Utica on NY 8 for about 57 miles. NY 8 parallels the lake's east side. CR 24 (Old Piseco Road) parallels the west side and boasts all the campgrounds.

CONTACT: New York State Department of Environmental Conservation Region 5.

97A. Point Comfort Public Campground

DESCRIPTION: This fee area offers 76 campsites, a paved boat launch with parking for six rigs, picnic areas, a sandy swimming beach, a bathhouse, and toilets. Open mid-May through Labor Day. Free day use permitted off-season.

DIRECTIONS: On Old Piseco Road, about 1.5 miles from its western terminus at NY 8.

97B. Little Sand Point Public Campground

DESCRIPTION: This fee area offers 78 campsites, more than half on the lakeshore, a paved boat launch with parking for six rigs, a picnic area, a swimming beach, a bathhouse, toilets, and a trailer dumping station. Open mid-May through Labor Day. Off-season day use permitted.

DIRECTIONS: On Old Piseco Road, 3.5 miles east of its western terminus at NY 8.

97C. Poplar Point Public Campground

DESCRIPTION: This fee area offers 21 campsites—all but 3 on the beach—a paved boat launch with parking for 15 rigs, a sandy beach, a bathhouse, and toilets. Open mid-May through Labor Day. Day use allowed off-season.

DIRECTIONS: On Old Piseco Road, 4.4 miles east of its western terminus at NY 8.

98. SACANDAGA LAKE

KEY SPECIES: Brown trout, chain pickerel, smallmouth bass, largemouth bass, and yellow perch.

DESCRIPTION: This 1,600-acre lake's entire northern half is in the Jessup River Wild Forest. Averaging 28 feet deep, it has a maximum depth of 60 feet and is connected to Lake Pleasant by a navigable channel.

TIPS: Don't confuse this lake with its mighty offspring, Great Sacandaga Lake.

THE FISHING: Like all lakes they've infiltrated, rainbow smelt "have changed Sacandaga . . . Walleye and rainbow trout fishing have vanished," reports retired state fisheries biologist Rich Preall. "Smallmouth bass and yellow perch love all the new smelt to eat and are now abundant, fat, and happy." Bronzebacks range from 1 to 5 pounds, and respond well to scented tubes and curly-tailed grubs bounced or dragged on bottom. Yellow perch average 10 inches and like minnows, worms, and small jigs. Chain pickerel averaging 18 inches cruise shallow, weedy areas and strike fast-moving silver spoons, ThunderSticks, and Rooster Tail spinners. The lake is experiencing the development of largemouth bass fishery. However, it's unlikely the species will gain too much ground because their preferred habitat is very limited.

Still, bucketmouths up to 5 pounds are available and will strike all the usual suspects, particularly spinnerbaits and jerkbaits worked around cover in shallow water.

The rainbow smelt invasion notwithstanding, the authorities haven't given up on the place and manage it as a two-story fishery, stocking it annually with hundreds of brown trout (1,280 9-inchers in 2015). Survival is good and the general population averages 12 inches, with fish measuring over 20 inches and weighing up to 5 pounds caught regularly. Jigging minnows on bottom in spring and fall works best, but trolling minnow-imitating crankbaits scented with fish oil also fills live wells. John Fieroh says lakers have been stocked regularly since 2009 (2,800 7-inchers in 2014), but he hasn't heard too much about them from anglers. Rumor has it some keepers are taken incidentally by anglers flatlining spoons and minnowbaits for browns in the spring and fall.

In an effort to reintroduce walleyes, DEC stocked 32,000 1.5-inchers in 2014, and it's likely they'll continue stocking them regularly over the next few years.

Fishing is prohibited in the lake's tributaries and outlet from March 16 until opening day of walleye season.

DIRECTIONS: From Thruway exit 27 (Amsterdam), head north on NY 30 for about 24 miles to Speculator, then west on NY 8 for about 2 miles. Turn right on Page Street and travel for about a mile.

ADDITIONAL INFORMATION: Moffitts Beach Campground, on the lake's northwestern arm, is a fee area offering 261 campsites, a beach launch with parking for 30 rigs, hot showers, and picnic areas. A day-use fee is charged noncampers when the campground is open, mid-May through mid-October. Free day use permitted off-season. The road is plowed in winter.

CONTACT: Hamilton County Tourism and New York State Department of Environmental Conservation Region 5.

99. LAKE PLEASANT

KEY SPECIES: Smallmouth bass, brown trout, lake trout, and walleyes.

DESCRIPTION: This 1,504-acre lake has an average depth of 29 feet and a maximum depth of 65 feet. Although surrounded by roads, it is far enough off the beaten path to discourage crowding. It is connected to Sacandaga Lake by a channel.

TIPS: The largest walleyes are most active at night.

THE FISHING: This lake's inlet allows its fish to intermingle with Sacandaga Lake's, making the fisheries almost identical. "Same smelt story as Sacandaga," claims retired fisheries biologist Rich Preall, adding, "Rainbow and salmon policies were canceled." The state stocks roughly 1,300 brown trout averaging 8.5

inches annually. They generally average 12 inches, with quite a few taken each year weighing up to 5 pounds. Minnows and worms work best, but trolling minnow-imitating crankbaits scented with fish oil also works well. With all the smelt around, "smallmouth bass swarm the lake," says Preall. Smallies typically run from 1 to 4 pounds, and talking about them in area bars is a local pastime. They like crayfish and minnows, 3-inch plastic worms dropshotted near shore and around the island, and soft jerkbaits ripped around boat docks and other cover. Although smelt have done a number on the walleye population by feeding on their fry, DEC is fighting back by stocking thousands regularly (29,000 1.5-inchers in 2014). Surprisingly, some monster eyes are still around, providing unexpected thrills to anglers who take them incidentally on jigs and minnowbaits targeting bass. "Yellow perch are big," boasts Preall. They average 10 inches and respond to minnows, worms, and small lures, especially curly-tailed grubs worked around cover.

Trout season is open year-round. Fishing is prohibited in all tributaries from March 16 until the first Saturday in May to protect spawning walleyes. As with its sister lake above, Lake Pleasant has a developing largemouth bass fishery.

DIRECTIONS: From Thruway exit 27 (Amsterdam), head north on NY 30 for about 24 miles to Speculator.

ADDITIONAL INFORMATION: A beach launch with parking for 10 cars is located near the NY 30/NY 8 bridge crossing the outlet. Camping is available at Moffitt Beach Public Campground on adjoining Sacandaga Lake (**site 98**).

CONTACT: Hamilton County Tourism and New York State Department of Environmental Conservation Region 5.

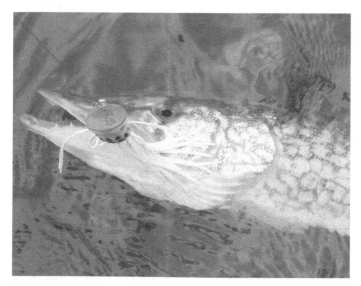

Fly fishing with large poppers for bass in places like Lake Pleasant (site 99) will generally produce feisty, tasty pickerel, too.

100. WEST BRANCH SACANDAGA RIVER

KEY SPECIES: Brook trout and brown trout.

DESCRIPTION: Springing from the Silver Lake Wilderness, this branch runs a bony course for roughly 20 miles before joining the main stem at the Sacandaga Public Campground.

TIPS: Two-year-old browns are stocked at the Sacandaga Public Campground.

THE FISHING: Most of this stream gets too warm to hold trout in summer. However, the stretch from Jimmy Creek downstream boasts tolerable temperatures most of the time. Each spring, the state stocks this area with about 700 browns and 800 rainbows ranging from 7 to 8 inches. They hit worms, minnows, and cork flies imitating food pellets early and late in the season, flies and in-line spinners during warm weather.

DIRECTIONS: From its intersection with Buttermilk Hill Road in Wells, head south on NY 30 for just short of 0.5 mile, turn right on CR 5, travel about 0.5 mile, turn left on West River Road, continue for about 1.5 mile, and turn left on Black Bridge Road.

ADDITIONAL INFORMATION: Nestled in a stand of old-growth white pines, Sacandaga Public Campground is the oldest in the state. This fee area offers 143 campsites, hot showers, and a trailer dump station. A day-use fee is charged noncampers when the campground is open, mid-May through Labor Day. Free day use is permitted off-season.

CONTACT: New York State Department of Environmental Conservation Region 5.

100A. Jimmy Creek

DESCRIPTION: Skinny by any measure, this tributary's frigid waters help keep the West Branch Sacandaga River cool enough to support trout.

THE FISHING: Native brookies up to 10 inches occupy this stream's cool waters. They hit worms, minnows, small lures, and flies.

DIRECTIONS: About a mile upstream from the Black Bridge.

101. EAST BRANCH SACANDAGA RIVER

KEY SPECIES: Brook trout and brown trout.

DESCRIPTION: This river pours out of the west side of Gore Mountain, snakes through the Siamese Ponds Wilderness, then comes to NY 8 and follows it south for a good 10 miles before feeding the main stem Sacandaga River at the NY 8/NY 30 junction, 8 miles east of Speculator.

TIPS: Wear a Bug-Out Sportswear head net in the spring to keep blackflies from bugging you.

THE FISHING: Hardy trout purists willing to take the long hike find wild brookies ranging from 4 to 10 inches in the cool, wilderness headwaters. They take worms early in the year, brown and tan nymphs in summer. A few brown trout enter the lower portion of the stream from the main river fall through spring but hightail it out when the water gets too warm, generally in early June.

DIRECTIONS: Head east out of Speculator on NY 30/NY 8 for about 8 miles, then continue on NY 8, which parallels it for about 10 miles.

ADDITIONAL INFORMATION: This branch feeds the main stem just upstream of the bridge at the NY 8/NY 30 junction.

CONTACT: New York State Department of Environmental Conservation Region 5.

102. SACANDAGA RIVER

KEY SPECIES: Brown trout, smallmouth bass, chain pickerel, northern pike, walleyes, and fallfish.

DESCRIPTION: Spawned as the outlet of Sacandaga Lake, this stream starts off as a short drink of water, flowing a few hundred yards before being swallowed by Lake Pleasant. Gently passing through, it comes out the north end, crawling at first, then quickly picking up speed and tumbling down the mountain like a respectable river. And while its path pours over dynamite-looking trout habitat, much of it gets too warm in summer to support salmonids.

TIPS: The best trout fishing runs for about a mile upstream and downstream of Sacandaga Public Campground.

THE FISHING: Close proximity to NY 8/NY 30 qualifies this stream for some heavy stocking. Roughly 3,500 brown trout averaging 8 inches are released annually, with several hundred two-year-olds thrown in every couple of years or so to keep things interesting (many of the larger trout are released at the Sacandaga Campground, reveals retired fisheries biologist Rich Preall). They provide a lot of excitement for fly fishermen casting mayflies, caddis, and other terrestrial patterns until early summer, before water temperatures get too warm and they beat fins for spring holes, tributaries, or Great Sacandaga Lake (**site 103**). Smallmouth bass ranging from 12 to 14 inches, and chain pickerel averaging 18 inches, inhabit the entire stream. Both take minnows, spinnerbaits, and crankbaits like Bass Pro Shops XPS Minnows. Northern pike up to 36 inches and walleyes ranging from 18 to 23 inches are available in the lower reaches—the closer you get to Great Sacandaga Lake, the better your chances of catching one. The northerns are partial to spoons and in-line spinnerbaits, and walleyes have a taste for worms pulled slowly upstream, on bottom, or retrieved slowly on a spinner-rigged harness. Both respond to bucktail jigs. While some trout purists consider the fallfish "white trash," they deserve some respect. Typically running from 4 to 12 inches, with some going over 16 inches, willing to strike flies and streamers as eagerly as worms, then follow through with a feisty, trout-like fight, these guys often save the day when the river's more glamorous species have lockjaw.

From March 16 through the first Saturday in May, fishing is prohibited from Bridge Street in Northville upstream to the NY 30 bridge to protect spawning walleyes.

DIRECTIONS: NY 30 parallels the entire river north of the hamlet of Northville.

ADDITIONAL INFORMATION: Several pull-offs punctate NY 30. Sacandaga Public Campground, a fee area located on NY 30, a couple of miles south of Wells, offers 143 campsites, picnic sites, hot showers, and a dump station. A user fee is charged noncampers when the campground is open, mid-May through Labor Day. Free day use is permitted off-season. Ron Kolodziej, a local outdoor writer, says the most efficient way to fish the productive stretch from Sacandaga Campground to Great Sacandaga Lake is by canoe.

CONTACT: New York State Department of Environmental Conservation Region 5.

102A. Lake Algonquin

DESCRIPTION: Brushing the west side of the hamlet of Wells, this 224-acre impoundment was "drained in 2011 to prevent damage from Hurricane Irene," says Preall. "The bass took a ride downstream, but the pickerel stayed put. It'll take a while for the bass to recover." He's quick to add, however, "Locals stock largemouth into Lake Algonquin using mitigation money they get from the power company." These predators all hit Mepps Aglias, Jr. ThunderSticks, soft jerkbaits. and $\frac{1}{16}$- and $\frac{1}{24}$-ounce Hula Poppers.

ADDITIONAL INFORMATION: This lake has access with parking on both sides of the NY 30 bridge.

DIRECTIONS: Off NY 30, 13.6 miles south of Speculator.

103. GREAT SACANDAGA LAKE

KEY SPECIES: Northern pike, pickerel, walleyes, smallmouth bass, largemouth bass, brown trout, and rainbow trout.

DESCRIPTION: Formed by a dam built in 1930 on the Sacandaga River, this 26,860-acre lake averages 32 feet deep and has a maximum depth of 74 feet. Subject to wildly fluctuating water levels, it's a dangerous place for boats, especially during low water, when its numerous shoals reach propeller level. The reservoir is totally contained within the Adirondack Park; ancient peaks loom over its northern horizon.

TIPS: Fish the mouths of tributaries with large suckers and shiners suspended below bobbers.

THE FISHING: This lake has broken several northern pike state records and surrendered the current holder, a 46-pound, 2-ounce monster. Trophy northerns didn't get that way by being stupid, and catching one is a real challenge. Ron Kolodziej, a retired guide who specialized exclusively in hunting these wolves of the aquatic world, suggests using minnows "one-third the size of the fish you're after; a 10-inch minnow for a 30-inch pike, and so on." However, many large pike are taken serendipitously on smaller minnows targeting walleyes and bass. Walleyes generally range from 15 to 20 inches, "and there's a lot of 'em," adds Kolodziej. They respond well to ThunderSticks and bucktail jigs fished plain or tipped with minnows or worms. The Great Sacandaga Lake Fisheries Federation, a private group, is trying to increase walleye numbers and has stocked thousands of 6- to 8-inchers over the years. "I don't know how successful their efforts have been, but a good way to find walleyes is to follow northern burps; pike love stockie-sized walleyes," chuckles Kolodziej. Smallmouth bass stretching the tape from 12 to 20 inches are plentiful and hang out along the old river bottom on the lake's long, eastern arm, where they are popularly targeted with minnows, crayfish, curly-tailed grubs, and tubes. Largemouths grow up to 5 pounds and can be taken on stickworms and spinner baits worked in shallow cover. Perch ranging from 7 to 11 inches take small minnows and Beetle Spins. Local clubs stock rainbow and brown trout. Former state aquatic biologist Rich Preall says the impoundment has "a thin zone where some trout can survive. Most of the stockies are stressed for their entire time here, and eventually end up in the mouth of a northern pike." Still, trout ranging from 8 to 14 inches are available and are mostly taken on worms, minnows, spoons, and bucktail spinners fished in and around tributary mouths, early and late in the season.

Catfish, ranging from eating-sized to 20-pound trophies, thrive in Great Sacandaga Lake (site 103).

From March 16 until opening day of walleye season, fishing is prohibited in the outlet and all tributaries from their mouths upstream to the first highway bridge to protect spawning walleye. Trout can be taken any size, year-round.

DIRECTIONS: Take NYS Thruway exit 27 (Amsterdam) and get on NY Route 30 north, which parallels the west shore; CR 110 (it turns into CR 7 at the county line) skirts the east bank.

ADDITIONAL INFORMATION: Northhampton Beach Public Campground, off NY 30, about 3 miles south of Northampton, is a fee area offering 224 no-frills campsites, public showers, handicapped access, a hard-surface boat launch, a picnic pavilion, a playground, and parking for 100 rigs. A day-use fee is charged noncampers when the campground is open, early May through mid-October. Free day use allowed off-season.

CONTACT: New York State Department of Environmental Conservation Region 5 and Fulton County Chamber of Commerce.

103A. Northville Boat Launch

DESCRIPTION: This handicapped-accessible site offers a hard-surface ramp and parking for 60 rigs.

DIRECTIONS: On NY 30 in the village of Northville.

103B. Broadalbin Boat Launch

DESCRIPTION: This site has a hard-surface launch and parking for 70 rigs.

DIRECTIONS: Off CR110, 3 miles north of the village of Broadalbin.

103C. Edinburg Boat Launch

DESCRIPTION: This site has a hard-surface ramp and parking for 44 rigs.

DIRECTIONS: Off CR 4, 5 miles north of Edinburg.

104. SARATOGA LAKE

KEY SPECIES: Largemouth bass, smallmouth bass, chain pickerel, northern pike, walleyes, black crappies, and panfish.

DESCRIPTION: This 3,762-acre lake averages 25 feet deep and has a maximum depth of 96 feet.

TIPS: In early summer, flatline rattling minnowbaits a half hour on either side of dawn and dusk, in 5 to 15 feet of water, for walleyes.

THE FISHING: Although smallmouths are more plentiful, this lake is best known for bucketmouths ranging from 1 to 4 pounds. They hang out in weeds and respond to 4-inch worms on jigheads tossed into the openings, spinnerbaits worked along the edges, and buzzbaits ripped over the top. Smallmouths ranging from 0.75 to 3 pounds are common on rocky bottoms and like Carolina-rigged finesse worms and bucktail jigs tipped with scented plastics. Pickerel in the 1- to 2.5-pound class are plentiful and react with extreme violence to fat-bodied crankbaits, surface baits, and night crawlers on spinner harnesses worked quickly through openings in the weeds and along their edges. Retired fishing guide Ron Kolodziej says, "Working your way down the lake while casting spinnerbaits will result in mixed bags of largemouth and smallmouth bass, northern pike, and pickerel. The lake is ringed with camps and the owners mow the weeds in front of their docks, creating all kinds of exciting opportunities." Recently, the state has been supplementing the natural walleye population by releasing millions of fry annually: 26 million in 2013. Typical eyes range from 2 to 5 pounds and respond to rattling lures like Rat-L-Traps and LiveTarget Smelt worked around tributary mouths in the fall and spring, and on summer evenings. Sunfish and rock bass ranging from 0.5 to 1 pound are numerous and respond to worms and small poppers. Yellow perch running 7 to 10 inches and black crappies from 9 to 12 inches are abundant and hit small minnows and scented 2-inch curly-tailed grubs; in spring, the hot spot for crappies is around the NY 9P bridge. A state survey in 2008 revealed that the lake is loaded with bullheads running from 9 to 15 inches. They like worms fished on bottom on cloudy days and at night.

The limit on sunfish (bluegill, pumpkinseed, and redbreast) is 15.

DIRECTIONS: Take I-87 north out of Albany for about 20 miles to Saratoga Springs exit 14, then take NY 9P east for about 3 miles.

ADDITIONAL INFORMATION: Saratoga Lake boat launch, located on the north end, off NY 9P, has a hard-surface ramp and parking for about 100 rigs. There is no camping on the lake, but a lot of folks stay at Moreau Lake State Park, 10 miles north.

CONTACT: New York State Department of Environmental Conservation Region 5.

105. EAST CAROGA LAKE

KEY SPECIES: Splake, rainbow trout, chain pickerel, largemouth bass, smallmouth bass, black crappies, and panfish.

DESCRIPTION: This 198-acre lake averages 13 feet deep and has a maximum depth of 48 feet. A little over half its shoreline is developed with private residences. It's connected to West Caroga Lake (**site 106**) by a channel.

TIPS: Work Beetle Spins over weed beds.

THE FISHING: Some splake come in through the channel from West Caroga Lake. Ranging from 8 to 12 inches, they're usually taken incidentally by anglers casting spoons or spinners for smallmouth bass. Rainbow trout are stocked to the tune of 1,200 averaging 8.5 inches annually. The habitat is decent, and they grow to average 14 inches. They'll take thin silver spoons flatlined along shore in the spring and fall, dry flies matching the hatch on calm summer evenings. Chain pickerel are the dominant warmwater predator. They typically go from 15 to 20 inches and strike spoons and surface baits. Largemouth bass running from 1 to 6 pounds, and bronzebacks averaging 14 inches—with quite a few reaching 18 inches and better—eagerly take it all, from spinnerbaits and wide-bodied crankbaits to Carolina-rigged worms and Zara Spooks. Black crappies ranging from 9 to 11 inches love Beetle Spins worked around weeds and waterlogged timber. Yellow perch average 8 inches, pumpkinseeds typically go 5 to 7 inches, and bullheads reach 14 inches. The perch like small Beetle Spins and 2-inch Berkley Power Grubs, the sunfish go for wet flies and poppers, and they all, including the bullheads, love worms.

Trout season is open year-round.

DIRECTIONS: From NYS Thruway exit 29 (Canajoharie), head north on NY 10 for about 15 miles.

ADDITIONAL INFORMATION: Caroga Lake Public Campground is a fee area offering 161 campsites (some handicapped accessible), a boat launch with a paved ramp and parking for 10 rigs, a swimming beach, picnic tables, hot showers, and a trailer dumping station. A day-use fee is charged noncampers when the campground is open, mid-May through Labor Day. Free day use is allowed off-season.

CONTACT: New York State Department of Environmental Conservation Region 5.

106. WEST CAROGA LAKE

KEY SPECIES: Splake, smallmouth bass, chain pickerel, and yellow perch.

DESCRIPTION: Oval-shaped with symmetrical contours steadily sliding into its deep center, this 275-acre lake's average depth is 13 feet deep, and it has a maximum depth of 74 feet. Its shoreline is largely developed with private residences. It's connected to East Caroga Lake (**site 105**) by a navigable channel.

TIPS: Ice fish with minnows.

THE FISHING: This lake is one of the state's top splake hot spots. About 5,000 8.5-inchers are stocked regularly. Most grow to average 11.5 inches, but there are some over 25 inches down there. Locals ice fish for them by jigging minnows plain or on Swedish Pimples. Smallmouth bass range from 12 to 15 inches and hit scented curly-tailed grubs or tubes dragged on bottom in 10 to 20 feet of water. Chain pickerel up to 20 inches provide explosive action on worms retrieved rapidly over weed beds on spinner-rigged harnesses. Yellow perch range between 7 and 10 inches and hit worms, minnows, and scented 2-inch curly-tailed grubs.

DIRECTIONS: From Thruway exit 29 (Canajoharie), head north on NY 10 for about 17 miles.

ADDITIONAL INFORMATION: Camping and a boat launch are available at Caroga Lake Public Campground on neighboring East Caroga Lake.

CONTACT: New York State Department of Environmental Conservation Region 5.

BOG RIVER FLOW AREA

This canoe route boasts two lakes and two ponds connected by the Bog River and Horseshoe Lake's outlet. It is highly popular with backwoods anglers, canoeists, and earth travelers because it offers numerous beach campsites, in a wilderness setting, close to the road. The waterway owes it navigability to two dams on the Bog River. Lows Lake, the largest impoundment, is one of the state's most productive loon nesting sites. Other rare birds likely to be sighted include bald eagles, ospreys, and spruce grouse.

107. HORSESHOE LAKE

KEY SPECIES: Tiger muskies, walleyes, largemouth bass, smallmouth bass, and yellow perch.

DESCRIPTION: Nestled in the Horseshoe Lake Wild Forest, this 384-acre lake averages 9 feet deep and has a maximum depth of 16 feet. Its shoreline is completely forested.

TIPS: Retrieve a large bucktail spinner at a steady clip; when it comes to within a yard of the boat, sink your rod tip into the water and make some figure eights to trigger strikes from followers.

THE FISHING: This lake is the best norlunge spot in NYSDEC Region 6. The state stocks tigers periodically—2,100 8-inchers in 2014. They typically run 7 to 12 pounds, but 18-pounders are caught regularly. They respond to large baits: minnows, bucktail spinners, spoons, and crankbaits like Bomber Long A's. The state also regularly stocks walleyes—8,500 1.5-inchers in 2014. "They are doing very well," says retired fisheries biologist Rich Preall. "Several of my angler contacts fish there often for eyes which range from 15 to 22 inches." They'll take worms dragged slowly on bottom, jigs, and minnowbaits. Preall says the "lake can produce largemouths up to 6 pounds." Smallmouths are also plentiful, and can go up to 3 pounds. Both bass strike crayfish, minnows, and just about every lure imaginable, but are most exciting to catch on poppers and darters worked over a calm surface. Yellow perch average 9 inches and are often caught on crayfish and minnows targeting smallmouths. Many are also taken by drifting worms and jigging 2-inch scented, curly-tailed grubs.

Fishing for black bass out of season is prohibited. The minimum length for walleye is 18 inches.

DIRECTIONS: From Long Lake village, take NY 30 north for about 14 miles, turn west on NY 421, and travel for about 5.5 miles.

ADDITIONAL INFORMATION: A cartop launch with parking for about five cars, two handicapped-accessible campsites with pads (one has a privy), several primitive campsites, and a fishing pier are off NY 421, on the southern half of the lake. Camping is only permitted in sites designated by CAMP HERE disks.

CONTACT: New York State Department of Environmental Conservation Region 6 and St. Lawrence County Chamber of Commerce.

108. HITCHINS POND

KEY SPECIES: Largemouth bass and yellow perch.

DESCRIPTION: This 147-acre pond averages 12 feet deep and has a maximum depth of 33 feet.

TIPS: The north basin is the deepest part.

THE FISHING: A decent largemouth bass fishery has developed here over the past decade or so. Bucketmouths typically range from 1.5 to 3.5 pounds and react violently to anything noisy, from poppers to rattling crankbaits. Yellow perch from 6 to 10 inches are abundant and hit worms and 2-inch spinner-rigged soft plastics like curly-tailed grubs. "Emigrant tiger muskies from Horseshoe Lake occasionally petrify bass anglers," advises Rich Preall. In addition, according to the retired fisheries biologist formerly assigned to the beat, "Brook trout pile up in the rapids downstream of Hitchins Pond in the spring and sometimes fall."

DIRECTIONS: Paddle down Horseshoe Lake's (**site 107**) outlet for about a mile to its confluence with the Bog River, then head upstream (west) on the Bog for about a mile.

ADDITIONAL INFORMATION: The pond offers five primitive beach campsites.

CONTACT: New York State Department of Environmental Conservation Region 6.

109. LOWS LAKE (BOG RIVER FLOW)

KEY SPECIES: Largemouth bass and brook trout.

DESCRIPTION: Its western half set in the deep woods of the Five Ponds Wilderness, fringed in spots with vast bogs and marshes, this 2,844-acre lake averages 5 feet deep and has a maximum depth of 55 feet.

TIPS: Store food away from the campsite to prevent visits from bears.

THE FISHING: Largemouth bass in a wilderness setting is the lake's major draw. Bucketmouths typically range from 1 to 5 pounds. Ron Kolodziej, retired outdoor columnist for the *Amsterdam Recorder*, suggests working buzzbaits and spinnerbaits along weed edges at dusk. On the other hand, Rich Preall, a former state fisheries biologist, says the bass hang out near or under floating bog mats, adding, "They are very abundant, and catches of 30 to 50 in an evening are common. Chuck a Senko or Fluke, or twitch a Rapala near the mats for quick action." Brook trout from 6 to 14 inches occupy deep spring holes. These wild fish will take a worm or streamer trolled behind a wobbler or small dodger.

Possession or use of baitfish is prohibited. No motors allowed.

DIRECTIONS: Head south on NY 30 for about 7 miles out of Tupper Lake village and turn west on NY 421. Travel for about 4 miles, skirting the south shore of Horseshoe Lake, and at the end, take the gravel road heading south to the lower dam. Launch on the Bog River and head upstream. If a barrier prevents access to the gravel road, continue on NY 421 to Horseshoe Lake's (**site 107**) outlet, launch there, and paddle downstream to the confluence with the Bog River, then head upstream. You will have one short portage around the upper dam.

ADDITIONAL INFORMATION: There are 39 primitive campsites spread around the lake, some with pit privies. Beach camping is only permitted in sites designated by a disk. Several islands and points are off-limits to the general public from June through August.

CONTACT: New York State Department of Environmental Conservation Region 6.

110. GRASSY POND (GRASSE AND GRASS)

KEY SPECIES: Brook trout and largemouth bass.

DESCRIPTION: This 125-acre pond averages 20 feet deep and has a maximum depth of 30 feet.

TIPS: Dead-drift nymphs at the mouths of tributaries.

THE FISHING: Native brook trout ranging from 6 up to 16 inches are available in the mouths of tributaries, in the deep hole off the northwestern tributary, and in the deep center. They hit worms and Muddler Minnows trolled about 8 inches behind an attractor. Largemouth bass up to 4 pounds roam the shallow shoreline and the outlet channel. They hit rattling crankbaits and plastic worms, fished on Texas rigs or skipped over the surface around vegetation and windfalls.

Use or possession of baitfish is prohibited.

DIRECTIONS: This pond is at the tip of the north arm on Lows Lake's (**site 109**) west end.

ADDITIONAL INFORMATION: This pond has five beach campsites, three with pit privies.

CONTACT: New York State Department of Environmental Conservation Region 6.

111. BOG RIVER

KEY SPECIES: Brook trout and largemouth bass.

DESCRIPTION: Gathering the flows from Lows and Horseshoe Lakes, Hitchins and Grassy Ponds, this river tumbles over a dam and flows east for about 7 miles to feed Tupper Lake's south end.

TIPS: Scout all rapids.

THE FISHING: Downstream of the Bog River Flow's lower dam, the state stocks about 700 brookies averaging 8.5 inches annually. They typically reach 10 to 12 inches and respond to worms, in-line spinners, and Phoebes. Some largemouth bass are also available near the mouth. Ranging from 1 to 2.5 pounds, they can be taken in holes on crayfish, by fly fishing with bass streamers and $\frac{1}{24}$-ounce Hula Poppers tight to vegetation and structure, and by walking topwater lures like Zara Spooks over open water.

DIRECTIONS: Head south on NY 30 for about 8 miles out of Tupper Lake village and turn west on NY 421. Travel for about 4 miles, skirting the south shore of Horseshoe Lake, turn left on the gravel road heading south, and continue for a mile to the dam.

ADDITIONAL INFORMATION: The best way to fish here is to float in a rubber raft or white-water canoe. Always scout rapids: While most of this stream flows gently, it has some stretches of technical Class III rapids, along with a Class V and a killer Class VI waterfalls. Primitive camping is allowed in the state forest lining most of both banks.

CONTACT: New York State Department of Environmental Conservation Region 6.

112. SHALLOW LAKE

KEY SPECIES: Brook trout and smallmouth bass.

DESCRIPTION: Located deep in the Pigeon Lake Wilderness, this 268-acre lake averages 11 feet deep and has a maximum depth of 30 feet.

TIPS: "Fish Shallow Lake on a calm day; its east–west orientation and shallow water combine for boat-rocking whitecaps on windy days," suggests Rich Preall, a retired fisheries biologist formerly assigned to the beat.

THE FISHING: The state air-drops about 6,400 brook trout averaging 4.5 inches regularly. They typically end up ranging from 6 to 15 inches, but Rich Preall says he's seen brookies here that go 3 pounds. They take streamers trolled 100 feet behind the canoe in a figure-eight pattern. Smallmouth bass ranging from 12 to 14 inches are common and also hit streamers. However, they are just as likely to hit spinnerbaits, worms, and crayfish.

Use or possession of baitfish is prohibited.

DIRECTIONS: Head northwest for 1.5 miles on the footpath at the north end of Lower Brown Tract Pond Campground (**site 113**).

CONTACT: New York State Department of Environmental Conservation Region 5.

113. LOWER BROWN TRACT POND

KEY SPECIES: Brook trout, smallmouth bass, largemouth bass, and panfish.

DESCRIPTION: Located on the seam of the Pigeon Lake Wilderness and the Moose River Plains Wild Forest, this 156-acre pond averages 14 feet deep and has a maximum depth of 33 feet.

TIPS: Work leech patterns with a sinking line.

THE FISHING: A few brook trout find their way here via tributaries. Ranging from 6 to 14 inches, they are often caught serendipitously by surprised campers targeting bullheads and pumpkinseeds with worms. According to retired NYSDEC fisheries biologist Rich Preall, "The famous fish culturist Seth Green introduced smallmouth bass into the Adirondacks via stocking into Lower Browns Tract Pond in 1872." They found the place desirable and prospered, currently ranging from 12 to 14 inches. A few largemouths up to 18 inches are also available. Both take surface lures and spinnerbaits. "Upper and Lower Brown Tract Ponds are leech havens, and lures imitating them would no doubt appeal to bass," adds Preall. Brown bullheads averaging 9 inches and pumpkinseeds up to 8 inches are common and strike worms fished on bottom.

Motors are prohibited.

DIRECTIONS: Head west out of Raquette Lake village for about a mile on Uncas Road.

ADDITIONAL INFORMATION: Brown Tract Pond Public Campground, a fee area, offers 90 campsites, picnic areas, vault toilets, and a hard-surface boat launch. A day-use fee is charged noncampers when the campground is open, mid-May through Labor Day. Free day use is permitted off-season.

CONTACT: New York State Department of Environmental Conservation Region 5.

Ladies unwinding on Lower Brown Tract Pond (site 113).

114. UPPER BROWN TRACT POND

KEY SPECIES: Largemouth bass and brown bullheads.

DESCRIPTION: This 51-acre pond is totally surrounded by woods, averages 14 feet deep, and has a maximum depth of 33 feet.

TIPS: Walk Zara Pooches on calm days.

THE FISHING: Largemouth bass range from undersized to 16 inches. They take in-line spinners and crankbaits. Brown bullheads average 9 inches and take worms fished on bottom.

Motors are prohibited.

DIRECTIONS: About 0.5 mile west of Lower Brown Tract Pond (**site 113**) on Uncas Road.

CONTACT: New York State Department of Environmental Conservation Region 5.

115. BLUE MOUNTAIN LAKE

KEY SPECIES: Lake trout, landlocked Atlantic salmon, brook trout, and smallmouth bass.

DESCRIPTION: Less than 20 feet from the road in spots, punctuated by several forested islands, shaded to the east by its 3,759-foot-high namesake, this 1,220-acre lake averages 25 feet deep and has a maximum depth of 102 feet. Its bottom is pitted with deep holes ranging from 60 to 100 feet deep.

TIPS: Fishing is best in June.

THE FISHING: Lake trout are the bread-and-butter species here. Unfortunately, they're generally undersized—a 2013 state survey resulted in 44 averaging 16 inches, though there were several keepers, including a 27-incher. The state stocks roughly 600 7-inchers most years; and survival is good on the lake's numerous smelt. Dramatic depth changes make trolling impractical, so most anglers target the lakers by jigging spoons or fishing live suckers on bottom. Atlantic salmon are also stocked regularly: 1,300 6.5-inchers in 2013. They easily reach their 15-inch size limit on the smelt, too, and are mostly targeted by trolling streamers like Black Nose Dace, Gray Ghosts, and Crystal Woolly Buggers around tributary mouths during April's smelt runs. Smallmouths ranging from 12 to 15 inches, with quite a few going 4-something pounds, thrive in the rocky, relatively shallow southwestern corner. They hit minnows and crayfish drifted along breaklines and drop-offs, and bucktail jigs worked on bottom in 15 to 30 feet of water. Surplus brook trout are stocked periodically. Ranging from 6 to 12 inches, they hit worms fished near tributary mouths, early and late in the season; lures and flies in summer.

Trout season is year-round; the limit for lake trout is two; and ice fishing is permitted.

DIRECTIONS: Head south out of the hamlet of Long Lake on NY 30 for about 9 miles.

ADDITIONAL INFORMATION: There is a cartop launch next to the public beach on NY 28 in the village of Blue Mountain Lake, and a couple of commercial marinas with launches are nearby. Primitive camping is allowed in the Blue Ridge Wilderness, on the south side of NY 28, about 2 miles west of the village of Blue Mountain Lake. The divide separating the Hudson and St. Lawrence River drainages is about a mile east of the hamlet.

CONTACT: New York State Department of Environmental Conservation Region 5 and Hamilton County Tourism.

Public access to the water is found on NY 28, in the hamlet of Blue Mountain Lake.

116. RAQUETTE LAKE

KEY SPECIES: Lake trout, largemouth bass, brook trout, smallmouth bass, black crappies, lake whitefish, and panfish.

DESCRIPTION: Covering 4,927 acres, this lake averages 44 feet deep and has a maximum depth of 96 feet. The largest natural lake in the Adirondacks, its numerous points stretch its shoreline to 99 miles. Its banks are punctuated with numerous cottages, including several Great Camps, fabulous log palaces constructed by industrialists and robber barons between 1870 and 1930.

TIPS: The best time to troll for lakers in summer is a couple of hours each side of high noon.

THE FISHING: Lake trout are the most common game fish in Raquette Lake. They typically range from 2 to 5 pounds, but lunkers over 10 pounds are present. May is the best month to fish for the species because the water is still uniformly cold and they hang out in relatively shallow water, within range of anglers casting spoons and minnowbaits, especially around Beecher Island on the north end. In summer, they go deep and respond to minnows and spoons trolled near bottom behind flashers and Christmas tree rigs. While the lake isn't exactly swimming in bucketmouth habitat, the little it has—primarily in its shallow, weedy bays—is loaded with largemouths ranging from 1.5 to 5 pounds. Indeed, a local fish and game club that holds annual potluck fishing tournaments has seen lake trout pushed out of the top spot the past few years by largemouths. They'll take soft jerkbaits like Slug-Gos worked around fallen timber, weed beds, and lily pads; and 4-inch Texas-rigged tubes worked along the edges of bulrushes and cattail mats. Every now and then, the state stocks thousands of brook trout to supplement natural populations. Those that avoid the jaws of lakers and bass end up averaging about 8 inches, and lunkers over 16 inches are available. They take worms, minnows, Mepps Aglias, and Panther Martins. Although smallmouth bass numbers are down lately, there are still enough 12- to 15-inchers around to make targeting them worthwhile. They hit jigs, minnows, crayfish, and diving crankbaits. Lake whitefish average about 2 pounds and are usually taken incidentally in summer by anglers targeting perch and bass with minnows, on bottom, in deep water. They come in shallower in winter and respond to ice jigs tipped with a minnow, fish belly, or insect larva. Yellow perch in the 6- to 12-inch range, sunfish averaging 6 inches, and brown bullheads up to 13 inches are plentiful and respond to worms. Retired fisheries biologist Rich Preall claims, "A Johnny Crappieseed introduced black crappies about seven years ago"; rock bass have also made it into the system recently, and anglers report catching them with increasing frequency. They'll hit small jigs, poppers, flies, and minnows.

The limit for lake trout is two per day. Trout can be taken year-round.

DIRECTIONS: Head north out of Inlet on NY 28 for about 7 miles.

ADDITIONAL INFORMATION: The Raquette Lake Supply Co. in the hamlet of Raquette Lake operates a hard-surface ramp with parking for several rigs. A no-fee canoe launch is on NY 28, 2.5 miles east of Raquette Lake village. Big island, due east of the village, has three primitive lean-tos. Several other lean-tos are on the lake's west and north shores. These structures are available to the public on a first-come, first-served bases, for one night. Golden Beach Public Campground, a fee area on NY 28, about 3 miles east of the hamlet of Raquette Lake, offers 205 no-frills sites, many on the beach, a paved launch suitable for small trailered craft, parking for 15 rigs, shore fishing, hot showers, picnic areas with fireplaces, and a swimming beach. A day-use fee is charged noncampers during camping season, mid-May through Labor Day. Free day use allowed off-season.

CONTACT: New York State Department of Environmental Conservation Region 5.

Paddling into Raquette Lake (site 116) via the Lower Brown Tract Pond (site 113) outlet.

116A. Tioga Point Public Campgrounds

DESCRIPTION: This fee area has 15 lean-tos, 10 no-frills sites, picnic tables, and fireplaces. No potable water. Open from mid-May through Labor Day.

DIRECTIONS: Accessible only by water, this facility is on the third point on the east bank as you head north up the lake.

RAQUETTE RIVER

Running for 136 miles, mostly through the Adirondack Park, this river bears two distinct personalities: free and controlled. For this reason, it will be covered in upper and lower sections. The upper reach, the free section, tumbles over waterfalls and careens down some awesome rapids on its journey to Carry Falls Reservoir. North of the impoundment, the stream is tamed by a series of dams, which create numerous reservoirs and quiet wide-waters all the way to its mouth on the St. Lawrence River.

117. UPPER RAQUETTE RIVER

KEY SPECIES: Brown trout, walleyes, northern pike, largemouth bass, smallmouth bass.

DESCRIPTION: Spawned as the outlet of Raquette Lake, this stretch of the river feeds and drains Forked and Long Lakes, Simon and Raquette Ponds, and Piercefield Flow. It comes to rest in Carry Falls Reservoir.

TIPS: Douse yourself in insect repellent and wear a head net in late spring.

THE FISHING: The headwaters to a couple of miles below Raquette Falls are generally fast-flowing coldwater habitat. The state stocks about 1,050 brown trout running from 8 to 13.5 inches (30 percent are two-year-olds) annually to supplement naturally occurring populations of brook trout. Both species take worms during spring runoff and after summer rains, nymphs and in-line spinners the rest of the time.

Downstream of Raquette Falls, the river is primarily a warmwater fishery. Northern pike normally range from 3 to 5 pounds, but larger ones show up all the time. They hit best on large minnows but also take spinnerbaits, crankbaits, and in-line spinners dressed in bucktail. Walleyes ranging from 18 to 23 inches grow progressively more common the closer you get to Tupper Lake and respond well to bucktail jigs, 3-inch curly-tailed grubs, and tubes worked on bottom in holes and along undercut banks. Smallmouths

The Raquette River and its reservoirs are loaded with walleyes like this beauty.

running from 0.5 to 1.5 pounds are also well represented. They share habitat with the walleyes and will take the same baits. In addition, bronzebacks react violently to anything flashy like a spoon or spinnerbait whipping past them. Lately, largemouths ranging from 1 to 4 pounds have been threatening to knock smallmouths from their lofty position as the river's top bass. Search for them with large poppers, buzzbaits, and soft plastic jerkbaits worked around vegetation and windfalls in oxbows and backwaters.

DIRECTIONS: North Point Road, which strikes southwest from the hamlet of Deerland, skirts the headwaters; NY 3 parallels the river from Tupper Lake north to Sevey; and NY 56 hugs it from there to Carry Falls Reservoir.

ADDITIONAL INFORMATION: This section of river is a popular canoe route and is spotted with numerous lean-tos. The state's free brochure *Adirondack Waterways 2014* contains a map of this stretch.

CONTACT: New York State Department of Environmental Conservation Region 5.

117A. Buttermilk Falls Public Access

DESCRIPTION: This site has shoulder parking for about five cars and access to the river above and below one of the most beautiful waterfalls in the Adirondack Park.

THE FISHING: Brown and brook trout are present above and below the falls. Bass and northern pike occupy holes just upstream of Long Lake.

DIRECTIONS: Take NY 28 north out of Raquette Lake Village for about 13 miles to the hamlet of Blue Mountain Lake and head north on NY 30/28N. When you pass the Adirondack Museum on the edge of town, continue for 6.4 miles to the sharp curve in Deerland, take a left on North Point Road, and travel for about 2 miles.

ADDITIONAL INFORMATION: There are three public lean-tos near the falls—one above and two below. They are available to the public for one night per group, first come, first served.

117B. Public Access

DESCRIPTION: Parking for about 10 cars and river access at the entrance to the state campground.

THE FISHING: This stretch of river has native brook trout ranging from 5 to 12 inches and brown trout averaging 14 inches. They take worms and nymphs.

DIRECTIONS: Continue heading down North Point Road from the above site for about 2 miles and turn into the Forked Lake State Campground.

117C. Axton Landing

DESCRIPTION: Parking for 10 cars and a beach launch for cartop craft.

THE FISHING: Walleyes, northern pike, and smallmouth bass occupy this relatively quiet section of river that runs through a massive marsh whose habitats include steep shorelines, undercut banks, blowdowns, cattail mats, bulrush colonies, lily pads, and tributary mouths. Minnows, crankbaits, and spinnerbaits are effective for bass and northerns; worms and jigs are popularly used for the bronzebacks and walleyes.

DIRECTIONS: From the village of Tupper Lake, head east on NY 3 for about 7 miles, turn south on Coreys Road, and continue for about 1.5 miles.

ADDITIONAL INFORMATION: Raquette River falls is about 3 miles upstream.

117D. Raquette River Public Access

DESCRIPTION: "Locals call this site the Crusher because launching a boat here during high water can lead to wild results," says retired fisheries biologist Rich Preall. The state added jetties in 2011 to protect boats during launching. Located downstream of Raquette Falls, it has a double-wide ramp, two lots with parking for over 50 rigs, and toilets.

THE FISHING: The river is aimless here. Flowing slowly, quietly through one of the largest wetlands in the Adirondacks, it looks like a watery web whose strands of creeks, backwaters, and oxbows shoot out in all directions. This navigable network of channels is home to good populations of northern pike, smallmouth bass, bucketmouths, and walleyes.

DIRECTIONS: Head north out of the village of Tupper Lake on NY 30/3 for about 3 miles.

ADDITIONAL INFORMATION: Much of this section, in both directions, runs through or along the High Peaks Wilderness Area, where primitive camping is allowed.

118. FORKED LAKE

KEY SPECIES: Largemouth bass, smallmouth bass, yellow perch, pumpkinseeds, brown bullheads, brook trout, lake trout, and landlocked salmon.

DESCRIPTION: Set in deep woods, this crooked, 1,248-acre lake averages 10 feet deep and drops down to 40 feet in one spot.

TIPS: Work soft plastic jerkbaits around tree stumps and submerged logs.

THE FISHING: This warmwater fishery is loaded with smallmouths ranging from 12 to 16 inches, and bucketmouths running from 12 to 20 inches. They respond to tubes, stickworms, soft swimbaits, Texas-rigged worms, jig-n-pigs, crankbaits—all the usual suspects. Concentrate your efforts around fallen timber. Yellow perch thrive here, reaching up to 12 inches. They take minnows and small lures. Pumpkinseeds ranging from 4 to 7 inches and bullheads averaging a whopping 13 inches are also abundant and love worms. Up until recently, this lake's deepest area, a hole east of the west end's Squirrel Point, was acidic and devoid of fish. Remedial efforts panned out and now, according to fisheries biologist Rich Preall, "lake trout, salmon, and brookies show up there—mostly migrants from Raquette Lake or Brandreth Lake." They'll take spoons and minnows jigged on bottom.

Lake trout and landlocked salmon can be taken all year; the daily limit for lakers is two.

DIRECTIONS: Head north on NY 28 out of Raquette Lake Village for about 13 miles to the hamlet of Blue Mountain Lake. Get on NY 30/28N and head north for about 8 miles to Deerland. Turn west on North Point Road, travel for about 3 miles, turn right on Forked Lake Campsite Lane, and travel for about a mile.

ADDITIONAL INFORMATION: Forked Lake State Campground has 80 no-frills campsites, a boat launch, picnic facilities, canoe and boat rentals, hiking trails, and pit toilets. Open from mid-May through Labor Day. A day-fee is charged noncampers during the season; free day use is permitted off-season.

CONTACT: New York State Department of Environmental Conservation Region 5.

118A. Canoe Carry Access

DESCRIPTION: This beach launch is suitable for small trailered craft; parking for about 10 rigs.

DIRECTIONS: Head southeast for about 5 miles on North Point Road from its intersection with the campground entrance road, then turn right.

119. LONG LAKE

KEY SPECIES: Smallmouth bass, largemouth bass, and northern pike.

DESCRIPTION: Really just a long, wide pool in the Raquette River, this 4,000-something-acre wide-water stretches for 14 miles, averages 13 feet deep, and has a maximum depth of around 50 feet.

TIPS: Find habitat and you'll find fish.

THE FISHING: This lake is poor in habitat. While the shoreline may look fishy, the lake floor is mostly barren. Still, there's a good population of 1- to 2.5-pound smallmouth bass. They are especially numerous around the north end's two sets of islands—the deepest part of the lake—where they respond to scented tubes, 3-inch curly-tailed grubs, and 4-inch finesse worms on dropshot rigs. First appearing about 20 years ago, largemouth bass took a liking to the place and prospered. Typically ranging from 1 to 4 pounds, most are taken on Rat-L-Traps, Zara Spooks, and jerkbaits worked around everything from docks and fallen timber to lily pads. The northern pike fishery, the lake's former main attraction, is holding its own. They used to range from 3 to 8 pounds but now typically go from 2 to 5 pounds. They hang out anywhere there is cover and respond to live minnows, spinnerbaits, and crankbaits.

DIRECTIONS: Take NY 28 north out of Raquette Lake village for 12 miles to Blue Mountain Lake, then head north on NY 30/28N for about 7 miles.

ADDITIONAL INFORMATION: The Long Lake fishing access site, located on Dock Road right in the heart of Long Lake village (turn east at the flashing light on NY 30), has a boat launch with a triple-wide paved ramp, parking for 40 rigs, and toilets.

CONTACT: New York State Department of Environmental Conservation Region 5.

120. TUPPER LAKE

KEY SPECIES: Northern pike, walleyes, largemouth bass, smallmouth bass, lake trout, landlocked Atlantic salmon, and yellow perch.

DESCRIPTION: Covering roughly 4,000 acres, averaging 39 feet deep, and having a maximum depth of 100 feet, half of this two-story fishery's shoreline is heavily developed and includes the village of Tupper Lake, one of the largest in the Adirondacks.

TIPS: Be creative with presentations so your bait stands out.

THE FISHING: It's fitting that this lake was named after a surveyor who drowned while fishing it. Abundant rainbow smelt support large populations of a variety of game species. Trophy northern pike are the most famous. Normally ranging from 3 to 15 pounds, with 20-pounders caught fairly regularly, they're mostly taken through the ice with large minnows. Walleyes ranging from 2 to 10 pounds are the lake's best-kept secret. In fact, Richard Preall, a state biologist, says he wouldn't be surprised if a new state record is loose in the lake. Locals quietly take quite a few at night by flatlining minnowbaits and casting crankbaits around the islands. Smallmouth bass range from 0.75 to 3 pounds. They congregate around island drop-offs and rocky points, and respond with alacrity to crayfish, minnows, salted tubes, and spinnerbaits. Preall says this lake, like many on the Raquette River, is experiencing an explosion of largemouth bass. Bucketmouths ranging from 2 to 4 pounds are common, and 5-pounders, even bigger, are landed often. They hang out in the lake's bays and stream mouths and are mostly taken on spinnerbaits, buzzbaits, and Texas-rigged worms. Yellow perch range from 6 to 14 inches and hit worms, minnows, and scented, 2-inch curly-tailed grubs.

Anywhere from 10,000 to 15,000 lake trout averaging 6.5 inches are stocked every couple of years—it used to be annually but DEC cut back when surveys revealed 20 percent of the lakers are naturally reproduced. Ranging from 20 to 30 inches, they're generally caught through the ice on minnows fished on bottom. Heavy stocking of Atlantic salmon was discontinued for about eight years early in this century. "We kept the tradition alive by stocking a few surplus fish about every other year," says retired fisheries biologist Rich Preall. The state resumed a serious stocking program when numerous anglers presented photographic evidence of salmon up to 8 pounds taken during the lean period. Currently, several thousand Atlantics averaging 7 inches are released most years. They typically grow to range from 15 to 22 inches, and are taken early in the season by trolling off the mouth of the Bog River or by lobbing gobs of worms suspended below bobbers into the current below the falls and letting the bait get swept into the lake. In summer, they take tandem streamers and crankbaits flatlined in open water.

It is often said big fish didn't get that way by being stupid. Tupper Lake is an exception to that rule. Here the fish grow huge because of the unusually abundant forage base. In fact, the population of rainbow smelt is so vast, the biggest problem anglers face is presenting their bait so game fish can see it. Preall says one guide he knows solved the situation by trolling 4- to 5-inch minnowbaits "just under the smelt schools, which can be a half mile long."

Lake trout can be taken year-round.

DIRECTIONS: NY 30 parallels the lake's east bank south of Tupper Lake Village.

ADDITIONAL INFORMATION: Tupper Lake Boat Launching Site, on NY 30, about 2 miles south of the village, has a paved, four-lane ramp, parking for about 75 rigs, shore-fishing access, handicapped access, and toilets. Numerous inns and motels line NY 30.

CONTACT: New York State Department of Environmental Conservation Region 5 and Tupper Lake Chamber of Commerce.

121. RAQUETTE POND

KEY SPECIES: Northern pike, walleyes, yellow perch, and possibly black crappies.

DESCRIPTION: Created by a dam built on the Raquette River, a couple of miles downstream of Tupper Lake, this pond is difficult to differentiate from the main lake—but the natives insist on calling it Raquette Pond. Covering 1,180 acres, it averages 5 feet deep and has a maximum depth of 12 feet.

TIPS: Troll the channel winding down the center.

THE FISHING: Northern pike ranging from 3 to 15 pounds prowl the weed edges and hit large minnows, curly-tailed grubs (yellow is especially effective), and spinnerbaits. Walleyes running from 3 to 10 pounds are available in the spring and autumn and respond to bucktail jigs worked along the channel drops, worms drifted on harnesses (plain and spinner-rigged), and curly-tailed grubs. Yellow perch run up to 12 inches and take worms, minnows, and 2-inch scented grubs swimmed on plain jigheads or tipped on bucktail jigs and bounced on bottom.

DIRECTIONS: NY 3 parallels the pond's north shore in the hamlet of Tupper Lake.

ADDITIONAL INFORMATION: The municipal park on NY 3 has a beach launch suitable for small trailered craft.

CONTACT: New York State Department of Environmental Conservation Region 5 and Tupper Lake Chamber of Commerce.

122. SIMON POND

KEY SPECIES: Northern pike, walleyes, largemouth bass, and yellow perch.

DESCRIPTION: This 689-acre body of water averages 10 feet deep and has a maximum depth of 36 feet. It is connected to Tupper Lake by a canal-like, navigable channel.

TIPS: Ice fish with minnows in the weedy areas on the northwestern corner.

THE FISHING: While this pond offers great fishing year-round, its greatest claim to fame is its ice bite. Northerns ranging from 5 to 7 pounds are plentiful, and pike up to 15 pounds are taken each winter. They like plain minnows fished in weed clearings, freelined or weighted down; or tipped on spoons and jigged on bottom. Walleyes ranging from 3 to 8 pounds are also taken through the ice on minnows, primarily in the deep eastern corner. Perch up to 13 inches occupy the entire pond and hit minnows and grubs. In summer, largemouth bass up to 5 pounds hang out in the weeds, eagerly ambushing poppers chugging along, gurgling and spitting; jig-n-pigs tossed into slop, weed openings, and edges; and soft jerkbaits ripped across any water deep enough to cover their backs.

DIRECTIONS: On the east side of the NY 30 bridge, just south of the village of Tupper Lake.

ADDITIONAL INFORMATION: The annual Northern Challenge Ice Fishing Derby, held on the first Saturday in February, draws "800–1,000 ice fishermen for the great prizes and social atmosphere," says retired fisheries biologist Rich Preall. The access site most favored by ice fishermen is the local rod and gun club's gravel boat launch on Lake Simond Road. Parking for 10 cars.

CONTACT: New York State Department of Environmental Conservation Region 5 and Tupper Lake Chamber of Commerce.

123. PIERCEFIELD FLOW

KEY SPECIES: Northern pike, smallmouth bass, largemouth bass, and walleyes.

DESCRIPTION: This 365-acre impoundment averages 7 feet deep and has a maximum depth of 50 feet. Surrounded by forest, it is littered with numerous, barely submerged stumps.

TIPS: Fish the fast water downstream of the Setting Pole dam (on the Raquette River, about 0.5 mile upstream of its mouth) for early- and late-season walleyes.

THE FISHING: This water body is loaded with northern pike habitat. They range from 18 to 30 inches and eagerly take minnows and spinnerbaits. Bronzebacks ranging from 12 to 14 inches and bucketmouths up to 18 inches are abundant. The smallies respond to jigs; the largemouths like spinnerbaits; and both hit 3- and 4-inch scented minnows worked on dropshot rigs and Texas-rigged worms worked in timber. Walleyes range from 15 to 22 inches and strike bucktail and marabou jigs, and minnow-imitating crankbaits. Retired fisheries biologist Rich Preall reports: "I found 85 feet of water in a big hole about 0.5 mile down from the Setting Pole dam . . . Caught walleye, smallmouth, and largemouth."

DIRECTIONS: Take NY 3 south out of the village of Tupper Lake for about 4 miles and turn right on Pumphouse Road.

ADDITIONAL INFORMATION: Primitive camping is allowed at Setting Pole dam. A beach launch for cartop craft is on NY 3; the current is usually pretty strong here, so avoid being swept over the dam by making sure your motor is working before launching.

CONTACT: New York State Department of Environmental Conservation Region 6 and St. Lawrence County Chamber of Commerce.

124. CARRY FALLS RESERVOIR

KEY SPECIES: Northern pike, walleyes, smallmouth bass, and brown bullheads.

DESCRIPTION: This 3,170-acre impoundment averages 18 feet deep and has a maximum depth of 50 feet. Its shoreline is almost entirely forested.

TIPS: Fish for walleyes on moonless nights.

THE FISHING: Northern pike ranging from 2 to 6 pounds are the primary predator. They respond to minnows, large bucktail spinners, spinnerbaits, and minnowbaits like Rapalas and ThunderSticks. Walleyes go anywhere from 15 to 26 inches and hang out on the deep end of drop-offs and at the dam by day; over shallow shoals and around the mouth of the Raquette River by night and during low-light conditions. They take worms drifted or trolled on spinner harnesses when the sun's high, and minnowbaits worked over shoals and along the shoreline from dusk until midmorning. Smallmouth bass typically go from 12 to 15 inches, like to hang out over boulder fields on flats and drop-offs, and respond to crayfish, minnows, and scented and salted tubes. Brown bullheads ranging from 8 to 12 inches are plentiful and hit worms fished on bottom, especially on cloudy days and at night.

DIRECTIONS: Head south out of Potsdam on NY 56 for about 18 miles to the hamlet of Stark. Turn east on Stark Road, travel for about 1.5 miles, turn right on Carry Falls Road and continue for about 2 miles (you'll pass Start Falls Reservoir, site 125).

ADDITIONAL INFORMATION: A hard-surface launch ramp with parking for about five cars is next to the dam. Parmenter Camp (315-267-2640), a fee area run by Brookfield Power off NY 56, 10 miles south of Colton, offers 16 primitive sites and a boat launch. Open Memorial Day through Labor Day.

CONTACT: New York State Department of Environmental Conservation Region 6 and the St. Lawrence County Chamber of Commerce.

RAQUETTE RIVER RESERVOIRS

Downstream of Carry Falls Reservoir all the way to Raymondville, a distance of about 50 miles, the Raquette River is straddled by several dams, transforming it into a staircase of impoundments punctuated by short sets of rapids. Pools below the dams hold walleyes early in the season.

Kayak fishing and sun worshippers.

125. STARK FALLS RESERVOIR

KEY SPECIES: Northern pike, walleyes, smallmouth bass, largemouth bass, brown bullheads, and yellow perch.

DESCRIPTION: Formed at the base of the Carry Falls dam, this 650-acre impoundment averages 24 feet and has a maximum depth of 50 feet.

TIPS: Work jerkbaits along the shoreline.

THE FISHING: Northerns run 2 to 6 pounds and are quick to strike 3- to 4-inch scented curly-tailed grubs swimmed steadily or jerked. Walleyes ranging from 15 to 22 inches hit bucktail jigs tipped with minnows or worms and bounced slowly on bottom, in 15 to 20 feet of water. The breaklines at the mouths of bays hold good numbers of smallmouths up to 16 inches. They respond well to 3- and 4-inch soft baits worked on dropshot rigs. Largemouth bass ranging from 12 to 16 inches are being reported with increasing frequency. They hit soft jerkbaits worked over and around windfalls and vegetation, and Texas-rigged worms dragged slowly down drop-offs. Brown bullheads and yellow perch range from 7 to 11 inches and are the local remedy for cabin fever right after ice-out. The bullheads take worms fished on bottom at night, and on overcast or rainy days; and the perch go for small jigs tipped with Berkley Honey Worms, and small minnows suspended below tiny bobbers and fished 3 to 15 feet deep, on sunny days, spring through autumn.

DIRECTIONS: Carry Falls Road (see Directions to site 124) skirts the west bank.

ADDITIONAL INFORMATION: A hard-surface ramp, with parking for about five rigs, is at the dam. While reversing out of the launch area, watch out for boulders on the left.

CONTACT: New York State Department of Environmental Conservation Region 6 and St. Lawrence County Chamber of Commerce.

126. BLAKE FALLS RESERVOIR

KEY SPECIES: Walleyes, smallmouth bass, northern pike, yellow perch, and brown bullheads.

DESCRIPTION: This 642-acre impoundment averages 7.2 feet deep and has a maximum depth of 45 feet. Large bays are numerous and relatively shallow. The deepest part is a narrow, 10.5-mile-long trench running right down the middle.

TIPS: Work crankbaits in the bays, especially the one north of Blake McNeil Campground.

THE FISHING: Walleyes range from 2 to 5 pounds and respond well to minnows fished deep on a Lindy rigs. In the evening, they rise to the bays and hit shallow and deep-diving crankbaits worked at a steady clip, and jerked every now and then to make them more interesting. A popular daytime method for taking eyes is to drift worms on bottom, in the old channel. Smallmouth bass from 12 to 14 inches are abundant, and fish up to 18 inches are available. They respond to crayfish, minnows, tubes, and diving crankbaits. Northerns ranging from 18 to 26 inches are targeted by anglers casting spinnerbaits, drifting large minnows, or suspending them below bobbers and letting them "walk along" as Cousin Staash likes to say. Bullheads and perch can reach 13 inches and take worms.

DIRECTIONS: Head east out of South Colton on Raquette River Road for just under 7 miles.

ADDITIONAL INFORMATION: Blake McNeil Campground (315-262-2640), a fee area on Raquette River Road, offers 58 sites, a hard-surface launch ramp, and toilets.

CONTACT: New York State Department of Environmental Conservation Region 6 and St. Lawrence County Chamber of Commerce.

Even with a shorter growing season, North Country lakes can produce huge smallmouth bass.

127. RAINBOW FALLS RESERVOIR

KEY SPECIES: Walleye, smallmouth bass, northern pike, yellow perch, and brown bullheads.

DESCRIPTION: This 717-acre impoundment's south shore is heavily developed in cottages, but its north shore is heavily wooded. It averages 7 feet deep, drops to a maximum depth of 45 feet, and has a huge island along with several smaller ones.

TIPS: Work buzzbaits over the tops of weeds, especially on the southern end.

THE FISHING: Walleye ranging from 15 to 22 inches are plentiful. Most are taken on bucktail jigs fished plain or tipped with minnows, or scented 3-inch curly-tailed grubs. Smallmouths can go as large as 3 pounds, but 1-pounders are the norm. They like to hang out near the islands, off rocky points and the drop-offs below the dam. They hit baited jigs but are just as inclined to strike fat-bodied crankbaits worked in the upper reaches of drop-offs; soft jerk-baits ripped around windfalls and docks; and Carolina-rigged finesse worms dragged slowly on bottom in 10 to 20 feet of water. Northerns rule the lake's weed beds. They respond well to a tube jigs baited with minnows and worked along weed edges hugging drop-offs.

DIRECTIONS: Head south on NY 56 from the hamlet of South Colton for about 0.5 mile, turn left onto East Hill Road, and travel for about 2.5 miles to Raquette River Road, which parallels the reservoir.

ADDITIONAL INFORMATION: A public boat launch with a hard-surface ramp and parking for 10 rigs is located on Raquette River Road.

CONTACT: New York State Department of Environmental Conservation Region 6 and St. Lawrence County Chamber of Commerce.

128. FIVE FALLS RESERVOIR

KEY SPECIES: Walleyes, northern pike, and smallmouth bass.

DESCRIPTION: Smallest of the Raquette Lake impoundments, this place is shallow with vast weed beds and little shoreline development—characteristics that make it look more like a beaver pond than a hydroelectric reservoir.

TIPS: Work the rapids at the mouth of the Raquette River with jigs tipped with scented soft plastics for walleyes and scrappy smallmouths.

THE FISHING: Walleyes often range anywhere from too little to just big enough, and a 23-incher is considered a trophy. They hang out in the channel and the fast water at the Raquette River's mouth in spring and autumn and around the dam in summer. They take worms drifted on bottom along current edges, crankbaits cast into eddies, and jigs and diving crankbaits at the dam. Smallmouths generally hang out in the same places and take tubes, crayfish, and worms drifted for walleyes; the eyes get even by hitting crankbaits targeting bronzebacks. This whole lake is northern pike territory. While 20-pounders are present, lunkers running between 28 and 36 inches are realistic goals; be prepared for a lot of smaller ones. They like minnows and soft jerkbaits worked over and around weeds.

DIRECTIONS: At the bend (and end) of Three Falls Lane (aka Raquette River Road), northeast of the hamlet of South Colton.

ADDITIONAL INFORMATION: A public launch site with a hard-surface ramp and parking for five cars is on Raquette River Road.

CONTACT: New York State Department of Environmental Conservation Region 6 and St. Lawrence County Chamber of Commerce.

129. SOUTH COLTON RESERVOIR

KEY SPECIES: Walleyes, northern pike, and smallmouth bass.

DESCRIPTION: Almost entirely in private hands, this 230-acre reservoir's shoreline is spotted with cottages. Averaging 14 feet deep, it has a maximum depth of 47 feet. Several islands poke out of its waves on the north end.

TIPS: Drag worms on harnesses, on bottom, along the edges of the Morgan Rapids at the mouth of the Raquette River in spring and fall for walleyes.

THE FISHING: Walleyes average 18 inches and respond to scented curly-tailed grubs, minnows, bucktail jigs (plain or tipped with worms), and crankbaits ranging from Rat-L-Traps to Bass Pro Extreme Minnows. Northern pike run from 20 to 28 inches and tear into rattling crankbaits and buzzbaits with extreme prejudice bordering on fanaticism. The biggest northerns, however—36 inches, even better—are taken through the ice on minnows. Smallmouth bass can run anywhere from too small to 18 inches. Most of the time, the bigger ones hang out in quiet water between 10 and 25 feet deep, where they strike crayfish, minnows, and Texas- and Carolina-rigged worms. Scrappy, 12- to 14-inch youngsters love the rapids between the reservoirs, responding with relish to streamers swung through the current and salted tubes tossed into eddies and pockets.

DIRECTIONS: Head east out of South Colton on Raquette River Road for about 0.5 miles; the road parallels the impoundment.

ADDITIONAL INFORMATION: Undeveloped fishing access and a beach launch for cartop craft are on Three Falls Lane.

CONTACT: New York State Department of Environmental Conservation Region 6 and St. Lawrence County Chamber of Commerce.

130. HIGLEY FLOW RESERVOIR (HIGLEY FALLS RESERVOIR)

KEY SPECIES: Northern pike, smallmouth bass, largemouth bass, walleyes, black crappies, yellow perch, and brown bullheads.

DESCRIPTION: This 693-acre impoundment averages 11.5 feet deep and has a maximum depth of 32 feet. Its shoreline is heavily developed with private residences.

TIPS: Walleyes hang out in the deep water around the dam all summer long.

THE FISHING: Northern pike ranging from 18 to 36 inches rule this pond, especially the shallow, southern half near the mouth of the Raquette River. They respond violently to spinnerbaits, buzzbaits, and minnowbaits, but will take just about any lure, prompting cost-conscious anglers to use steel leaders (you'll get more hits without a leader, however). Smallmouth bass ranging from 12 to 20 inches, and walleyes averaging 17 inches, reign in the northern half where they share the drop-offs. The walleyes like it a little deeper during day, between 20 and 30 feet in summer. Both species respond well to minnows, worms, and bucktail jigs. At night, they move into shallow water, within reach of minnowbaits cast from shore. Largemouth bass are also plentiful, with quite a few going 20 inches or even better. They hit spinnerbaits and jerkbaits worked in and around cover, as well as 4-inch tubes bounced off branches and docks, or pitched along weed edges. Panfish are a big draw, particularly around the south shore. This is the best Raquette River reservoir for crappies ranging from 9 to 12 inches. They respond to scented tubes like

Berkley Atomic Teasers, and to spinner-rigged, 2-inch curly-tails fished along weed edges. Yellow perch range from 6 to 8 inches, and brown bullheads in the 6- to 10-inch range are also plentiful. Perch take the same small lures as crappies and, like bullheads, are fond of worms fished on bottom.

DIRECTIONS: Head south out of Potsdam on NY 56 for about 10 miles.

ADDITIONAL INFORMATION: A paved boat launch with parking for about five rigs is on Pine Road (off Gulf Road), just south of Colton. Higley Flow State Park, a 1,250-acre fee area, occupies much of the south shore. It offers a single-lane paved launch, 135 campsites (43 with electric hookups), playing fields, a swimming beach, and hiking trails. Open from Memorial Day through Labor Day. Although free day use is permitted off-season, a barrier prevents vehicles from entering.

CONTACT: New York State Department of Environmental Conservation Region 6 and the St. Lawrence County Chamber of Commerce.

131. COLTON FLOW

KEY SPECIES: Northern pike, largemouth bass, yellow perch, and panfish.

DESCRIPTION: Slow moving and river-like, this weedy, 154-acre impoundment averages 4 feet deep and has a maximum depth of about 10 feet. A lattice-work of channels flows through grass islands dotting the southern half. Pools at each end, its deepest spots, hold most of the game fish.

TIPS: Rip buzzbaits down the center of the channels cutting through emergent vegetation.

THE FISHING: Northern pike ranging from 18 to 22 inches are abundant and respond to soft and hard jerkbaits. Largemouth bass go 1 to 4 pounds and strike weightless plastic minnows jerked through weed openings, and jig-n-pigs pitched to the edges of emergent vegetation. Bluegills and pumpkinseeds averaging 5 inches, yellow perch up to 10 inches, and bullheads running 6 to 12 inches are plentiful, and respond enthusiastically to worms.

DIRECTIONS: Take NY 56 south out of Potsdam for about 8 miles to the village of Colton.

ADDITIONAL INFORMATION: A cartop launch and parking for five cars is located on Gulf Road (off NY 68), on the west bank. An informal bank-fishing access site with parking for about 20 cars is just past the NY 56 bridge.

CONTACT: New York State Department of Environmental Conservation and St. Lawrence County Chamber of Commerce.

132. HANNAWA FALLS FLOW

KEY SPECIES: Smallmouth bass, walleyes, and panfish.

DESCRIPTION: Its shoreline heavily developed with homes, this 200-acre impoundment averages about 6 feet deep and has a maximum depth of 15 feet.

TIPS: Cast perch-colored spoons.

THE FISHING: Smallmouth bass ranging from 12 to 14 inches respond well to 3-inch, scented curly-tailed grubs and salted tubes worked slowly on bottom. Walleyes are few and small and respond to minnowbaits, scented curly-tailed grubs jigged slowly on bottom, and worms dragged on bottom. Brown bullheads up to 12 inches and rock bass averaging 6 inches are plentiful and hit worms still-fished on bottom. In addition, rock bass respond to wet flies and poppers.

DIRECTIONS: Head south out of Potsdam on NY 56 for about 3 miles.

ADDITIONAL INFORMATION: Postwood Park (from Main Street turn south on Church Street, then right on Postwood Road) offers bathrooms, playgrounds, picnic tables, parking for about 100 cars, and beach access; launching cartop craft is permitted. You have to walk about 200 yards to get to the beach.

CONTACT: New York State Department of Environmental Conservation Region 6 and St. Lawrence County Chamber of Commerce.

133. POTSDAM FLOW

KEY SPECIES: Northern pike, smallmouth bass, yellow perch, and rock bass.

DESCRIPTION: This shallow, 540-acre "pocket wilderness" runs right through the middle of the village of Potsdam.

TIPS: Work soft jerkbaits through the channels between the marshy islands.

THE FISHING: Northern pike ranging from 18 to 22 inches are fairly common and respond to minnows and swimbaits. Smallmouth bass in the 12- to 14-inch range are available, but you'll have to go through 10 shorties to catch a keeper. They hit flashy stuff like spinnerbaits and spoons. Yellow perch between 5 and 9 inches, and rock bass up to 8 inches, are common and are popularly sought by family groups fishing on bottom with worms while picnicking in Ives (Water Street) and Fall Island Parks.

ADDITIONAL INFORMATION: There is no launch suitable for trailered craft, but the village parks mentioned above offer beach launching of canoes.

CONTACT: New York State Department of Environmental Conservation and St. Lawrence County Chamber of Commerce.

134. NORWOOD RESERVOIR

KEY SPECIES: Northern pike, smallmouth bass, walleyes, and panfish.

DESCRIPTION: Lapping the village of Norwood's southwestern corner, this 352-acre reservoir averages about 8 feet deep and drops to a maximum depth of 20 feet. The east shore is moderately developed with private residences; the west bank is a patchwork of forests, farms, and private residences.

TIPS: In May, work jigs and minnowbaits around the mouth of the Raquette River for walleye and northern pike.

THE FISHING: Northern pike ranging from 18 to 26 inches are plentiful, especially on the southern flats in spring, and have a taste for large minnows and spinnerbaits. Smallmouth bass running 12 to 15 inches, and walleyes up to 20 inches, like the 10- to 20-foot drop-off in the trench running down the middle on the north half of the lake. Both cotton to lipless crankbaits swimmed through the upper level of the range early and late in the season. Come summer, the bronzebacks hit crayfish and minnows drifted or bottom-fished in 15 to 30 feet of water, while the walleyes take worms drifted at the same depths on harnesses. Panfish include yellow perch running from 6 to 9 inches, rock bass averaging 6 inches, and brown bullheads up to 14 inches. The rockies and perch like minnows and, along with the bullheads, worms.

DIRECTIONS: Paralleled by Lakeshore Drive and River Road on the south side of the hamlet of Norwood.

ADDITIONAL INFORMATION: The village of Norwood has a hard-surface launch ramp and parking for about five cars off Lake Shore Drive.

CONTACT: New York State Department of Environmental Conservation Region 6 and St. Lawrence County Chamber of Commerce.

135. LOWER RAQUETTE RIVER

KEY SPECIES: Walleyes, northern pike, smallmouth bass, and muskellunge.

DESCRIPTION: Free of man-made barriers for its last 15 miles, from Raymondsville to the St. Lawrence River, this section of stream runs through low rolling hills, offering long stretches of flat water punctuated by rapids and waterfalls, ideal habitat for whitewater canoeists. The surrounding shoreline is mostly farmland and mixed bottomland forest.

TIPS: Obtain permission from the Indians before fishing their water at the mouth.

THE FISHING: The state stocks a couple million 0.5-inch walleyes periodically to supplement naturally reproduced fish. Those lucky enough to avoid being on a predator's menu easily reach between 18 inches and 12 pounds. Anglers target them by flatlining suspending and sinking minnowbaits in flat water. Northern pike up to 40 inches are possible and have a taste for large minnows, spinnerbaits, and buzzbaits. Although smallmouth bass exceeding 4 pounds are caught each year, they're the exception. Typical smallies run between 1 to 2 pounds, and bite best on minnows, crayfish, and Carolina-rigged worms. Though rare, muskellunge terrorize the lesser denizens of these waters. Usually ranging from 8 to 12 pounds, 20-something-pounders are landed regularly. They respond best to large minnows, bucktail spinners, and crankbaits.

DIRECTIONS: NY 56 parallels the river from Raymondsville north for about 3 miles, Raquette River Road (CR 40) parallels it to Massena, and NY 37 parallels it to a couple of miles south of the mouth.

ADDITIONAL INFORMATION: The last 5.6 miles of the river are on the St. Regis Indian Reservation, and you need permission from the sovereign nation to fish there.

CONTACT: New York State Department of Environmental Conservation Region 6, St. Lawrence County Chamber of Commerce, and the Mohawk Council of Akwesasne Conservation Department.

135A. Massena Springs Park

DESCRIPTION: This village park has a paved single-lane ramp, parking for 10 rigs, a fishing platform, a floating dock, and toilets.

THE FISHING: The slow stretches upstream and downstream are ideal habitat for walleyes, northerns, smallmouths, and muskies.

DIRECTIONS: Off Hatfield Street (CR 40), below the northwestern corner of the NY 420 bridge, in the village of Massena.

136. LAKE OZONIA

KEY SPECIES: Splake, Atlantic salmon, rainbow trout, brown trout, smallmouth bass, yellow perch, and brown bullheads.

DESCRIPTION: Just a few feet shy of 405 acres, this lake has an average depth of 20 feet and drops to a maximum depth of 60 feet.

TIPS: The most productive time to fish for splake is right after safe ice forms.

THE FISHING: Managed as a coldwater fishery, this lake boasts an above-average splake fishery. The state stocks about 3,000 8.5-inchers every other year or so, and a lot of them grow to 16 inches and better. The state also regularly stocks a lot of rainbow trout (3,000 averaging 9 inches in 2015) and Atlantic salmon (4,800 running from 2 to 8 inches in 2014). Recently, two-year-old brown trout have been added to the mix. While surveys show salmonid survival is good, most anglers have difficulty catching them. Savvy locals do best at ice time by staggering minnows below tip-ups, throughout the water column; and by jigging small silver spoons and marabou jigs tipped with minnows or insect larvae. In spring and fall, salmonids strike streamers and spoons flatlined along the shoreline, at the entrances to bays and around points, in anywhere from 5 to 15 feet of water; in summer, drag the same baits twice as deep. Smallmouth bass are plentiful. Easily reaching 20 inches, they like jigs and crayfish. The yellow perch fishing is outstanding, with 12-inchers caught regularly, though most run closer to 8 inches. They take minnows and scented 2-inch grubs in fall and spring; worms, small lures, and yellow streamers like Mickey Finns in summer. Bullheads run up to 12 inches and like worms still-fished on bottom, spring through fall.

Trout and salmon can be taken year-round. The minimum length for trout is 12 inches, and the daily limit is three.

DIRECTIONS: From its intersection with NY 72 in the hamlet of Hopkinton, head south on Lake Ozonia Road for about 8 miles.

ADDITIONAL INFORMATION: A DEC hand launch is off Lake Ozonia Road; motors are limited to 10 horsepower.

CONTACT: New York State Department of Environmental Conservation Region 6 and St. Lawrence County Chamber of Commerce.

137. LAKE EATON

KEY SPECIES: Landlocked Atlantic salmon, lake trout, brown trout, smallmouth bass, yellow perch, pumpkinseeds, and brown bullheads.

DESCRIPTION: Surrounded on three sides by the Sargent Ponds Wild Forest, this 558-acre lake's wooded shoreline is spotted with campsites. It averages 26 feet deep and drops to a maximum depth of 56 feet.

TIPS: Use cork flies imitating food pellets.

THE FISHING: The state stocks almost 1,000 landlocked salmon annually averaging 6.5 inches. They typically grow to range from 15 to 18 inches and respond to flatlined streamers. In autumn of some years, the local hatchery releases a few dozen brood-stock landlocked salmon up to 25 inches long. They provide cheap thrills for hatchery-truck chasers who fish for them below the stocking truck, sometimes before they can even hit the water. Come winter, survivors are taken through the ice on suspended minnows; in spring and summer, on minnowbaits and silver spoons, cast and trolled. Up to 2,500 lake trout averaging 7 inches are stocked regularly. Growth is good and anglers take quite a few keepers by casting spoons and crankbaits from shore in the spring and fall, jigging spoons on bottom in summer, and ice fishing with minnows on bottom in winter. Although the state hasn't stocked browns in several years, 20-something-inch survivors from earlier plantings are still around. They respond to minnows, worms, and crankbaits. Finally, anywhere from 1,800 to 3,100 rainbow trout running from 7 to 9.5 inches are stocked yearly. The habitat is good to them, and many reach 20-something inches. They take kernel corn, Berkley Trout Bait, and flies imitating food pellets. A few naturally spawned brook trout up to 14 inches are also available, and respond to dry flies and spinners. Smallmouth bass range from 12 to 14 inches and take crayfish, worms, jigs, and crankbaits. Perch averaging 7 inches, bullheads reaching up to 14 inches, and pumpkinseeds as big as 7 inches hit worms fished on bottom.

Trout and landlocked salmon can be taken year-round. Daily limit for lake trout is 2.

DIRECTIONS: Head north out of Long Lake village on NY 30 for 1.5 miles.

ADDITIONAL INFORMATION: Lake Eaton Public Campground, a fee area, offers 135 no-frills campsites (roughly half are beach sites), a hard-surface beach launch with parking for 12 rigs, boat and canoe rentals, hot showers, a swimming beach, and a trailer dumping station. A day-use fee is charged noncampers when the campground is open, mid-May through Labor Day. Free day use permitted off-season.

CONTACT: New York State Department of Environmental Conservation Region 5.

138. LAKE HARRIS

KEY SPECIES: Northern pike, smallmouth bass, largemouth bass, walleyes, brown bullheads, and yellow perch.

DESCRIPTION: Bordered on its entire north side by state land, this 301-acre lake averages 11.5 feet deep and has a maximum depth of 40 feet.

TIPS: From May to mid-June, fish for walleyes in the rapids entering the lake just north of the village of Newcomb.

THE FISHING: Northern pike range from 18 to 24 inches and are mostly caught on large shiners. Smallmouth bass run from 12 to 15 inches and take minnows, crayfish, and diving crankbaits. Largemouth bass go from 12 to 20 inches and strike spinnerbaits, buzzbaits, and plastic worms. In 2003, the DEC corrupted this natural fishery by introducing 5,600 walleyes over the next five years. "A 2012 survey caught 44 ranging 10–20 inches, with an average size of 14 inches," reports retired state fisheries biologist Rich Preall. "Natural reproduction seems to be occurring and walleye are now the most common game fish." Perch averaging 7 inches and bullheads up to 12 inches are abundant, and take worms fished on bottom.

The minimum length for walleyes is 18 inches, and the daily limit is 3.

DIRECTIONS: From the village of Long Lake, head east on NY 28N for about 14 miles to Newcomb, then north on the Campsite Road for about 1 mile.

ADDITIONAL INFORMATION: Lake Harris Public Campground is a fee area offering 89 no-frills campsites (57 beach sites), a boat launch, canoe and rowboat rentals, hot showers, picnic areas, and a trailer dump station. A day-use fee is charged noncampers when the campground is open, mid-May through Labor Day. Free day use is allowed off-season.

CONTACT: New York State Department of Environmental Conservation Region 5.

139. LITTLE TUPPER LAKE

KEY SPECIES: Brook trout and largemouth bass.

DESCRIPTION: Nestled in the William C Whitney Wilderness, this 2,305-acre pond is surrounded by forest, averages 10 feet deep, and drops to a maximum depth of 25 feet.

TIPS: Use lures with single hooks.

THE FISHING: This lake is famous for Little Tupper Lake brook trout, a rare strain scientists classify as genetically unique. Fishing is restricted to catch and release with artificial lures only. Like brook trout everywhere, these fish have an awesome appetite and will take properly presented flies, streamers, and lures. The tributaries have low densities of trout. Fishing is prohibited on the Charley Pond Outlet, the tributary at the southwestern corner, from July 1 through September 15. Other tributaries may be closed to fishing as well—check the *Fishing Regulations Guide*. Since trout fishing is catch and release, remove the fish from the water only when it's absolutely necessary—to pose for a "hero shot," for instance. Then—wetting your hands first—gently grasp the fish and hold it horizontally, supporting its belly with your hand. Do not insert your fingers under its gill plate.

Retired state fisheries biologist Rich Preall claims: "After the state acquired Little Tupper Lake and closed hunting camps there, the lake was illegally stocked with largemouth bass. The bass fishing can be outstanding, especially on the south end where there is a weed bed at the outlet of Rock Lake . . . Getting that far down the lake is a challenge, requiring strong paddling skills." The bucketmouths like spinnerbaits and wacky-rigged plastic worms.

The use or possession of baitfish is prohibited. No motors allowed.

DIRECTIONS: From Long Lake village, head north on NY 30 for roughly 7 miles, turn left onto Circle Road (CR 10A), travel for about 2 miles, and turn onto Sebattis Road (CR 10).

ADDITIONAL INFORMATION: A cartop launch and parking for about 10 cars is on Sebattis Road. There are 24 primitive beach campsites around the lake and on some islands. Beach camping is only allowed in sites designated with CAMP HERE disks.

CONTACT: New York State Department of Environmental Conservation Region 5.

140. LAKE LILA

KEY SPECIES: Lake trout and smallmouth bass.

DESCRIPTION: Set in the 19,500-acre William C. Whitney Wilderness, this 1,490-acre lake averages 25 feet deep and has a maximum depth of 75 feet. The largest body of water in the forest preserve totally bound by state land, it is named after railroad magnate William Seward Webb's wife—the adjoining township is named after the man himself.

TIPS: Beetle Spins work great for smallmouths.

THE FISHING: Lake Lila boasts a remarkable number of lake trout ranging from 15 to 30 inches; so many, in fact, that the state lowered the minimum length to 15 inches in the hope of thinning them out a bit. They are easiest to catch in the spring and fall when they cruise shallow water, within reach of anglers casting or flatlining spoons, streamers, and silver crankbaits. The lake's smallmouth fishery is just short of legendary. Rich Preall, a retired state aquatic biologist, says they range from 12 to 15 inches, and 50-fish days are possible. Mostly found in the rocky habitat on the northeastern end, they respond to spinnerbaits, diving crankbaits, and crayfish. From late June through early July, this place spawns massive mayfly hatches, offering some of the most exciting dry-fly fishing for smallmouths in these ancient hills. There are also some natural landlocked salmon and brook trout, scions of past stocking programs.

Use or possession of baitfish is prohibited. No motors allowed.

DIRECTIONS: Head north on NY 30 out of Long Lake village for 7 miles, turn left on Circle Road (CR 10A), travel about 2 miles, bear left on Sebattis Road (CR 10), go about 3 miles, turn left on Lake Lila Access Road, and continue south for roughly 5.5 miles. The trail to the canoe launch is about 100 yards before the barrier.

ADDITIONAL INFORMATION: This lake has a lean-to and 24 primitive campsites along the shore and on its islands. Beach camping is only allowed in sites designated by CAMP HERE disks. The state's free brochure *William C. Whitney Wilderness: Adirondack Forest Preserve Map and Guide* shows the locations of beach campsites.

CONTACT: New York State Department of Environmental Conservation Region 5.

BEAVER RIVER RESERVOIRS

Spawned free as the outlet of Lake Lila, the Beaver River quickly flows onto private property. While it's classified as navigable water, and boating on navigable waters is legal in the state (you just can't anchor on private riverbed or come ashore on private property), the authorities advise against canoeing on this stretch, explaining: "While recent court cases have established the public's right to traverse private lands by boat on specific waters in other parts of the state, the question of the legal right of the public to navigate any of the waters that enter private lands from the William C. Whitney Wilderness has not been resolved. Landowners may take legal action should you decide to proceed by boat beyond state land boundaries." In other words, the people who own the banks of the Beaver River, from about a mile south of its source to its mouth on Stillwater Reservoir, like their solitude and privacy. And though you have the right to float a boat on the state's navigable waters, fishing is a different matter, and you could find yourself in court (some of the landowners are lawyers) for reasons varying from touching bottom with your lure or sinker, to snagging private property like bushes and windfalls, and portaging around bony spots.

Besides the species listed in each site, natural brook trout are available in all tributaries and can be caught in the mouths, especially in the spring.

141. STILLWATER RESERVOIR

KEY SPECIES: Smallmouth bass, brook trout, splake, yellow perch, rock bass, and bullheads.

DESCRIPTION: This 6,034-acre impoundment averages 6.2 feet deep and has a maximum depth of 32 feet. Almost entirely surrounded by public woods, rich in points and islands, this impoundment is one of the most popular destinations for earth travelers in these mountains.

TIPS: Keep your eyes peeled for shoals, sandbars, and barely submerged stumps.

THE FISHING: Smallmouth bass ranging from 2 to 4 pounds are plentiful, and larger ones are available. Indeed, the reservoir was partially drained in the summer of 2001 for repairs on the dam, and numerous bronzebacks over 5 pounds were caught in the pools. Minnows and crayfish work best, but crankbaits and soft plastics will also do. Brook trout migrate into the reservoir when they outgrow the tributaries. Ranging from 12 to 16 inches, they hit spinners and spoons cast or flatlined along shore in spring and autumn, worms, minnows, and streamers deep-trolled behind Wabblers in summer, and minnows suspended a few feet below the ice. The state used to stock 1,500 splake annually into the Burnt Lake and Trout Pond (natural lakes that were "drowned" by the reservoir) sections on the northeastern corner. While

The public launch at Stillwater Reservoir (site 141).

they haven't been stocked lately, anglers regularly report catching splake, some over 20 inches. They respond to the same baits the brookies do. Yellow perch range from 6 to 9 inches, rock bass average a solid 5 inches, and bullheads can reach 14 inches; they all hit worms fished on bottom.

Trout season is year-round, the minimum length is 12 inches, and the daily limit is 3.

DIRECTIONS: Take NY 28 north out of Old Forge for about 9 miles to Eagle Bay. Turn north on Big Moose Road (CR 1) and travel for about 8 miles to the hamlet of Big Moose, where the pavement ends. Continue on the gravel road for about 10 miles and turn right, at the sign, into the state boat launch and parking area.

ADDITIONAL INFORMATION: The launch area has a double-wide paved ramp, a loading dock, parking for about 50 rigs, picnic tables, toilets, a convenience store, and a restaurant. The shoreline and islands are dotted with 46 hardened campsites. Campers must register at the state forest ranger headquarters at the boat launch.

CONTACT: New York State Department of Environmental Conservation Region 6.

141A. Informal Shoulder Access

DESCRIPTION: A no-name tributary forms a pond on the south side of Stillwater Big Moose Road before feeding the reservoir through a culvert. This site offers about 500 yards of bank-fishing access on both sides of the culvert. There's also a very primitive beach launch that "requires a lot of guts and skill to use," according to a local character who wouldn't identify himself but claimed, "I fish this spot a lot with my wife for rock bass."

DIRECTIONS: From the DEC boat launch, head south on Stillwater Road for a couple hundred yards, turn left on Stillwater Big Moose Road, and continue for about 3 miles.

BEAVER RIVER CANOE ROUTE

From Moshier Reservoir downstream to High Falls Reservoir, the Beaver River enters Brookfield Power territory. The privately owned utility regulates the river for profit, storing it in reservoirs, pushing it over dams, squeezing it through power pipes, even setting it free and allowing it to foam and froth in a couple of wild stretches. The power company has constructed canoe launches, parking areas, portage trails, canoe rests, primitive campsites, a couple of handicapped fishing platforms, a handicapped-accessible trail, and a fee campground along the 14-mile-long course. The utility's free brochure *Beaver River Canoe Route and Recreational Facilities* contains a detailed map of this fabulous recreational treasure (877-856-7466).

142. MOSHIER RESERVOIR

KEY SPECIES: Tiger muskies, smallmouth bass, yellow perch, brook trout, and splake.

DESCRIPTION: Spawned at the Stillwater Reservoir dam, this long, narrow, 280-acre impoundment averages 19 feet deep and has a maximum depth of 75 feet. The shoreline is largely forested.

TIPS: Suspend large shiners 3 to 5 feet below bobbers. Keep the floats as small as possible.

THE FISHING: Up until recently, this reservoir got stocked annually with 900 norlunge averaging 9.5 inches. Those that are still around go anywhere from 5 to 20 pounds and respond to large crankbaits and minnows. Smallmouth bass running from 1 to 2 pounds and yellow perch from 4 to 7 inches are typical and hit minnows, worms, and lures. Some brookies and splake, escapees from Stillwater Reservoir, go from 8 to 20 inches, and are mostly taken incidentally on worms, crankbaits, and in-spinners targeting bronzebacks.

DIRECTIONS: From the Stillwater Reservoir launch (**site 141**), continue west on Stillwater Road for about 3 miles, turn north on Moshier Road, and follow it for about 2.5 miles to the parking lot above the dam.

ADDITIONAL INFORMATION: The river between Moshier Reservoir and Beaver Lake runs fast and is popular with white-water kayakers and canoeists.

CONTACT: New York State Department of Environmental Conservation Region 6 and Brookfield Power.

143. BEAVER LAKE

KEY SPECIES: Chain pickerel, smallmouth bass, brown bullheads, and yellow perch.

DESCRIPTION: This 234-acre impoundment averages 8 feet deep and has a maximum depth of 30 feet. It has several back bays and a long narrow stretch.

TIPS: If you are fishing for perch and catch a small one, try another spot; keep moving until you catch one at least 8 inches long, then work the area thoroughly.

THE FISHING: Pickerel are the main predators. They range from 15 to 25 inches and respond well to worms on spinner harnesses retrieved at a moderate speed. Smallmouth bass typically range from 10 to 16 inches and like crayfish and scented curly-tailed grubs. Perch average 6 inches, but schools of fish ranging from 8 to 10 inches are present. They can be anywhere. A good technique is to drift around working a scented, 2-inch curly-tailed grub through the entire water column until you locate one—generally there will be more. Brown bullheads range from 6 to 12 inches and love worms still-fished on muddy bottom.

DIRECTIONS: Follow the above directions to Moshier Reservoir (**site 142**), but after turning from Stillwater Road to Moshier Road, only continue about 0.5 mile to the powerhouse.

ADDITIONAL INFORMATION: There is parking for about five cars at the power-house. If you want to launch a canoe, you'll have to portage about 0.25 mile, crossing Sunday Creek on a footbridge, to the beach launch.

CONTACT: New York State Department of Environmental Conservation Region 6 and Brookfield Power.

143A. Eagle Reservoir Public Access

DESCRIPTION: This site has parking for about three cars above the Eagle Falls dam.

DIRECTIONS: From the Beaver Lake access site above, get back on Stillwater Road and travel west to its end. Turn right (north) on Buck Point Road, then left (west) 0.5 mile later onto Adsit Trail, a hard-surface road. Travel for 2.6 miles, turn right, go downhill for 0.2 mile, and bear right to the launch site.

ADDITIONAL INFORMATION: This site is above the dam on Eagle Reservoir, a wide-water on the narrow, northern arm of Beaver Lake that is separated from the main body by a long strait widened in spots by bays.

144. SOFT MAPLE RESERVOIR

KEY SPECIES: Norlunge, smallmouth bass, and brown bullhead.

DESCRIPTION: This 326-acre impoundment averages 23 feet deep and has a maximum depth of 63 feet. A channel on the southwest side leads into its smaller kin, Lower Maple Reservoir. The islands offer just enough extra habitat to make this pond one of the most productive in the chain.

TIPS: Cast large, in-line bucktail spinners for tigers.

THE FISHING: This place gets stocked periodically with tiger muskies averaging 8.5 inches—1,600 in 2014. They end up stretching the tape to between 30 and 40 inches and respond well to large minnows, crankbaits, and Mepps Musky Killers. This is the best smallmouth water on the Beaver River system. Bronzebacks ranging from 10 to 18 inches are common, and numerous 20-something-inchers are taken each year. They like crayfish, minnows, jigs tipped with a little flavoring like Berkley Power Honey Worms, and spinner-baits. Brown bullheads average 10 inches and take worms fished on bottom.

DIRECTIONS: From **site 143A**, get back on the Adsit Trail and head northwest for about 0.7 mile to the canoe launch.

ADDITIONAL INFORMATION: The canoe launch at the foot of the powerhouse has parking for about five cars. The Soft Maple Recreation Area, about a mile farther west on Adsit Road, is a fee area offering campsites, picnic facilities, a canoe launch, and toilets. There are several free, no-frills campsites on the islands and on the long point poking into the northeastern corner.

CONTACT: New York State Department of Environmental Conservation Region 6 and Brookfield Power.

145. EFFLEY FALLS RESERVOIR

KEY SPECIES: Chain pickerel, smallmouth bass, brown bullheads, sunfish, and rock bass.

DESCRIPTION: This 339-acre impoundment is the first Beaver River impoundment outside of the Adirondack Park. Averaging 17 feet deep, its maximum depth is 31 feet.

TIPS: Fly fish with ¼-ounce poppers.

THE FISHING: Chain pickerel are plentiful. They range from 15 inches to 25 inches and respond well to poppers and worms on spinner-rigged harnesses retrieved a little below the surface at a moderate to rapid clip. Smallmouth bass average 12 inches but go as long as 20, and take buzzbaits, rubber worms, crayfish, and minnows. Pumpkinseeds, bluegills, and rock bass running 3 to 6 inches are typical and have a taste for surface poppers and dry flies. In addition, they, along with bullheads ranging from 8 to 11 inches, take worms fished on bottom.

DIRECTIONS: From **site 143A**, continue down Adsit Trail for about 2.5 miles.

ADDITIONAL INFORMATION: The cartop launch below the Soft Maple powerhouse has parking for five cars.

CONTACT: New York State Department of Environmental Conservation and Brookfield Power.

145A. Elmer Falls Reservoir

DESCRIPTION: This river-like, mile-long wide-water starts below the Effley Falls dam and runs west for about a mile to the Elmer Falls dam and powerhouse. At press time, the only road leading to it was private and closed to the public.

THE FISHING: Smallmouth bass typically run from 0.5 to 2 pounds and respond to jigs and minnowbaits. Look for them in the rapids early in the season and in the slower water just above the dam after mid-July. They like jigs and soft swimbaits. Rock bass up to 8 inches long hang out in eddies and the slower water at the end of the reservoir, where they take worms and small lures.

DIRECTIONS: Portages exist at the north end of Effley Falls dam and a few hundred yards east of the Elmer Falls dam and powerhouse.

146. TAYLORVILLE RESERVOIR

KEY SPECIES: Chain pickerel, smallmouth bass, and brown bullheads.

DESCRIPTION: This 95-acre impoundment averages 9 feet deep and has a maximum depth of 25 feet.

TIPS: Bottom-fish with worms in the spring for bullheads and bring lots of insect repellent.

THE FISHING: Chain pickerel ranging from 15 to 21 inches are plentiful. They respond well to a variety of soft plastics, but especially jerkbaits and curly-tailed grubs worked along the shoreline in 3 to 10 feet of water. Smallmouth bass are generally 10 to 15 inches and hang out a little deeper than the pickerel, up to 25 feet down, in fact. They respond best to crayfish but will also take Texas-rigged worms, 3-inch grubs, and fat-bodied crankbaits. Bullheads averaging 10 inches are plentiful. While they will hit a worm fished on bottom most any time of year, they are especially hungry—and plentiful near shore—from late April through May, and are popularly targeted by family groups at the Taylorville parking/picnic area on the northwestern corner of the reservoir.

DIRECTIONS: Head north out of Lowville on NY 812 for about 9 miles to just north of Croghan. Bear right onto CR 10 (Belfort Road) and travel a little over 2 miles to the north end of the hamlet of Belfort; turn right on Long Pond Road, then right again a few hundred feet later onto Taylorville Road. About 0.3 mile later, bear left onto Double Eddy Road and continue for 0.6 mile, along the huge pipe, to the dam.

ADDITIONAL INFORMATION: The Taylorville parking/picnic area has a canoe launch, shore-fishing access, picnic facilities, and toilets.

CONTACT: New York State Department of Environmental Conservation Region 6 and Brookfield Power.

147. BELFORT RESERVOIR

KEY SPECIES: Chain pickerel and yellow perch.

DESCRIPTION: Covering only about 40 acres, this impoundment averages 5 feet deep and has a maximum depth of 14 feet.

TIPS: Fly-fish with streamers.

THE FISHING: This small reservoir is seldom fished because it doesn't have many fish. However, some chain pickerel in the 15- to 18-inch range are available and respond to night crawlers on spinner harnesses, flashy crankbaits, buck-tail spinners, and just about anything bite-sized that whips past them. The perch are small, 5- to 7-inchers, and are a lot of fun to catch on worms and wet flies fished below tiny bobbers with ultralight tackle.

DIRECTIONS: In the hamlet of Belfort; follow the directions to Belfort in **site 146**.

ADDITIONAL INFORMATION: Some folks bank fish and launch canoes from the shoulder at the CR 10 bridge. A canoe launch at the end of Taylorville Road has parking for about five cars.

CONTACT: New York State Department of Environmental Conservation Region 6 and Brookfield Power.

148. HIGH FALLS RESERVOIR

KEY SPECIES: Smallmouth bass, rock bass, and brown bullheads.

DESCRIPTION: The last of the Beaver River impoundments, this 118-acre reservoir averages 5 feet deep and has a maximum depth of 40 feet.

TIPS: The area around the dam holds most of the bass.

THE FISHING: Smallmouths range from 10 to 14 inches. They respond to 3-inch curly-tailed grubs and 3-inch plastic minnows on dropshot rigs. Rock bass go anywhere from 5 to 8 inches. The larger ones hit minnows, worms, flies, and dropshotted soft plastic worms and minnows. Bullheads up to 12 inches hit worms fished on bottom. The formal and shoulder access sites at the culverts on Old State Road are local hot spots in the spring.

DIRECTIONS: Head west for 2 miles out of Belfort on Old State Road.

ADDITIONAL INFORMATION: A cartop launch at the Old State Road culvert has parking for about 10 cars, picnic facilities, and shore access. Primitive camping is allowed on the two largest islands.

CONTACT: New York State Department of Environmental Conservation Region 6 and Brookfield Power.

149. LOWER BEAVER RIVER

KEY SPECIES: Walleyes, smallmouth bass, and northern pike.

DESCRIPTION: Its upper reaches tamed by a number of reservoirs, the bottom of the Beaver River slowly snakes west for about 10 miles to feed the Black River a mile east of Castorland. Dark, deep, confined by steep banks loaded with windfalls, this stretch runs through relatively flat farm country and bottomland forests.

TIPS: Work minnows, worms, or scented curly-tailed grubs through the holes below log piles.

THE FISHING: Walleyes ranging from 15 to 22 inches are plentiful in these dark waters. Although they respond well to Rapalas and Bomber Long A's worked through the channels, daytime anglers have better luck casting live bait under structure and along steep banks. Smallmouths typically go from 10 to 16 inches, but 20-inchers are possible. They take 3-inch scented curly-tails, tubes, and Texas-rigged worms. Northerns prowl shallow areas. Fish in the 30-inch range are common and respond well to Rat-L-Traps bounced off emergent branches then worked tight to the submerged timber.

The minimum length for black bass is 10 inches.

DIRECTIONS: NY 126 and 812 parallel the river near the hamlet of Croghan.

CONTACT: New York State Department of Environmental Conservation Region 6 and Lewis County Chamber of Commerce.

149A. Public Access

DESCRIPTION: Located on the Black River (site 173), a few hundred feet downstream of the mouth of the Beaver River, this site offers a paved, single lane ramp, a hard-surface double-lane ramp, bank-fishing access, parking for 50 rigs and toilets.

DIRECTIONS: Head north out of Lowville on NY 26 for 6 miles. Turn east on NY 410, travel for 3.2 miles, cross the bridge, and turn left.

150. FRANCIS LAKE

KEY SPECIES: Chain pickerel, brown bullheads, yellow perch, and pumpkinseeds.

DESCRIPTION: Boasting an undeveloped shoreline, this weedy, 137-acre lake averages 5.2 feet deep and drops to a maximum depth of 18 feet.

TIPS: Cast a spinnerbait around windfalls and emergent vegetation for pickerel.

THE FISHING: Chain pickerel love ambushing prey along the edges of lily pads and over deep weeds. They hit spinner-rigged worms run at a fairly fast clip, bucktail spinners, and crankbaits. Though small, pumpkinseeds and yellow perch eagerly hit worms dangled in front of their faces. In addition, the perch like Mickey Finn streamers, and the sunnies take tiny surface poppers and dry flies. Bullheads hit worms, liver, and cut bait still-fished on bottom.

DIRECTIONS: From the heart of the village of Lowville, head east on River Street—which turns to Number Four Road at the edge of town. About 3.5 miles later, in the hamlet of Bushes Landing, the road turns left. Continue on Number Four Road for 9 miles to the hamlet of Number Four, turn right on Stillwater Road, and continue for 0.8 mile to the entrance of the public access site, which is straddled by two posts.

ADDITIONAL INFORMATION: A beach launch for cartop craft and a small dock are the lake's only signs of civilization. And that's cool with the local wildlife; the place is a popular hangout and nursery for loons. The state has issued a health advisory against eating the perch because of high mercury levels.

CONTACT: New York State Department of Environmental Conservation Region 6.

Francis Lake (site 150).

151. TWITCHELL LAKE

KEY SPECIES: Brook trout, lake trout, yellow perch, and brown bullheads.

DESCRIPTION: Averaging 10 feet deep, and dropping to a maximum depth of 30 feet, this 150-acre lake's shoreline is lightly developed with summer cottages.

TIPS: In May and June, work a Berkley Atomic Teaser tipped with a red Berkley Honey Worm slowly on bottom along the shoreline in 5 to 10 feet of water for brookies and yellow perch.

THE FISHING: State fisheries biologist Frank Flack says this lake has a history as an excellent brook trout fishery. Acid rain ruined it for a while in the last century, but anti-pollution legislation brought it back. Now the brookies face a different challenge: yellow perch. Flack says there's a chance the perch could wipe the brookies out. The state has kept a token presence by annually stocking 2,000 spring yearlings averaging 9 inches. They're easiest to catch from May through mid-July when they're close to shore and eagerly strike worms, small lures, and flies. Recently, the state has been experimenting with lake trout, stocking roughly 2,000 annually. By press time, it was too early to tell how they're doing. If they take, they'll hit spoons jigged or trolled on bottom in the deep water in the middle of the lake, especially on the north end. Perch average about 5 inches and take worms and small jigs. Bullheads run 6 to 12 inches and take worms still-fished on bottom, especially during a light drizzle.

Use or possession of baitfish is prohibited.

DIRECTIONS: From its intersection with NY 28 in Eagle Bay, head north on Big Moose Road (CR 1), travel 7.5 miles, turn right on Twitchell Road, and continue 2.1 miles.

ADDITIONAL INFORMATION: The fishing access site has parking for about five cars, a beach launch suitable for small trailered craft, and a small dock.

CONTACT: New York State Department of Environmental Conservation Region 6 and Town of Webb Tourist Information Center.

151A. Twitchell Creek

DESCRIPTION: From its source at the bottom of Twitchell Lake, this creek flows for about 10 miles through the northern wilds and feeds Stillwater Reservoir.

THE FISHING: Fisheries biologist Frank Flack says this creek contains wild brookies. They'll hit worms, nymphs, and small Mepps spinners.

DIRECTIONS: The stream is most easily accessible along Twitchell Road.

ADDITIONAL INFORMATION: There is no official stretch of public fishing rights, so pay attention to posted signs and leave if you're challenged.

152. BIG MOOSE LAKE

KEY SPECIES: Lake trout, brook trout, largemouth bass, smallmouth bass, yellow perch, pumpkinseeds, and brown bullheads.

DESCRIPTION: Spread over 1,242 acres, this lake averages 23 feet deep and drops to over 70 feet.

TIPS: Work streamers on a sinking line, near shore, at dusk and dawn, for brookies and yellow perch.

THE FISHING: Lakers typically run 3 to 5 pounds. From the opening month of the season they can be taken by casting spoons, minnowbaits, even streamers close to shore. May generally finds them at least 20 feet deep, by June they're 30 to 40 feet down, and deep summer sends them to the deepest water, primarily in the middle of the northern half of the lake. They'll hit cut bait and spoons fished deep and slow with Christmas tree rigs. Brook trout ranging from 6 to 16 inches are also present. They'll hit worms, small lures, and wet flies. On calm evenings they'll rise for dry flies. State fisheries biologist Roger Klindt says largemouths have found their way into the system but the fishery isn't "something to write home to Mother about." Still, there's enough of them around in the 12- to 15-inch range to make going after them with crayfish, stickworms, and swimbaits a good way to spend a sunny afternoon. Be prepared to latch into some smallmouths ranging from too small to 13 inches, too. Yellow perch averaging 6 inches and pumpkinseeds running about 4 inches are numerous and hit worms. Bullheads up to 12 inches are abundant and take worms and crayfish still-fished on bottom.

DIRECTIONS: From NY 28 in Eagle Bay, head north on Big Moose Road for 5.4 miles.

ADDITIONAL INFORMATION: Frank Flack, a state fisheries biologist assigned to the beat, says Moose Lake was the largest body of water in these ancient mountains to be acidified by acid rain back in the last century, and its recovery is very reassuring. This lake is the setting for the crime Theodore Dreiser fictionalized in his 1925 novel *An American Tragedy* and for the 1951 movie *A Place in the Sun.*

CONTACT: New York State Department of Environmental Conservation Region 6 and Town of Webb Tourist Information Center.

153. LAKE DURANT

KEY SPECIES: Tiger muskies, largemouth bass, pumpkinseeds, rock bass, and yellow perch.

DESCRIPTION: Named after William West Durant, a 19th-century developer famed as the father of the Adirondack Great Camp, this 293-acre impoundment averages about 8 feet deep and has a maximum depth of 20 feet.

TIPS: Fly-fish the back bays with large bass bugs.

THE FISHING: This lake's claim to fame is norlunge. The state stocks between 1,300 and 1,900 averaging 9 inches annually. Although few, if any, reach true trophy proportions, there's a lot of 5- to 7-pound fish, making this one of your best bets in the "Daks" for catching a tiger. They hit large bucktail spinners and crankbaits like ThunderSticks. Largemouth bass range from 3 to 5 pounds and respond to soft jerkbaits and spinnerbaits. Yellow perch go from 5 to 9 inches and can be counted on to hit worms and 2-inch scented, curly-tailed grubs. Pumpkinseeds and rock bass average 5 inches and like worms, wet flies, and tiny poppers.

DIRECTIONS: Take NY 28/30 for about a mile east of Blue Mountain Lake.

ADDITIONAL INFORMATION: Lake Durant Public Campground, a fee area, offers 61 no-frills sites, hot showers, a paved launch ramp with parking for 10 rigs, a handicapped-accessible fishing platform, hiking trails, and a sand beach. A day fee is charged noncampers when the campground is open, mid-May through Columbus Day. Free day use is permitted off-season.

CONTACT: New York State Department of Environmental Conservation Region 5.

154. LIMEKILN LAKE

KEY SPECIES: Splake, yellow perch, and panfish.

DESCRIPTION: Set in the northwestern corner of the Moose River Plains Wild Forest, under the shadow of Fawn Lake Mountain, this 460-acre lake is mostly ringed by forest, averages 20 feet deep, and has a maximum depth of 71 feet.

TIPS: Slowly troll a gray ghost streamer 12 to 24 inches behind a gold Wabbler.

THE FISHING: This lake is one of only a handful in the state that is stocked with splake—2,000 annually. These fish generally range from 0.5 to 1.5 pounds—and there are a lot of them—but specimens up to 9 pounds have been taken. Most are caught on streamers or worms trolled deep, behind attractors. Trout can be taken year-round. Yellow perch ranging from 6 to 10 inches are plentiful and hit small jigs and worms. Bullheads up to 12 inches and pumpkinseeds averaging 5 inches are also numerous, and both love worms.

Trout can be taken year-round. No motors allowed on the lake.

DIRECTIONS: Head north out of Utica on NY 12 for 24 miles to Alder Creek. Get on NY 28 north and travel for about 35 miles; go through the village of Inlet and turn right, about a mile later, onto Limekiln Lake Road. Travel for 1.5 miles, turn right onto Campsite Road, and continue for 0.5 mile.

ADDITIONAL INFORMATION: Limekiln Lake Public Campground is a fee area offering 271 no-frills tent and trailer sites, a gravel launch ramp, parking for 20 cars, a swimming area, canoe rentals, nature trails, and hot showers. A day-use fee is charged noncampers when the campground is open, mid-May through Labor Day. Free day use is allowed off-season.

CONTACT: New York State Department of Environmental Conservation Region 6.

FULTON CHAIN

Eight lakes in Herkimer and Hamilton Counties make up the Fulton Chain, one of the most popular canoe routes in the Adirondack Park. First through Fourth Lakes are connected by navigable channels. Fifth Lake is connected to Fourth by a shallow channel suitable only for canoes. A 0.5-mile portage is required to get to Sixth Lake from Fifth. Sixth and Seventh Lakes are the same body of water, separated by a bottleneck. And it takes a mile carry to get to Eighth Lake from Seventh.

155. OLD FORGE POND

KEY SPECIES: Largemouth bass, northern pike, tiger muskies, and rainbow trout.

DESCRIPTION: Covering about 30 acres, this pond averages 5 feet deep and has a maximum depth of 9 feet. A 0.5-mile-long channel averaging 3 feet deep connects it to First Lake.

TIPS: Spinnerbaits work well on all three warmwater species.

THE FISHING: Crowning the north end of Old Forge, this pond collects the combined flow of the Fulton Chain of Lakes and spits it out over a short dam, creating the Middle Branch Moose River. Gallon for gallon, it holds more than its fair share of northerns of truly pikeasaurus dimensions, and hawg bucketmouths. Rumors of 20-pound northerns have been circulating through the

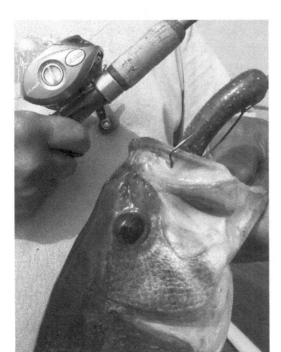

Hawg bucketmouths love 4-inch tubes worked along the edges of emergent vegetation.

watering holes of Old Forge since the end of the 20th century. While there's a good chance monsters that big are terrorizing the resident bait, they're rare. However, there's a lot of fish half that size around. Large minnows, flashy spinners, and noisy crankbaits spark their bloodlust, driving them to strike with extreme prejudice. Largemouth bass in the 1- to 3-pound range are common. They hang out under docks and in vegetation, responding well to Texas-rigged worms dragged over mud, and to fly-rod-sized poppers tossed onto inside lily pads and "bounced on the roof" to the water's edge. Tiger muskies in the 30- to 40-inch range are available, and Mepps Musky Killers trigger their aggression. The state stocks rainbow trout occasionally— roughly 550 9-inchers in 2014. Most end up in the bellies of bass and northerns, but those smart enough to avoid pike have been known to go up to 15 inches. They'll hit marshmallows, kernel corn, and worms.

DIRECTIONS: Head north out of Utica on NY 12 for about 22 miles to Alder Creek, bear right onto NY 28, and travel north for about 25 miles to Old Forge.

ADDITIONAL INFORMATION: A village park on NY 28, right at the wooden bridge on the north end of town, is suitable for bank fishing and launching canoes.

CONTACT: New York State Department of Environmental Conservation Region 6 and Town of Webb Tourist Information Center.

156. FIRST LAKE

KEY SPECIES: Smallmouth bass, largemouth bass, northern pike, and tiger muskies.

DESCRIPTION: This 736-acre lake averages 13 feet deep and has a maximum depth of 52 feet.

TIPS: Drift large minnows.

THE FISHING: Smallmouth bass ranging from 1 to 3 pounds are common here and are primarily targeted with tubes, bucktail jigs, and crayfish. Bucketmouths in the 1- to 4-pound range are plentiful and respond to jerkbaits worked in and around vegetation and submerged timber. While the monster pike taken early in the century are getting scarce (Frank Flack, a senior aquatic biologist with the state, claims a 34-pounder was caught here in September 2001, with several 20-pounders being reported since), northerns ranging from 4 to 8 pounds are plentiful. They hit large minnows, crankbaits, and spinnerbaits. The state stocks tiger muskies periodically, 2,800 averaging 10 inches in 2014. They grow to range a respectable 30 to 40 inches and relish the same baits northerns do.

Some landlocked salmon, rainbow trout, and brook trout are also available and respond to worms, spinners, and crankbaits. Salmonids can be taken year-round. Minimum size for trout is 9 inches.

DIRECTIONS: At the end of the main channel at the east end of Old Forge Pond (**site 155**).

CONTACT: New York State Department of Environmental Conservation Region 6 and Town of Webb Tourist Information Center.

157. SECOND LAKE

KEY SPECIES: Smallmouth bass, largemouth bass, northern pike, and tiger muskies.

DESCRIPTION: This 262-acre lake averages 51 feet deep and has a maximum depth of 85 feet.

TIPS: Work salted tubes off points.

THE FISHING: Smallmouth bass range from 12 to 15 inches. They take crayfish, minnows, and fat-bodied crankbaits. Largemouth bass go from 1 to 4 pounds and slam soft stickbaits jerked around docks and timber. Northern pike got into this system a little while ago, probably by a Johnny Pikeseed dumping a couple, and—as in all places when they first appear—reached gargantuan proportions feeding on trout. They hit large minnows, spinnerbaits, and hard jerkbaits. First Lake's muskies respect no boundaries, and tigers ranging from too small to 40 inches are available. They respond to the same baits northerns do.

Landlocked salmon along with rainbow, lake, and brook trout periodically wander in from adjoining lakes and tributaries and are caught incidentally by anglers targeting warmwater species. Salmonids can be taken year-round. The minimum size for trout is 9 inches.

DIRECTIONS: Just beyond the island on First Lake's (**site 156**) east end.

CONTACT: New York State Department of Environmental Conservation Region 6 and Town of Webb Tourist Information Center.

158. THIRD LAKE

KEY SPECIES: Lake trout, rainbow trout, smallmouth bass, largemouth bass, northern pike, tiger muskies, and yellow perch.

DESCRIPTION: This 179-acre lake averages 31 feet deep and has a maximum depth of 59 feet.

TIPS: Work propbaits and buzzbaits over the shallow shelves on the north and east banks, at dusk and dawn, for bucketmouths.

THE FISHING: Lake trout range from 21 to 25 inches and are usually taken near shore in spring and fall by flatlining spoons and crankbaits, and through the ice with smelt. The state stocks about 1,400 8-inch rainbow trout annually. For unknown reasons, they don't do too well (locals argue they're being eaten by the muskies and northerns), seldom growing over 10 inches. They'll hit worms, flies, and in-line spinners. Additionally, the state periodically plants a few hundred brook trout averaging 8.5 inches, most recently in 2014. They cruise the cool shallows in spring and fall, and respond to in-line spinners, streamers, and wet flies. In summer they go deeper, at least 15 feet down, and can be taken on jigs. Smallmouth bass ranging from 12 to 17 inches are common and respond to crayfish and Carolina-rigged finesse worms worked along breaklines. Bucketmouths in the 1- to 5-pound range thrive in the shallows and gentle drop-offs skirting the north and east banks; they respond to plastic worms and spinnerbaits. Northern pike run from 22 to 40 inches and love large minnows. Tiger muskies up to 40 inches can be taken on large minnows, crankbaits, and Mepps bucktail spinners. Yellow perch generally run from 4 to 10 inches and respond to minnows and small jigs.

Landlocked Atlantic salmon are present in small numbers and will hit flatlined tandem streamers and crankbaits like Bass Pro Shops XPS Extreme Minnows. Salmonids can be taken year-round. The minimum size for trout is 9 inches.

DIRECTIONS: Connected to the northeastern corner of Second Lake (**site 157**) by a channel.

CONTACT: New York State Department of Environmental Conservation Region 6 and Town of Webb Tourist Information Center.

159. FOURTH LAKE

KEY SPECIES: Landlocked Atlantic salmon, lake trout, rainbow trout, smallmouth bass, largemouth bass, northern pike, and tiger muskies.

DESCRIPTION: The largest and most popular lake in the chain, it covers 2,137 acres, averages 33 feet deep, and has a maximum depth of 85 feet.

TIPS: Ice fish with live smelt for lunker lake trout.

THE FISHING: This lake is a traditional ice-fishing hot spot for lake trout. Most years the state stocks thousands (9,200 averaging 6 inches in 2013). They grow to range from 2 to 10 pounds, with some reaching over 20 pounds. Most are taken by ice fishermen who first catch smelt by jigging, then use them for the lakers. Come warm weather, lakers are targeted with spoons trolled on Christmas tree or Seth Green rigs. Rainbow trout have fallen on hard times lately because of heavy predation by northerns and tigers, according to locals. Still, the state stocks thousands annually (7,270 averaging 9 inches in 2014), and early-bird anglers catch a bunch from May through mid-July on everything from worm/marshmallow combos fished on bottom, to flies and spoons. Some years the state also stocks landlocked Atlantic salmon— most recently in 2013 when 4,300 averaging 6.5 inches were planted. Enough manage to reach the 15-inch minimum length to make targeting them with streamers and crankbaits popular. The state stocks surplus brood stock in some years, usually in autumn, creating pleasant surprises for the coming season's ice fishermen.

Smallmouth bass can reach 18 inches. They hit minnows, crayfish, and salted tubes fished deep, especially around the islands. Largemouths up to 20 inches hang out in the back bays where they respond to jig-n-pigs worked in shallow slop and Texas-rigged 4-inch tubes flipped into vegetation and windfalls. Northerns up to 20 pounds are present, along with tiger muskies in the 30- to 40-inch range. Both love large minnows, crankbaits, and bucktail spinners. In addition, the northerns just can't seem to keep their mouths shut around a red-and-white spinnerbait.

Salmonids can be taken year-round. Minimum size for brook and rainbow trout is 9 inches. The state has issued a health advisory against eating any lake trout from this water because of high levels of DDT in their flesh, residues from the 1950s.

DIRECTIONS: Head north from Old Forge on NY 28 for about 12 miles to Inlet.

ADDITIONAL INFORMATION: The state launch on NY 28 in the village of Inlet has a paved double-wide ramp, loading dock, parking for 30 rigs, and toilets. Shore fishing is prohibited in the boat launch area. However, bank fishing is allowed in the village park, located in the heart of town, at the curve on NY 28. The park also offers a dock, picnic facilities, and toilets.

CONTACT: New York State Department of Environmental Conservation Region 6 and Town of Webb Tourist Information Center.

159A. Fourth Lake Picnic Area

DESCRIPTION: This site has a cartop boat launch and shore-fishing access; it's the reservation center for camping on Alger Island.

DIRECTIONS: Traveling north on NY 28 in Old Forge, turn right onto Gilbert Street (at the post office), then left onto Park Avenue. Follow Park Avenue to its end, turn right onto South Shore Road, and continue for almost 5 miles to Petrie Road. Turn left and travel for 0.75 mile.

159B. Alger Island Public Campground and Day Use Area

DESCRIPTION: This operation, located on a wooded, 40-acre island, is a fee area offering 15 lean-tos, two tent sites, outhouses, well water, picnic areas, a dock, and hiking trails. The campground is open mid-May through Labor Day. Free day use permitted off-season.

DIRECTIONS: Located on the west side of Fourth Lake.

160. FIFTH LAKE

KEY SPECIES: Smallmouth bass, largemouth bass, and rainbow trout.

DESCRIPTION: The runt of the chain, this lake covers 14 acres, averages 10 feet deep, and has a maximum depth of 20 feet.

TIPS: Drift with minnows or crayfish.

THE FISHING: Although any of the species found in its sister lakes can show up, this pond is mostly known for smallmouths. They run from 12 to 18 inches and respond to live bait, curly-tailed grubs, and salted tubes fished on bottom. Largemouth bass ranging from 12 to 18 inches claim the weedy areas on the west shore, where they can be taken with jerkbaits and weightless stickworms. In spring and fall, rainbows—and a few northerns—from Fourth Lake are drawn in by the current from Sixth Lake's outlet on the northeastern end. The trout respond to worms and nymphs; the northerns hit large minnows and loud, flashy lures.

DIRECTIONS: Although the lake is located on the south end of Inlet, right at the shoulder of NY 28, most get to it by paddling up the channel from Fourth Lake.

ADDITIONAL INFORMATION: An 0.5-mile portage up a hill and over NY 28 is required to get to Sixth Lake.

CONTACT: New York State Department of Environmental Conservation Region 5.

The channel between Fourth and Fifth Lakes (sites 159 and 160), Inlet, New York.

161. SIXTH LAKE

KEY SPECIES: Lake trout, landlocked Atlantic salmon, rainbow trout, and smallmouth bass.

DESCRIPTION: This 108-acre lake averages 12 feet deep and has a maximum depth of 38 feet. Separated from Seventh Lake by a navigable bottleneck created by an island and a point, "these lakes are the same, from a management standpoint," says Rich Preall, a retired state aquatic biologist.

TIPS: Flatline spoons parallel to shore, in 5 to 15 feet of water, in spring and fall.

THE FISHING: This lake is loaded with lake trout ranging from 18 to 20 inches. So many, in fact, that the state has reduced the minimum length to 18 inches in the hope of reducing populations a bit. Most are taken early and late in the season by casting or trolling spoons and crankbaits just off the shore. The state annually stocks about 1,000 rainbow trout averaging 9 inches. They quickly grow to at least 10 inches, and many reach 16 inches. Most accessible in spring and fall, when they cruise the shallows near shore, they respond to small spoons. Landlocked Atlantic salmon averaging 16 inches swim over from Seventh Lake all the time and are mostly taken by flatlining streamers. Smallmouths from 12 to 15 inches can be taken most anywhere by fishing crayfish on bottom, in 10 to 20 feet of water.

There is no closed season for trout and salmon.

DIRECTIONS: Head up NY 28 north out of Inlet for about 0.5 mile and turn left on Sixth Lake Road.

CONTACT: New York State Department of Environmental Conservation Region 5.

162. SEVENTH LAKE

KEY SPECIES: Lake trout, landlocked salmon, rainbow trout, brown trout, and smallmouth bass.

DESCRIPTION: This 851-acre lake averages 70 feet deep and has a maximum depth of 120 feet. Its shoreline is mostly ringed by forest.

TIPS: Use flies imitating food pellets for rainbows.

THE FISHING: In the recent past, the state stocked over 1,000 lake trout averaging 7 inches annually. They took. Before long, natural reproduction proved so fruitful that the authorities discontinued the program and reduced the minimum length for the species to 18 inches. Most lakers are taken by flatlining spoons near shore in the spring and fall. In summer, they are sought by anglers jigging spoons, or deep-trolling peanuts and spoons on Seth Green and Christmas tree rigs. Ice fishermen take quite a few on smelt. Roughly 800 landlocked salmon averaging 6.5 inches are stocked each year. They reach an average of 16 inches and like worms fished on bottom around tributary mouths in spring, fall, and after a summer rain. Surplus landlocked salmon brood stock are released here occasionally, always in the fall. Ranging from 5 to 15 pounds, these monsters are enthusiastically sought by ice fishermen suspending smelt or shiners a couple of feet below the hard water. Rainbow trout averaging 9 inches are stocked annually—3,000 in 2014. Most quickly reach 10 to 12 inches; they respond, from late spring through fall, to dry flies, streamers, and worms. Brown trout averaging 14 inches are stocked in some years. They can be caught in warm weather on worms, especially after a rain, and in winter by jigging smelt or suspending live minnows a couple of feet below the ice. Smallmouth bass ranging from 12 to 15 inches are popularly targeted by drifting minnows and crayfish close to shore in early summer; and from mid-June to the end of the season by dropshotting 4-inch finesse worms and jigging 3-inch curly-tailed grubs along drop-offs.

Trout and salmon can be taken year-round. The minimum size for lake trout is 18 inches.

DIRECTIONS: Take NY 28 north out of Inlet for about 3 miles.

ADDITIONAL INFORMATION: A fishing access site on NY 28 has a two-lane paved ramp and parking for 30 rigs.

CONTACT: New York State Department of Environmental Conservation Region 5.

163. EIGHTH LAKE

KEY SPECIES: Lake trout, landlocked Atlantic salmon, rainbow trout, and smallmouth bass.

DESCRIPTION: The last lake in the Fulton Chain, it covers 303 acres, averages 39 feet deep, and has a maximum depth of 81 feet. The shoreline is almost completely forested and undeveloped.

TIPS: Anchor at night and suspend a light over the side. Chum with kernel corn to attract trout, then fish for them with a worm, minnow, or fly.

THE FISHING: This lake is notorious for large lake trout. The state stocks hundreds regularly—790 7-inchers in 2013. Many grow to range from 6 to 10 pounds. Some make it all the way to 20 pounds. They respond to live smelt fished on bottom, and to spoons trolled behind Christmas tree and Seth Green rigs. Rainbows averaging 9 inches are stocked to the tune of 2,200 annually. Most grow to between 10 and 18 inches and are taken on worms, spoons, and spinners. Smallmouth bass go 12 to 16 inches and mostly hang out on the drop-offs along the rocky west bank; they're often found in water exceeding 20 feet. The best way to catch them is by fishing a crayfish or minnow on bottom, or with Carolina-rigged 4-inch worms.

DIRECTIONS: Six miles east of Inlet on NY 28.

ADDITIONAL INFORMATION: Eighth Lake Public Campground, a fee area on NY 28 on the southern tip of the lake, offers 126 tent and trailer sites, a hard-surface launch ramp, picnic areas, hiking trails, and showers. A day-use fee is charged noncampers in-season, mid-April through mid-November. Free day use is allowed during the off-season.

CONTACT: New York State Department of Environmental Conservation Region 5.

164. NICKS LAKE

KEY SPECIES: Brown trout, rainbow trout, largemouth bass, smallmouth bass, bullheads, sunfish, and rock bass.

DESCRIPTION: Set in the Black River Wild Forest, this 205-acre lake averages 8 feet deep and has a maximum depth of 17 feet.

TIPS: Mayfly and caddis patterns work great at dawn and dusk.

THE FISHING: This place is managed as a trout fishery. Recently the state has been stocking about 1,760 browns averaging 8.5 inches annually. Winter survival is average and anglers regularly report taking 3- to 4-pounders. The small, spirited ones will take dry flies, but fish over 10 inches generally hang low and respond to streamers and minnowbaits. Wild offspring of rainbows stocked in the past and native brookies are also present. The rainbows generally run 8 to 12 inches and respond to Krocodiles flatlined over 5 to 10 feet of water in spring and fall. Brookies run 6 to 10 inches, but some 18-inchers and better have been reported. They'll take in-line spinners and silver spoons. All the trout hit worms, especially after a rain. State fisheries biologist Frank Flack says keeper smallmouth and largemouth bass are present, and some reach monster proportions. Bronzebacks like the open water and bucketmouths are partial to shallows lined with brush or littered with fallen timber and emergent vegetation. Both hit spinnerbaits, rattling

Nicks Lake (site 164).

crankbaits and plastic worms dragged on bottom. Rock bass range from 4 to 8 inches, bullheads average 10 inches, and sunfish run from 3 to 6 inches. They all like worms fished on bottom.

No motors allowed. Use or possession of minnows is prohibited.

DIRECTIONS: From the post office on NY 28 in the heart of Old Forge, turn right on Gilbert Street, take the next right onto Park Avenue, then bear left at the next stop sign onto Joy Tract Road. Travel 0.7 mile, turn left onto Bisby, and continue for 0.6 mile to the campground sign on the right.

ADDITIONAL INFORMATION: Nicks Lake Public Campground (315-369-3314) offers a cartop boat launch, parking for about 10 cars, 112 campsites, hot showers, picnic facilities, ball fields, and hiking trails. A day-use fee is charged noncampers in-season, mid-May through late October. Free day use permitted off-season.

CONTACT: New York State Department of Environmental Conservation Region 6 and Town of Webb Tourist Information Center.

165. MASSAWEPIE LAKE (CONSERVATION EASEMENT)

KEY SPECIES: Lake trout and smallmouth bass.

DESCRIPTION: The largest body of water in the 3,700-acre conservation easement bearing its name, this 451-acre lake's average depth is 23 feet and its maximum depth, a little hole in the middle on the south end, is 70 feet.

TIPS: Work small, scented tubes on bottom, off points, for smallmouths.

THE FISHING: Lake trout are this lake's largest predator. Normally ranging from 21 to 25 inches, 30-inchers are possible. They respond to silver spoons jigged on bottom. Bronzebacks can reach 18 inches, though most run between 12 and 14 inches. They like spinners, spoons, and crankbaits.

Native brook trout can show up at any time—a 4-pound, 13-ounce former state record came out of nearby Deer Pond. The minimum length for trout is 12 inches, and the daily limit is three. Possession or use of bait fish is prohibited.

DIRECTIONS: Head east out of Sevey Corners on NY 3 for about 2 miles to Childwold, turn right (south) on Russell Road, and travel about a mile to Massawepie Road, which parallels the lake.

ADDITIONAL INFORMATION: Cartoppers can be launched off Massawepie Road. According to the NYSDEC website, this "property contains nine named lakes and ponds as well as a portion of the Massawepie Mire, the largest peatland in the state." The lake is closed for public recreation while the Boy Scout camp is in operation, June 15 through August 31.

CONTACT: New York State Department of Environmental Conservation Region 6.

166. CRANBERRY LAKE

KEY SPECIES: Brook trout, smallmouth bass, largemouth bass, northern pike, and rock bass.

DESCRIPTION: This 6,995-acre lake averages almost 6 feet deep, has a maximum depth of 38 feet, and has so many nooks and crannies, if you straightened out its shoreline it would stretch for 71.4 miles. Its north bay has a little development but the rest of the lake is largely ringed by wilderness.

TIPS: The hot spot for big brookies is Dead Creek Flow, the longest southern arm.

THE FISHING: Though this was traditionally a brook trout lake, the species was all but wiped out by acid rain late in the last century. After forcing industry to clean up its act, the state started stocking the Temiscamie hybrid strain of brook trout. A native of Canada known for its ability to tolerate acidic waters, the strain took, and fish ranging from 12 to 16 inches are common nowadays, with a few 4-pounders caught every year. They respond well to streamers like Muddler Minnows and worms trolled slowly behind wobblers. Smallmouth bass are plentiful but their numbers have been decreasing as brookie numbers increase. Still, bronzebacks ranging from 10 to 18 inches are plentiful over rocky areas and respond well to soft jerkbaits, scented tubes, and curly-tailed grubs. Recently, largemouths have made it into the lake. Running up to a whopping 5-something pounds, they like the stump fields in the flows (the lake's long arms) and respond to spinnerbaits, jerkbaits, and weightless, wacky-rigged worms cast to the edges of stumps and allowed to flutter to bottom. Someone dumped northern pike into the lake and the illegal aliens found the place to their liking, with many growing better than 20 pounds on the abundant forage. They have a taste for large minnows and spoons. The rock bass fishery sounds like a tall tale. Fish of 0.5 pound are typical, 0.75-pounders are plentiful, and 1-pounders are available. They hit worms, minnows, small spinners, spoons, flies—just about anything that moves and fits in their mouths.

Northern pike can be taken in any size.

DIRECTIONS: From Tupper Lake village, head west on NY 3 for about 21 miles.

ADDITIONAL INFORMATION: The Cranberry Lake Public Campground, located on Lone Pine Road, 1 mile south of NY 3, is a fee area offering 173 campsites, a handicapped-accessible fishing pier, hiking trails, a swimming beach, hot showers, picnic areas, and a trailer dump station. The state boat launch on Columbian Road (west side of the outlet bridge) has a paved double-wide ramp, loading docks, parking for 75 rigs, shore-fishing access, and overnight parking. In addition, there are 46 primitive clearings designated as campsites along the lakeshore and on Joe Indian Island.

CONTACT: New York State Department of Environmental Conservation Region 6 and the St. Lawrence County Chamber of Commerce.

167. OSWEGATCHIE RIVER

KEY SPECIES: Brook trout, brown trout, northern pike, walleyes, smallmouth bass, largemouth bass, muskellunge, channel catfish, yellow perch, and rock bass.

DESCRIPTION: Snaking up from the Five Ponds Wilderness to the St. Lawrence River, a distance of about 132 miles, this boulder-strewn stream offers a complete menu of angling adventures, from wilderness fly fishing for native brook trout under the gaze of bald eagles demonstrating their own version of catching fish on the fly, to trolling for trophy walleyes under the bridge in cosmopolitan Ogdensburg. It has numerous small impoundments.

TIPS: A canoe is the best way to tackle this river because the fishing always looks better on the other side.

THE FISHING: The headwaters are native brook trout territory. The state supplements their number by stocking about 880 brookies averaging 9.5 inches annually. You won't find the 5-pounders that used to lure robber barons into this fabulous backcountry following the Civil War, but 14-inchers—and better—are possible on worms dead drifted along submerged logs and undercut banks. This stretch is in the Five Ponds Wilderness, and the use of minnows as bait is prohibited.

Downstream from Cranberry Lake, the state annually stocks a couple thousand brook trout averaging 9 inches and about 2,400 brown trout averaging 8 inches. Another 250 or so two-year-old browns averaging 14 inches are thrown in to make things interesting. While trout can show up just anywhere on the river, their population thins progressively the farther downstream you go. The best trout water is from South Edwards upstream to Cranberry Lake. Salted minnows, worms, and in-line spinners work well.

Warmwater species thrive downstream of Cranberry Lake—the closer you get to the St. Lawrence River, the better. Smallmouth bass ranging from 10 to 18 inches respond well to minnows, 3-inch tubes, jerkbaits, and spinnerbaits. Come summer, the bigger ones migrate to impounds above dams where they take crayfish worked along drop-offs. Largemouth bass range from 1 to 4 pounds and strike topwater lures like Zara Spooks and buzzbaits on calm days; soft jerkbaits ripped through vegetation, Texas-rigged 4-inch tubes worked around timber, and Carolina-rigged worms bounced down drop-offs when the water's choppy. Northern pike ranging from 3 to 20 pounds claim quiet stretches and impoundments where they will take large minnows, and minnow-imitating crankbaits and spinnerbaits. Walleyes range from 2 to 6 pounds and hit jigs worked through pockets in fast water, minnowbaits and lipless crankbaits cast in slow-moving runs, worms on spinner harnesses, and diving crankbaits worked in stream mouths by day, as well as shallow-diving minnowbaits run on the shelves of impoundments at night.

Channel catfish ranging from 3 to 10 pounds—20-pounders are possible—hug the floor in deep holes and respond to cut bait, minnows, shrimp, and gobs of worms. While not plentiful, purebred muskellunge in the 5- to 25-pound class rule the lower reaches up to Heuvelton and are primarily taken incidentally on large minnows, spinnerbaits, crankbaits, and surface baits targeting northerns. Yellow perch ranging from 6 to 12 inches and rock bass from 4 to 8 inches are found in most impoundments and slow stretches, and love worms, minnows, and small lures.

Fishing is prohibited from the NY 68 bridge upstream to the dam in Ogdensburg from March 16 until opening day of walleye season.

ADDITIONAL INFORMATION: This stream is riddled with canoe-eating rapids, waterfalls, and dams. Head for shore to scout your course whenever you hear rushing water up ahead. Most communities on the river have informal public access with shoulder parking. They include Newton Falls, Fine, South Edwards, Edwards, Hailesboro, Gouverneur, Elmdale, Dekalb, Grandview, and Heuvelton.

CONTACT: New York State Department of Environmental Conservation Region 6 and St. Lawrence County Chamber of Commerce.

167A. Public Access

DESCRIPTION: This site, known as the Inlet, is in the Five Ponds Wilderness, and offers a beach launch and parking for 50 cars.

THE FISHING: The native brook trout in this section generally range from 4 to 14 inches and will take worms, in-line spinners, streamers, and flies, especially caddis variations. No baitfish or motors allowed.

DIRECTIONS: Head west on NY 3 for about 9 miles out of Cranberry Lake village. Turn south on Sunny Lake Road, then immediately turn left onto Inlet Road, and continue for 3.5 miles on the hard-surface road.

167B. Cranberry Lake Dam

THE FISHING: The state stocks the stretch of water downstream of NY 3 heavily, and one of the river's hottest trout spots is below this dam.

DIRECTIONS: On the west side of the village of Cranberry Lake.

ADDITIONAL INFORMATION: There's no developed access specifically for fishing below the dam. Anglers usually park along the shoulder of Columbian Road or in the state boat launch parking lots above the dam.

167C. Reliant Power's Flat Rock Public Access

DESCRIPTION: This site has a canoe launch, parking for five cars, shore-fishing access, and picnic facilities.

THE FISHING: This tiny reservoir's waters hold ideal habitat for smallmouth bass, northern pike, yellow perch, and rock bass.

DIRECTIONS: On NY 3, about 16 miles west of Cranberry Lake.

167D. Grandview Park

DESCRIPTION: Located on the Middle Branch, above the dam in the hamlet of Harrisville, this manicured park offers several hundred yards of fishing access on roaring rapids and quiet water, and parking for 10 cars.

THE FISHING: While this water looks like dynamite trout habitat, and you can even catch some early in the season, by June it reaches temperatures trout can't tolerate. Still, catching its smallmouth and rock bass, especially in the rapids, is a real thrill. Both species take worms, streamers, bucktail jigs, and tube jigs.

DIRECTIONS: Below the NY 3 bridge in the hamlet of Harrisville.

Middle Branch Oswegatchie River (site 167) at Grandview Park, Harrisville.

167E. Eel Weir State Park

DESCRIPTION: This fee area offers 38 campsites, bathrooms, picnic area, a paved launch ramp, and 600 feet of shore-fishing access. Open Memorial Day through Labor Day.

THE FISHING: This site sits between the river's mouth and the hamlet of Heuvelton, a stretch known for walleyes, bucketmouths, monster catfish, and a few muskies. The bass, walleyes, and muskies hit bucktail spinners and minnowbaits; the catfish like worms, shrimp, and cut bait.

DIRECTIONS: Head south out of Ogdensburg on NY 812 for about 3 miles, turn right (west) on CR 4, and travel for about 2 miles.

168. GRASS RIVER

KEY SPECIES: Brown trout, brook trout, walleyes, northern pike, smallmouth bass, largemouth bass, fallfish, and muskellunge.

DESCRIPTION: Springing from the foothills of the Adirondacks, this stream's three branches gather together to form the main stem east of Russell, and it slices north for about 50 miles, most of it canoeable, to feed the St. Lawrence River at Massena.

TIPS: The best water for large muskies is the 21-mile stretch from Morley to Louisville.

THE FISHING: The state stocks this river's upper reaches around Russell with about 2,550 brown trout averaging 8.5 inches annually. They join native brook trout to offer decent angling for fish ranging from 8 to 14 inches. Trout habitat extends as far north as the village of Pyrites and the fish will take worms, salted minnows, flies, and spinners.

From here downstream, the habitat is strictly warmwater. Smallmouth bass range from too short to about 13 inches, "but there's a lot of 'em," says local guide and author Mike Seymour. "Good numbers are caught on crayfish, worms, and minnows, or casting spinners and small crankbaits." A few largemouth bass in the 12- to 18-inch range are found in the slow water, primarily in the section from Madrid to the mouth. They respond to spinnerbaits worked around vegetation and windfalls all the time, and to darters and buzzbaits on calm days. Northerns running from 18 to 30 inches rule all the way to Massena. They hit minnows and their imitations worked along the edges of emergent vegetation and over the tops of drop-offs. Walleyes from 18 to 22 inches are typical, but 25-something-inchers are caught occasionally. They'll hit jigs in the main channel and deep holes, and worms trolled deep on spinner harnesses by day; minnowbaits worked on shelves during low light and at night. Purebred muskies are available, but they're few. Still, dream-sized muskies are landed every year. The vast majority are taken in the most exciting and personal way: casting large crankbaits and bucktail spinners. Fallfish are one of the river's most important foods for its big game. These natives seldom get respect from anglers but they deserve it. Reaching up to a whopping 16 inches—even bigger, according to local tales—these scrappy little fighters will take a worm as readily as a streamer, a spinner as eagerly as a small spoon, and fight so hard you'll think you hooked a bragging-sized trout.

Minimum length for black bass is 10 inches.

ADDITIONAL INFORMATION: This stream is largely accessed at bridge crossings and spots where it comes close to the road.

CONTACT: New York State Department of Environmental Conservation Region 6.

168A. Informal Canoe Access

DESCRIPTION: This bridge crossing is on the Middle Branch, about 0.75 mile upstream of its confluence with the Southern Branch.

THE FISHING: Brown trout, wild brook trout, and bronzebacks are available.

DIRECTIONS: Head north out of Cranberry Lake on Tooley Pond Road for about 16 miles to Degrasse, and take CR 27 north for 2 miles.

168B. Fishing Access

DESCRIPTION: This state site, located on the eastern edge of the Upper and Lower Lakes State Wildlife Management Area, offers a hard-surface launch ramp and parking for 25 rigs.

THE FISHING: For 2 miles downstream of the boat launch, the river is flat water averaging 4.5 feet deep, providing good northern pike, smallmouth bass, and walleye habitat.

DIRECTIONS: On NY 68, about 3 miles north of Canton.

168C. Fishing Access

DESCRIPTION: This site has a paved ramp and parking for five rigs above the dam.

THE FISHING: The slow, relatively deep water holds northerns, black bass, and panfish.

DIRECTIONS: On the west side of the NY 345 bridge in the hamlet of Madrid.

168D. Fishing Access

DESCRIPTION: This site is suitable for launching handheld craft.

THE FISHING: Smallmouth like the fast water downstream of the bridge just about anytime; walleyes hang there in spring and fall. Both species respond to jigs, in-line spinners, and rattling crankbaits.

DIRECTIONS: From the east side of the NY 345 bridge in Madrid, head north on River Street.

168E. Massena Municipal Boat Launch

DESCRIPTION: Although this site has a paved ramp, the water is often way below it, making it suitable only for hand-carried craft. There's parking for about 25 cars. The adjacent park has picnic tables and toilets.

THE FISHING: This stretch's shallow areas are good northern pike habitat, and the deep holes and channels contain walleyes and smallmouth bass. Some muskies are also available.

DIRECTIONS: Behind the Firehouse on Andrews Street.

169. LONG LAKE (ONEIDA COUNTY)

KEY SPECIES: Black bass, walleyes, black crappies, yellow perch, rock bass, and brown bullheads.

DESCRIPTION: Also called Little Long Lake, this body of water covers a surface area of 152 acres in the northeastern corner of the county, averages 9 feet deep, and has a maximum depth of 35 feet. Its shoreline is lightly developed with cottages.

TIPS: Cast stickworms around vegetation and submerged timber on the north end for bucketmouths.

THE FISHING: This warmwater fishery has a good population of largemouth bass averaging 2 pounds. Larger fish up to 5 pounds, even better, are available. They respond to spinnerbaits and large plastic worms free-floated to bottom. While not numerous, walleyes are around in sufficient quantities to draw the attention of anglers, who target them specifically by working bucktail jigs along the south end's drop-offs during daylight, and casting crankbaits like Bass Pro XPS Extreme Minnows onto shallow shelves around dusk and dawn. Keeper black crappies and yellow perch ranging from 5 to 8 inches are targeted by locals with minnows in the spring. Rock bass and bullheads are the favorite fare of leisure-time anglers in summer.

DIRECTIONS: From the Adirondack Scenic Railroad Station in Thendara, head south on NY 28 for 15.1 miles, turn right on Round Lake Road (CR 63), travel 0.5 mile, bear right onto Long Lake Road, and continue 1.1 miles to the parking area on the right.

ADDITIONAL INFORMATION: The access site is wheelchair accessible and offers a canoe launch, bank-fishing access, and campsites.

CONTACT: New York State Department of Environmental Conservation Region 6.

170. WOODHULL CREEK

KEY SPECIES: Brook trout and brown trout.

DESCRIPTION: Like most streams that flow through the deep forests of the western Adirondacks, this scenic midsized creek is loaded with trout. Fortunately for the fish, the deep, undercut, alder-skirted banks provide cover capable of frustrating even the most savvy wilderness angler.

TIPS: The fishing is easiest in May.

THE FISHING: Native brookies rule the entire length of the stream. Browns join them about halfway down its course, growing more common the closer you come to the mouth. Both species hit worms in May and after summer rains. They also respond to in-line spinners worked through pools and along undercut banks, and dark streamers ripped quickly across rapids.

ADDITIONAL INFORMATION: The state owns 3.4 miles of public fishing rights, mostly downstream of the Horton Road bridge.

CONTACT: New York State Department of Environmental Conservation Region 6.

170A. Horton Road Access

DESCRIPTION: Parking in a clearing for about five cars and shoulder parking for an additional five cars.

DIRECTIONS: From the NY 28 bridge in Forestport, head north on NY 28 for 1.9 miles, turn right on Horton Road, and travel for 0.7 mile.

171. NORTH LAKE

KEY SPECIES: Tiger muskies, splake, brook trout, rainbow trout, yellow perch, and brown bullheads.

DESCRIPTION: This 307-acre reservoir is the major source of the Black River. Averaging about 18 feet deep, and having a maximum depth of roughly 50 feet, its shoreline is mostly forested. The bottom is strewn with rocks and huge boulders. The lake suffered acidification problems late in the last century, wiping out all the trout and most of the other species. Strict air pollution laws have resulted in the condition remedying itself, and wild brookies, migrants from its tributaries, started setting the fishery back on its feet again.

TIPS: Cast Mepps bucktail spinners for tiger muskies.

THE FISHING: The state stocks norlunge regularly, most recently in 2014 when it released 2,200 8.5-inchers. Currently tigers range 32 to 38 inches and hit minnows, bucktail spinners, and crankbaits. Splake have been stocked when available since 2008. Three thousand averaging 7.5 inches were stocked in 2014, and the state plans on releasing equal amounts annually. By press time there should be some 5-pounders around. They like worms trolled a few inches behind wobblers, in deep water, near bottom. Brook trout, native offspring of fish stocked early in the century and stockies released by the state in 2008, run anywhere from 3 inches to 3 pounds and like the same bait splake do, as well as jigs and in-line spinners. Rainbows were released in 2007, and the few remaining can run up to 20 inches. They'll take shiny spoons, wet flies, and streamers. Yellow perch get big, reaching better than 10 inches. They bite best on minnows and 2-inch, scented curly-tailed grubs. Bullheads only average 8 inches but there are enough of them to make going after a bullhead dinner worthwhile. They like worms fished on bottom.

DIRECTIONS: Head north out of Utica on NY 12 for about 22 miles to Alder Creek. At the transition, get on NY 28 north and travel for about 2 miles to Forestport. Cross the bridge, take the first right onto Woodhull Road (CR 72), and continue for about a mile into Forestport Station. When you cross the Railroad Tracks, continue straight onto North Lake Road (CR 214) and travel for about 14 miles.

ADDITIONAL INFORMATION: Several campsites with shore-fishing access punctuate the east and west banks. North Lake Road bears left at the dam and skirts the sites on the west shore. Those on the east shore can only be reached on foot or by boat.

CONTACT: New York State Department of Environmental Conservation Region 6.

Black River (site 173B) in Forestport.

172. SOUTH LAKE

KEY SPECIES: Brook trout and brown bullheads.

DESCRIPTION: This 486-acre reservoir is the second source of the Black River. It averages about 25 feet deep and has a maximum depth of 60 feet. Its shoreline is moderately developed with private camps.

TIPS: Early in the season, work weighted streamers slowly at right angles to shore.

THE FISHING: This lake has suffered major damage from acidification in the past. Currently the situation is reversed and fish can thrive once again. The state started stocking brook trout, the lake's bread-and-butter species, late in the last century and continues releasing them as needed, the last time in 2012. They generally run 3 to 14 inches, but, according to aquatic biologist Dick McDonald, 18-inchers are present. It's likely some, though not many, lakers and Atlantic salmon from former stocking programs are still present. They've been known to hit crankbaits and spoons targeting brookies in the spring. Bullheads generally go 5 to 8 inches and hit worms and smelly baits fished on bottom in shallow water.

DIRECTIONS: After reaching its namesake, North Lake Road (see the site above) turns left and South Lake Road continues straight for 2.3 miles to South Lake.

ADDITIONAL INFORMATION: A beach launch suitable for small trailered craft is located on South Lake Road. In addition, there are three beach campsites just off the road.

CONTACT: New York State Department of Environmental Conservation Region 6.

173. BLACK RIVER

KEY SPECIES: Brook trout, brown trout, rainbow trout, smallmouth bass, northern pike, walleyes, chain pickerel, rock bass, sunfish, and bullheads.

DESCRIPTION: Running for over 100 miles, this river contains three distinct fisheries. The upper section pours out of the western Adirondack Mountains and supports coldwater species, including native brook trout. The middle section, from the base of Lyons Falls to Watertown, is famed for warmwater species, particularly smallmouth bass, northern pike, and walleyes. The lower section, from the Mill Street dam in Watertown to the mouth, is warm water but supports seasonal runs of Lake Ontario salmonids. Only the first two sections are covered here; the lower river is covered in the sister guide *Fishing the Great Lakes of New York* (Burford Books, 201 pages, $16.95).

TIPS: Wild brook trout and brown trout are available in all tributary mouths in the spring.

THE FISHING: This river is one of the state's wildest. Dammed at least 25 times, it still manages a stiff current, punctuated with several sets of awesome rapids, for much of its course. Brook trout ranging from 6 to 10 inches, with a smattering of brown and rainbow trout a few inches longer, occupy the headwaters below North and South Lakes all the way to Kayuta Lake. Rainbow and brown trout ranging from 8 to 14 inches, and brook trout averaging 8 inches, are available from Forestport to Lyons Falls. These fish hit worms and salted minnows from opening day through mid-June and after a summer rain; they take spinners and flies during the dog days of summer.

While a few smallmouth bass are available in the upper reaches, the greatest numbers are found in the quiet stretches downstream of Forestport. Generally ranging from 10 to 13 inches, they are fond of worms, crayfish, minnows, and just about every lure imaginable. Pickerel share the river from Forestport to Lyons Falls with the smallmouths. They can reach 25 inches and are usually caught incidentally by guys casting lures for bass or trolling worms on spinner-rigged harnesses for walleyes. However, their savage strike and spirited fight endear them to a faithful following of anglers who target them with spoons and in-line spinners.

Below Lyons Falls, smallmouths range from 10 to 15 inches. Northern pike up to 36 inches become available and hit large minnows and their imitations. Although a smattering of walleyes has been caught as far upstream as the Denley dam, they reach fishable populations downstream of Lyons Falls. Ranging from 15 to 23 inches, eyes generally hang out in fast water—including rapids—from opening day through mid-July, and in autumn, when they hit minnow-imitating crankbaits run across the current, and worms—fished plain or tipping jigs—dragged slowly upstream, on bottom, along current edges, and in pockets. Come summer, they like the deep, quiet pools, especially off the mouths of tributaries, and respond to worms trolled slowly on spinner harnesses, bucktail jigs and 3-inch grubs gently bounced

Father and sons fishing on the Black River (site 173) below the dam in Forestport.

on bottom, and hard minnowbaits worked near shore at dusk and dawn. Panfish thrive in the impoundments, growing more numerous the farther downstream you go. Rock bass and sunfish run from 0.5 pound to 0.75 pound and hit worms, poppers, and flies. Bullheads ranging from 6 to 14 inches can't resist a fat, juicy worm squirming on bottom.

Upstream of the Dexter dam the minimum length for black bass is 10 inches; and fishing for bass, even catch and release, is prohibited when the season is closed.

DIRECTIONS: NY 12 parallels the river.

ADDITIONAL INFORMATION: Much of NY 12 was built over the old Black River Canal, an Erie Canal–era waterway that ran for 35 miles, connecting Carthage with Rome. Thirty-five locks lowered the boats down the mountain. Today their aging walls of cut limestone peek from the shoulder of NY 12 north of Boonville, and NY 46 south of the hamlet, giving silent testimony to the ambitions of 19th-century entrepreneurs and the skill of period stonemasons.

CONTACT: New York State Department of Environmental Conservation Region 6.

173A. Farr Road Bridge Access

DESCRIPTION: Shoulder parking for about five cars.

DIRECTIONS: From its transition with NY 12 in Alder Creek, head north on NY 28 for about a mile, cross the bridge over the Black River, and take a right onto Woodhull Road (CR 72). About a mile later, in Forestport Station, continue straight onto North Lake Road (CR 73) for about 9 miles and turn right onto Farr Road.

173B. Forestport Public Access

DESCRIPTION: This site straddles a dam, offering parking for about 30 cars and bank-fishing access to the pool above the dam and the rapids below.

DIRECTIONS: From NY 28 north in Forestport, take a left on River Road (just before the bridge) and travel for a couple hundred yards.

173C. Edmonds Road Bridge Access

DESCRIPTION: This informal access is at the foot of an abandoned bridge. There's shoulder parking for about five cars.

DIRECTIONS: From **site 172B** above, continue on River Road for about 4 miles to its end, turn left, and travel about 1,000 feet.

173D. Edmonds Road Public Access

DESCRIPTION: This formal site has parking for about five cars.

DIRECTIONS: Head downstream from **site 173C** for about 0.7 mile.

173E. Hawkinsville Public Access

DESCRIPTION: This formal site has parking for about 10 cars and access above and below the dam.

DIRECTIONS: From NY 12 on the south side of Boonville, head east on Woodgate Drive (CR 61) for about 2 miles to the hamlet of Hawkinsville, cross the bridge, turn right onto Edmonds Road and continue to the site at the dam.

173F. Norton Road Public Access

DESCRIPTION: This formal site has parking for three cars.

DIRECTIONS: Head north on NY 12 out of Boonville for 3.7 miles. Turn east on Norton Road and travel for 1 mile.

173G. Denley Power Project Dam Public Access

DESCRIPTION: This site offers parking for five cars and shore-fishing access above and below the dam.

DIRECTIONS: Head north out of Booneville on NY 12 for about 5 miles and turn right on the gravel road about 100 yards after the road narrows to two lanes.

173H. East Main Street Bridge, Port Leyden

DESCRIPTION: A village park on the southwestern corner of the bridge offers bank-fishing access at the bridge and upstream for a couple hundred feet, ending in a deep hole at the bend. There's parking for 10 cars and a picnic table.

DIRECTIONS: On East Main Street in the hamlet of Port Leyden.

173I. Upper Lyons Falls Public Access

DESCRIPTION: This site is designed as a canoe launch and portage but can handle small trailered craft. The Moose River joins the Black River here. Shore-fishing access on both rivers and parking for about 20 cars.

TIPS: During summer's low water levels, the current is slow here. Work a bait tight to the old bridge abutments in the mouth of the Moose River for small-mouth bass.

DIRECTIONS: In Lyons Falls, head south on Center Street to its intersection with Laura Street and turn left. Cross the bridge, turn left on CR 39, and the access site will be on the left.

173J. Lower Lyons Falls Public Access

DESCRIPTION: This site was specifically designed as a canoe launch but will accommodate small trailered craft. There is a long stretch of shore-fishing access, including to the massive plunge pool below the 60-something-foot-high falls. Parking for about 10 cars.

THE FISHING: The pool below the falls is a good spot for walleyes and bullheads in May.

DIRECTIONS: Head downstream on Lyons Falls Road (CR 39) for a few hundred yards from **site 173I.**

173K. High Towers State Forest

DESCRIPTION: Primitive camping is permitted in this large woods.

DIRECTIONS: On CR 39, a little over a mile north of Lyons Falls.

173L. Burdicks Crossing Public Access

DESCRIPTION: This park-like site has picnic facilities, a canoe launch, and shore access.

DIRECTIONS: Head north on NY 12 from Lyons Falls for about 4 miles, turn east on Burdick Crossing Road (CR 36), and travel about 0.8 mile.

173M. Public Fishing Access Site

DESCRIPTION: This site has a paved ramp, picnic facilities, and parking for about 20 rigs.

DIRECTIONS: Head south on NY 12 from Lowville for about 3 miles to Glenfield. Get on Main Street, turn east on Greig Road (CR 40), cross the bridge, and take an immediate left to the launch site.

173N. Public Fishing Access

DESCRIPTION: This site has a paved launch, parking for 10 rigs, and toilets.

DIRECTIONS: Head east on River Street out of Lowville. When it turns to Number Four Road (CR 26) outside of town, continue for 1.6 miles.

173O. Dadville Accessible Fishing Deck

DESCRIPTION: This wooden platform is about 10 feet above a slow-moving section of the river. The railings have holes for resting your rod. Parking for five vans.

DIRECTIONS: Head north on NY 812 for 0.8 mile out of Lowville. Turn east on Waters Road, then left a couple hundred feet later and travel for about 200 feet to the platform at the end of the road.

173P. Castorland Public Fishing Access Site

DESCRIPTION: This site has a paved single-lane ramp and a hard-surface, unpaved double-wide ramp right next to it. Parking for 50 rigs, along with toilets.

THE FISHING: Located a few hundred feet downstream of the mouths of the Beaver River and Negro Creek, this area's mix of water and currents always draws fish, including trout.

DIRECTIONS: Take NY 26 north out of Lowville for about 5 miles. Turn east on NY 410, travel for 3.2 miles, cross the bridge, and turn left.

173Q. NY 3 Fishing Access Site

DESCRIPTION: This site, provided by Brookfield Power, offers fishing access above a dam. There's a beach launch for cartop craft, parking for 20 cars, and a handicapped fishing platform.

DIRECTIONS: On the east side of the NY 3 bridge, just over Watertown's eastern boundary.

174. KAYUTA LAKE

KEY SPECIES: Brook trout, smallmouth bass, largemouth bass, chain pickerel, yellow perch, and panfish.

DESCRIPTION: This 422-acre Black River impoundment averages 10 feet deep and has a maximum depth of 22 feet.

TIPS: The area around the mouth of the Black River always holds fish.

THE FISHING: Wild brook trout enter this impoundment from the Black River and several smaller tributaries. Ranging from 8 to 15 inches, they'll hit worms, spinners, and spoons. The Adirondacks' short growing season keeps bass small. Bronzebacks range from 8 to 14 inches. Fat and feisty, they take jigs and spinners, and provide memorable action when caught on ultralight tackle. While not as plentiful as smallies, bucketmouths up to 18 inches are available. They'll hit all the usual baits and are especially fond of offset spinnerbaits and darters. Pickerel do pretty well here, reaching up to 25 inches. They'll hit soft plastic jerkbaits ripped over the surface, in-line spinners, and worms worked on spinner-rigged harnesses. Yellow perch ranging from 6 to 12 inches, bullheads between 6 and 14 inches, and sunfish and rock bass up to 7 inches are plentiful. They'll all hit worms during warm weather; and the perch and rock bass will take small lures, too. Ice fishermen catch pickerel, perch, and sunfish with tiny jigs tipped with insect larvae.

DIRECTIONS: Head north out of Utica on NY 12 for about 22 miles to Alder Creek. Get on NY 28 and travel for 2 miles to Forestport. Cross the bridge and turn right onto Woodhull Road. About a mile later, bear right (south) on Bardwell Mills Road (CR 72) and travel 2.8 miles.

ADDITIONAL INFORMATION: There is a shoulder parking area big enough for about two cars before you cross the bridge.

CONTACT: New York State Department of Environmental Conservation Region 6.

174A. Kayuta Hydro Recreation Boat Launch Area

DESCRIPTION: This site has a concrete ramp above the dam, parking for 10 rigs, and shore-fishing access above and below the dam.

DIRECTIONS: Take NY 12 north out of Utica for about 24 miles and bear right on NY 28 at Alder Creek. While still in the transition, turn right on Old State Dam Road and travel for 0.8 mile.

175. FORESTPORT RESERVOIR

KEY SPECIES: Largemouth bass, smallmouth bass, chain pickerel, yellow perch, and bullheads.

DESCRIPTION: This 117-acre Black River impoundment averages 18 feet deep and has a maximum depth of 50 feet. Its north end is flanked by the hamlet of Forestport.

TIPS: Work loud surface baits like Hula Poppers and buzzbaits on calm summer days.

THE FISHING: This impoundment is primarily warmwater habitat. Largemouth bass ranging from 10 to 14 inches are common and hang out around weed beds and emergent vegetation where they eagerly take jerkbaits, spinnerbaits, and noisy surface lures. Chain pickerel running between 15 and 22 inches occupy the same range and hit the same offerings. Smallmouths typically go 8 to 12 inches and like hanging out over rocky points and moving water—below Kayuta Lake's dam, for instance. They take crayfish, minnows, and jigs. Yellow perch up to 12 inches can turn up just about anywhere and respond to worms, minnows, crayfish, and small lures. Bullheads running from 6 to 10 inches scour bottom for crayfish and juicy night crawlers.

DIRECTIONS: Head north out of Utica on NY 12 for 22 miles, then bear north on NY 28 for about 2 miles.

ADDITIONAL INFORMATION: A fishing access site on River Road (west side of the NY 28 bridge) has two parking lots next to each other—one above the dam, one below—with combined parking for about 15 cars. Woodhull Road, at the other end of the bridge, offers access with parking for about 10 cars just south of the intersection.

CONTACT: New York State Department of Environmental Conservation Region 6.

176. MOOSE RIVER (MAIN STEM)

KEY SPECIES: Brown trout and smallmouth bass.

DESCRIPTION: Formed by the union of the South and Middle Branches a little north of the NY 28 bridge near the hamlet of McKeever, this stream snakes wildly for about 15 miles, tumbling over numerous spectacular waterfalls before pouring into the Black River at Lyons Falls.

TIPS: Work streamers at the heads and tails of pools, and through deep runs.

THE FISHING: The state stocks the section along the Moose River Road downstream of McKeever with 2,800 brook trout annually. "This is a fast, late-spring fishery, with most being caught quickly," says Frank Flack, a state fisheries biologist familiar with the stream. Survivors move to spring holes as the weather warms up, providing dynamite summer fishing to locals who know where the cool spots are located. Smallmouth bass occupy the entire stream and respond to lures, minnows, and crayfish. Huge brown trout rule the waters downstream of Fowlersville and take spoons and minnow-imitating crankbaits like Jr. ThunderSticks. From the dam in Kosterville to its mouth, the stream contains all the popular warmwater species, including walleyes.

DIRECTIONS: Moose River Road parallels the stretch from McKeever downstream for about 3 miles—shoulder parking. Lyonsdale Road parallels the lower 2 miles.

ADDITIONAL INFORMATION: Running over some of the most rugged area imaginable, the river carves an incredibly scenic path, drawing numerous daytrippers to the cataracts punctuating it from Fowlersville to Lyons Falls. Above McKeaver, the river has three branches (North, South, and Middle), each offering wild brookies under wilderness-like conditions.

CONTACT: New York State Department of Environmental Conservation Region 6.

176A. Kosterville Road

DESCRIPTION: This hard-surface road follows the river for a little over a mile, from Lyons Falls to the dams at Kosterville, offering shoulder parking and trails down to the water.

DIRECTIONS: From NY 12 on the south side of Lyons Falls, get on Franklin Street and head north (left) into the village. Turn right onto Laura Street, cross the Black River, and turn left onto Lyons Falls Road. Cross the Moose River a couple hundred yards later and immediately turn right onto Kosterville Road.

176B. Lyons Falls Hydroelectric Portage

DESCRIPTION: This official portage gives you access to the rapids below the dam. Shoulder parking.

DIRECTIONS: From the stop sign at the eastern end of Kosterville Road, turn left and travel about 100 yards.

176C. Moose River Hiking Trail

DESCRIPTION: This 0.5-mile-long trail leads to Agers Falls, past some of the fishiest rapids, waterfalls, and pools imaginable. Parking for four cars.

DIRECTIONS: Head east out of Lyons Falls on Laura Street and continue straight (east) onto CR 39 for about 1.5 miles to the parking area on the north shoulder.

176D. Agers Falls Access

DESCRIPTION: This site offers access to the rapids below Agers Falls, and parking for about 10 cars right at the river. In addition, there's a picnic area, Jonny on the spot, canoe portage, and the ruins of an old mill.

DIRECTIONS: From **site 176C** above, continue east 0.6 mile.

176E. Project Operation "Run of the River"

DESCRIPTION: Located just above the dam at the Burrows Paper Corporation's Lyonsdale Facility, this site offers parking for about 10 cars, portage, shore-fishing access, hiking trails, and a large map showing all the spots.

DIRECTIONS: From **site 176D** above, continue east on Lyonsdale Road for a few hundred yards.

177. FISH CREEK (LEWIS COUNTY)

KEY SPECIES: Brook trout and brown trout.

DESCRIPTION: This rift-pool stream flows for about 11 miles and feeds the Black River. In its upper reaches the bottom is sand, gravel, and boulders, and the lower portion is loaded with windfalls and tangles of woody debris.

TIPS: The biggest trout are in the lower section.

THE FISHING: This stream's brown and brook trout are wild. Brookies range from 6 to 12 inches, and the browns go from 6 to 20 inches. These fish will take worms early in the season and a gently presented dry fly in late spring. Worms still work well after a summer rain, while Muddler Minnows and Black Nose Dace, stripped rapidly across the surface around dawn and dusk, produce during the dog days of summer. The state owns 5.05 miles of public fishing rights downstream of North South Road.

DIRECTIONS: From NY 12 on the south side of Lyons Falls, take Franklin Street. Turn left at the stop sign about 0.1 mile later, travel 0.2 mile, turn right on Laura Street, cross the bridge, and turn left onto Lyons Falls Road (CR 39). Travel for 3.9 miles and cross the creek; Fish Creek Road parallels it to the east.

CONTACT: New York State Department of Environmental Conservation Region 6.

177A. Public Access

DESCRIPTION: Bridge access and parking on the shoulder.

DIRECTIONS: On River Road, roughly 100 yards west of its intersection with Lyons Falls Road (CR 76).

177B. Public Access

DESCRIPTION: Parking for about five cars.

DIRECTIONS: About 100 feet east on Fish Creek Road from its intersection with Lyons Falls Road (CR 76).

177C. Public Access

DESCRIPTION: Parking for about five cars.

DIRECTIONS: From **site 177B** above, head east on Fish Creek Road for about a mile to Jones Road, turn right, and travel a few hundred feet.

ADDITIONAL INFORMATION: This site has a 3-foot drop at the culvert, and another waterfall twice as tall a few feet farther downstream.

177D. Singing Waters Picnic Area

DESCRIPTION: This scenic county park has picnic facilities, two footbridges crossing the creek, and parking for 10 cars.

DIRECTIONS: From **site 177C**, continue east on Fish Creek Road for about 0.5 mile.

177E. Public Access

DESCRIPTION: Parking for about five cars.

DIRECTIONS: From **site 177D**, travel east about 1.5 miles on Fish Creek Road, bear right onto an unmarked, unpaved road, and continue about 0.1 mile to its end and the access site on North South Road, across from its terminus.

178. OTTER CREEK

KEY SPECIES: Brook trout and brown trout.

DESCRIPTION: Spawned by Big Otter Lake, this stream rushes down the relatively gentle slopes of the western Adirondacks for about 15 miles and feeds the Black River north of the hamlet of Glenfield.

TIPS: Both species of trout respond enthusiastically all summer long to nymphs dead-drifted through rapids and pockets.

THE FISHING: Frank Flack, a state fisheries biologist familiar with this beat, says the stretch from the mouth to Eatonville Road is primarily brown trout water and gradually transitions into brookie habitat the farther you go upstream. The state stocks roughly 2,650 yearling browns and 250 two-year-olds annually. The brookies are wild.

DIRECTIONS: From its intersection with NY 12 in the hamlet of Glenfield, head up Main Street for just under 0.5 mile, turn right onto Greig Road (CR 40), travel 0.5 mile, turn left onto Otter Creek Road (CR 56), and follow it for 1.4 miles to its intersection with Pine Grove Road (CR 39).

ADDITIONAL INFORMATION: At the above intersection, the creek brushes the road, and the shoulder is wide enough to park three cars.

CONTACT: New York State Department of Environmental Conservation Region 6.

178A. Dam Access

DESCRIPTION: Shoulder parking and fishing access to the mill pool above the dam and the rapids below.

DIRECTIONS: From its intersection with Otter Creek Road, head north on Pine Grove Road, take the next right onto Chases Lake Road, and continue for 0.5 mile to Otter Creek dam.

178B. Rockslide Access

DESCRIPTION: Some of the most promising trout holes are located at the "Rockslide," a gentle waterfall located at a bridge in the heart of the state forest named after the creek.

DIRECTIONS: From its intersection with Otter Creek Road, head south on Pine Grove Road for a few hundred yards, turn east on Eatonville Road, and travel for 1.4 miles (the pavement ends in 0.2 mile, and the hard-surface road has some rough spots).

ADDITIONAL INFORMATION: This section is part of the New York State Department of Environmental Conservation's hugely popular Otter Creek Horse Trails system. Several hardened campsites are near the bridge.

179. CRYSTAL CREEK

KEY SPECIES: Brook trout and brown trout.

DESCRIPTION: This rift-pool stream flows for about 12 miles and feeds the Black River.

TIPS: Cast spinners into the backwashes and pools below the fallen willows and woody debris downstream of New Bremen.

THE FISHING: Frank Flack, the local state fisheries biologist, considers this the best trout stream in Lewis County. Like all the Black River tributaries, it has native brook trout in its upper reaches. Flack claims a lot of browns are up there, too; they're just a lot savvier and harder to catch. From New Bremen, downstream, the state annually stocks about 800 browns averaging 8.5 inches, and 250 averaging 12 inches. Flack says this section has a nice combination of wild and stocked fish, many over 2 pounds, and has a 5-pound brown hanging on his wall to prove it.

DIRECTIONS: This creek runs through the village of New Bremen.

ADDITIONAL INFORMATION: The state owns public fishing rights on 10.6 miles of the stream.

CONTACT: New York State Department of Environmental Conservation Region 6 and Lewis County Chamber of Commerce.

179A. Public Access

DESCRIPTION: This informal site has parking for about four cars.
DIRECTIONS: Take NY 812 south out of New Bremen for about 0.5 mile, turn right onto Van Amber Road, and continue to the bridge.

179B. Crystal Pond

DESCRIPTION: This millpond park offers easy bank-fishing access.
DIRECTIONS: At the crossroads of CR 37 and NY 812 in the hamlet of New Bremen.

179C. Public Access

DESCRIPTION: This site offers access at a bridge and parking for five cars.
DIRECTIONS: Head east out of New Bremen on NY 812 for 0.8 mile and turn right on Tillman Road. Travel for 1.3 miles, turn right onto Lomber Road, cross the bridge 0.1 mile later, and park in the lot on the left.

179D. Public Access

DESCRIPTION: This site offers access at a bridge and parking for five cars.
DIRECTIONS: Continue east on Tillman Road (see **site 179C**) for about 0.9 mile to the access at the old bridge.

179E. Public Access

DESCRIPTION: Stream access, parking for eight cars, and a handicapped-accessible platform.
DIRECTIONS: From **site 179D**, continue east on Tillman Road for several hundred feet to its end. Turn right on Baker Road, travel 0.2 mile, and turn left onto Ossont Road. Turn left again onto Muncy Road 0.7 mile later and travel 0.1 mile to the access site.
ADDITIONAL INFORMATION: The handicapped-accessible platform is 0.15 mile in the woods, along a groomed path.

180. SUGAR RIVER

KEY SPECIES: Brook and brown trout.
DESCRIPTION: Like most of the streams trickling out of the Tug Hill Plateau, this tributary of the Black River is creek-sized and mild-mannered most of the time, but rages when swollen with runoff.

TIPS: Fish nymphs at a dead-drift under rocks at the heads of pockets.

THE FISHING: Brown trout migrate into this stream from the Black River, reaching as far as the falls just upstream of the NY 12D bridge. Wild brookies reign upstream of the falls all the way to the source.

DIRECTIONS: Slicing through the east side of Lewis County for roughly 95 percent of its length, this stream runs through the village of Constableville and the hamlet of Tolcottville.

ADDITIONAL INFORMATION: One of the reasons the state doesn't stock this stream is because there's no official public access. Still, anglers have been accessing the stream for years from the NY 26 bridge and the south side of the NY 12D bridge.

CONTACT: New York State Department of Environmental Conservation Region 6.

The Sugar River (site 180) just upstream of the NY 12D bridge.

181. WEST CANADA CREEK

KEY SPECIES: Brown trout, brook trout, and smallmouth bass.

DESCRIPTION: This stream springs from the western Adirondacks, runs for about 75 miles, and pours into the New Erie Canal at Herkimer. Along the way, it fills and drains Hinckley and Prospect Reservoirs.

TIPS: Use Elk Hair Caddis in autumn.

THE FISHING: The size of a small river, this is one of the most popular trout streams in the state. Curiously, the stretch feeding Hinckley Reservoir is pretty much a washout. The state stocks this section with about 3.000 brown trout and 10,500 brook trout averaging 8.5 inches annually. The stream is austere and acidic, however, and survival isn't easy for the browns; they don't grow much. Brookies do a little better: 12-inchers are available, and larger ones are possible. Both species take worms, salted minnows, in-line spinners, and flies.

Downstream of the Hinckley Reservoir is a different story. The fishery improves immediately (see Prospect Reservoir, **site 183**) and remains top-notch all the way to the mouth. Each year, the state stocks roughly 42,000 brown trout averaging 8.5 inches and 2,400 averaging 13.5 inches. Survival is good, and trout typically range from 10 to 18 inches; 19- to 23- inchers are common, and some stretching the tape over 24 inches are caught each year. Although the biggest fish are taken on worms and minnows, fly fishermen catch a lot up to 20 inches on wet flies, streamers, and nymphs. "I get them just as big on dries like mayflies and caddis," claims Jack Zasada, a local intimately familiar with just about every inch of this creek. Brook trout from 8 to 14 inches are also available, primarily near the mouths of the tributaries they outgrew. Most are taken on worms, minnows, and spinners.

Smallmouth bass are available in the lower part of the stream. They typically run between 12 and 14 inches, but 16-inchers are possible. Their numbers are sufficient to warrant locals targeting them specifically with crayfish, Dardevle spoons, and crankbaits like Excalibur Fat Free Shallow Divers.

The author fly fishing on West Canada Creek (site 181) in Nobleboro.

The stretch from the bridge at Trenton Falls downstream for 2.5 miles to the first bridge (Comstock Bridge) below the mouth of Cincinnati Creek is open year-round to catch-and-release trout fishing with artificial lures only.

DIRECTIONS: NY 28 parallels the creek from the village of Herkimer (Thruway exit 30) north for about 20 miles to Gravesville. NY 365 parallels the stream for about 8 miles upstream of Hinckley Reservoir. Parking areas are plentiful along both highways.

ADDITIONAL INFORMATION: Easement rights, public land, and agreements with private property owners open most of the creek to public fishing. Downstream of Hinckley dam, the river's level is manipulated by utilities, so be on the lookout for fast-rising waters. Zasada says, "The most important thing about fishing this stream is water levels. It's most productive and easiest to fish when it's running at 600 cfs or less." For a water flow report go to www.h2oline.com or call 00-452-1742 (code 365124). Motels and several commercial campgrounds are located along the river on NY 28.

CONTACT: New York State Department of Environmental Conservation Region 6.

181A. Public Access

DESCRIPTION: Algonquin Power Systems fisherman access, parking for 20 cars, and access to the plunge pool at the base of the dam and the rapids below it.

DIRECTIONS: On NY 28, 2.9 miles north of Thruway (I-90) exit 30 in Herkimer.

181B. Kast Bridge Public Access

DESCRIPTION: Parking for three cars and a trail down to the water.

DIRECTIONS: From **site 181A**, head north on NY 28 for 1.3 miles, turn right onto West End Road, and cross the bridge; the parking spot is on the left.

181C. Public Access

DESCRIPTION: An abandoned hard-surface road runs for about a mile between NY 28 and the creek, offering easy access to numerous pools and runs.

DIRECTIONS: Head back to NY 28 from **site 181B**, turn right, and travel about 0.2 mile.

181D. Public Access

DESCRIPTION: This paved pull-off is straddled by two pools; a deep run skirts the parking area.

DIRECTIONS: On NY 28, 3.8 miles north of Kast Bridge (**site 181B**).

181E. Public Access

DESCRIPTION: Access at a bridge.

DIRECTIONS: On Fairfield Street in the village of Middleville.

ADDITIONAL INFORMATION: A couple of commercial mines where you can dig for Herkimer diamonds—double-terminated quartz crystals so beautiful the Indians used them in religious ceremonies—are located on NY 28, about a mile south of Middleville.

181F. Public Access

DESCRIPTION: State fishing access site with parking for 20 cars.

DIRECTIONS: Get back on NY 28 from **site 181E** and head north for 0.8 mile.

181G. Public Access

DESCRIPTION: This public park offers access to a mill pool above a dam, an ideal spot for casting streamers, bottom-fishing with bait, or casting lures.

DIRECTIONS: Bridge Street in the village of Newport.

ADDITIONAL INFORMATION: Built in 1853 of cut limestone, the arched bridge was put on the National Register in 1992.

181H. Public Access

DESCRIPTION: This state site offers parking for about 20 cars.

DIRECTIONS: NY 28 just south of Poland.

181I. Public Access

DESCRIPTION: Parking for 15 cars.

DIRECTIONS: On NY 28, about 2 miles north of Poland.

181J. Public Access

DESCRIPTION: This state site offers parking for 20 cars.

DIRECTIONS: From the NY 8/NY 28 intersection in Poland, head north on NY 28 for 2.7 miles, turn right on Gravesville Road, then immediately left on Partridge Hill Road.

ADDITIONAL INFORMATION: Partridge Hill Road runs for about 2 miles and offers a couple of informal, shoulder access sites along its course. It ends at Dover Road, a few hundred feet from the bridge crossing the creek in the hamlet of Trenton Falls.

181K. Harvey Bridge Road Access

DESCRIPTION: Located on the upper creek above Hinckley Reservoir, this bridge offers parking for about 10 cars on its southeastern corner and trails down to a wide, shallow stretch of creek. The most efficient way to fish this area is by casting lures like Mepps spinners.

DIRECTIONS: From its intersection with NY 365, take Harvey Bridge Road south for 0.2 mile, turn right at the stop sign, cross the bridge, and park on the left.

181L. Haskell Road Scenic Overlook

DESCRIPTION: This site offers parking for five cars and a trail down to the creek. You'll have to scramble over some large boulders at the water's edge.

DIRECTIONS: On the west side of the NY 8 bridge in the hamlet of Nobleboro, turn north on Haskell Road, then take a right about 100 yards later.

ADDITIONAL INFORMATION: This spot's relatively deep, fast water looks dynamite but it's a tough bite, especially after the middle of summer when most of the stockies have been caught. Still, some wild brookies are always available if you have the patience and know-how to get them.

181M. Haskell Road Terminus

DESCRIPTION: Haskell Road is only paved for 0.3 mile, and continues slicing through the woods as a hard-surface road for another 2.4 miles, ending at a gate with a clearing big enough to park 20 cars. The gate is generally open, but the road narrows and softens into a logging trail—signs warn, WATCH FOR LOGGING TRUCKS. The creek cascades alongside it, offering scenic pocket water sparsely populated with brook trout.

ADDITIONAL INFORMATION: A trail down to the river is located behind some ruins at the northeastern corner of the clearing. At the bottom it turns into boggy ground littered with broken glass. Climb down carefully.

DIRECTIONS: Continue on Haskell Road from **site 181L.**

182. HINCKLEY RESERVOIR (KUYAHOORA LAKE)

KEY SPECIES: Rainbow trout, brook trout, brown trout, smallmouth bass, pickerel, perch, and rock bass.

DESCRIPTION: Measuring 13 miles long by 0.5 mile wide, this 2,800-acre body of water averages about 28 feet deep and drops to a maximum depth of about 75 feet. Its main tributary and outlet is West Canada Creek. Its waters are acidic and infertile, making it one of the most austere reservoirs in the state. What few nutrients it gets are washed away during winter drawdown. Indeed, the state Department of Environmental Conservation classifies this fishery as marginal, and finding someone willing to say something positive about it is challenging.

TIPS: Fish the mouths of tributaries after a rain.

THE FISHING: The state stocks about 4,000 rainbow trout averaging 9 inches annually. They're joined by brookies and browns fleeing the austere waters of West Canada Creek, only to find the reservoir even stingier. However, anglers realize modest success trolling with spoons, catching rainbows averaging 12 inches. Browns running from 8 to 14 inches and brookies averaging 6 inches are targeted mainly in the spring by bank anglers bottom-fishing with worms or suspending minnows below bobbers. Smallmouth bass are plentiful but they're cookie cutters, averaging 12 inches. Still, these little guys are feisty, and a lot of fun to catch on jigs and small crankbaits. Pickerel typically grow to 22 inches, but most are a lot smaller. They'll take just about anything that moves and fits in their mouths, but are especially fond of flashy stuff like spinners.

Trout season is year-round; the minimum length is 12 inches and the daily limit is three.

DIRECTIONS: Head north out of Utica on NY 12 for 14 miles. Turn east on NY 365 and travel for about 4.5 miles.

ADDITIONAL INFORMATION: Close proximity to the road makes this scenic reservoir a very popular recreational spot. The boat launch on NY 365, 0.3 mile east of the dam, a fee area operated by the New York Power Authority, offers a hard-surface ramp and parking for about 40 rigs.

Primitive camping is allowed on the large island.

CONTACT: New York State Department of Environmental Conservation Region 6.

182A. Public Access

DESCRIPTION: This scenic overlook offers parking for about 10 cars and several hundred feet of bank-fishing access.

DIRECTIONS: On NY 365, right at the dam.

182B. Public Access

DESCRIPTION: This informal site offers parking for about 10 cars and bank-fishing access to a shallow mudflat that reaches over 100 yards into the lake.

DIRECTIONS: On NY 365, 1.5 miles east of the dam.

182C. Hinckley Day Use Area

DESCRIPTION: Run by the state Department of Environmental Conservation, this fee area is for day use during summer. There's a beach launch for cartop craft, ample shore-fishing access, a swimming beach, playing fields, hiking trails, picnic tables, a bathhouse, toilets, and parking for 100 cars. Open from Memorial Day through Labor Day.

DIRECTIONS: From its intersection with NY 385 just below the dam, take South Side Road (CR 151) for about 4 miles to the stop sign, turn left on Grant Road (CR 90), travel for 0.6 mile, and turn left. Turning into a seasonal highway 0.2 mile from South Side Road, Grant Road doesn't get plowed.

183. PROSPECT RESERVOIR

KEY SPECIES: Brown trout and rainbow trout.

DESCRIPTION: This reservoir starts directly below the Hinckley Reservoir dam and stretches for a little over a mile to the power dam.

TIPS: Drift the fast water below Hinckley dam with live bait.

THE FISHING: The state stocks 3,000 brown trout averaging 9 inches annually. Survival is decent and they range from stockies to a whopping 10 pounds. Some rainbows, scions of former stockings, are present and can run up to 2 feet long. The rainbows like flies, shiny spoons, and spinners; the browns respond best to minnows, worms, and minnowbaits.

Trout season is year-round; the minimum length is 12 inches and the daily limit is 3.

DIRECTIONS: Head north on NY 12 from Utica for 14 miles, turn east on NY 365, and travel 3.9 miles.

ADDITIONAL INFORMATION: Reliant Energy Company's West Canada Creek Recreation Area access site on NY 365 has a hard-surface ramp and parking for about 15 rigs. Open Memorial Day through Labor Day. Motors exceeding 10 hp are prohibited.

CONTACT: New York State Department of Environmental Conservation Region 6.

183A. Public Access

DESCRIPTION: Popular with bank anglers, this site offers parking for 15 cars.

DIRECTIONS: At the South Side Road bridge, 1.3 miles east of the launch mentioned above.

ADDITIONAL INFORMATION: A 4-foot drop at the bank makes launching cartoppers tough during low water.

184. LANSING KILL

KEY SPECIES: Brown trout and brook trout.

DESCRIPTION: This skinny stream pours out of the hills near Booneville, flows south for about 10 miles, and feeds the Mohawk River in the hamlet of Hillside. But don't let its diminutive size fool ya; it boasts so many big fish, the state protects them by limiting your catch of trout over 12 inches to two per day.

TIPS: Cast white caddis early in the evening.

THE FISHING: The state stocks over 3,700 brown trout averaging 8.5 inches annually. Growth is good and many reach 12 inches, even more. They take worms, flies, and in-line spinners. Natural brook trout, scions of tiny tributaries, migrate into the stream when they outgrow their natal turf. Ranging from 4 to 10 inches, they take worms and flies.

DIRECTIONS: NY 46 parallels the stream.

ADDITIONAL INFORMATION: The state owns public fishing rights on 2.5 miles of the stream, and informal access at bridges and off the shoulder of the road is plentiful. Abandoned locks and other structures of the old Black River Canal punctuate the roadside north of Hillside.

CONTACT: New York State Department of Environmental Conservation Region 6.

184A. Public Access

DESCRIPTION: This site has shoulder parking for about five cars.

DIRECTIONS: From its intersection with Golf Course Road below the Delta Lake dam, head north on NY 46 for 6.3 miles, turn left on Hillside Road (it's unmarked), and travel 0.1 mile to the bridge.

ADDITIONAL INFORMATION: The stream feeds the Mohawk River at the next bridge, 0.2 mile downstream.

184B. Formal Public Access

DESCRIPTION: This site has parking for about 10 cars.

DIRECTIONS: On NY 46, about 2 miles above its intersection with the northern terminus of Hillside Road.

184C. Pixley Falls State Park

DESCRIPTION: The Lansing Kill's 50-foot waterfall is the park's greatest attraction. The plunge pool below is a favorite early-season spot among locals.

DIRECTIONS: The park is on NY 46, about 2.7 miles north of **site 184B**.

ADDITIONAL INFORMATION: The park offers restrooms, hiking trails, shelters, and picnic facilities. The Old Black River Canal, an Erie Canal–era waterway that carried trade from Rome into the North Country, runs through the park.

185. UPPER MOHAWK RIVER

KEY SPECIES: Brown trout, brook trout, norlunge, northern pike, and walleyes.

DESCRIPTION: This section covers the coldwater portion of the Mohawk River, stretching from its headwaters to the New Erie Canal in Rome.

TIPS: Swing large streamers through the deep runs downstream of the Delta Lake dam for monster trout and northern pike.

THE FISHING: The state stocks about 8,000 brown trout averaging 8 inches into the river above Delta Lake annually. Habitat is good, and the trout easily reach 12 inches. Indeed, state fisheries biologist Frank Flack believes there are enough big browns here to warrant raising the minimum length to 12 inches. A relatively wide, open stream, this is good water to fly fish; many big trout are taken on nymphs and streamers.

An exciting mix of coldwater and warmwater species is found below the Delta Lake dam. The state annually stocks in excess of 10,000 brown trout averaging 8.5 inches, and about 1,200 averaging 14 inches. Some years see a couple hundred stretching the tape to 17 inches thrown in to make things interesting. Huge brook trout also like this spot. The state stocks some occasionally, and 2-pounders are caught with surprising regularity; 4-pounders have been reported. Both species take worms, minnows, in-line spinners, Rapalas, and Bass Pro Shops XPS Minnows. Walleyes run from 1 to 5 pounds and are taken on worms, jigs, and the same minnowbaits the trout like. While a few northern pike ranging from 26 to 40 inches are present in the river's mouth at Delta Lake, they're notorious in the lower stream. They'll hit minnows, crankbaits, and large in-line spinners dressed in bucktail skirts. The state stocks tiger muskies every now and then. They grow to over 36 inches and respond to the same baits the northerns do.

DIRECTIONS: NY 46 parallels much of the river.

ADDITIONAL INFORMATION: Special trout seasons stretching from April 1 to November 30 are in effect from the bridge in Westernville upstream to its confluence with the Lansing Kill, and from Delta dam downstream to the New Erie Canal. The state owns several miles of public fishing rights, designated by yellow steel signs nailed to trees; and informal access is plentiful off the shoulder of the road.

CONTACT: New York State Department of Environmental Conservation Region 6.

The Mohawk River (site 185) above Northwestern.

185A. Public Access

DESCRIPTION: This official parking area offers access to the headwaters of the East Branch of the Mohawk.

DIRECTIONS: On NY 26, about 2 miles north of West Leyden.

ADDITIONAL INFORMATION: Located in 1,210-acre Mohawk Springs State Forest, named for the cold springs that spawn the river, the stream is nothing more than a skinny brook here, but its colorful native brookies make the 0.25-mile hike to the water worth the effort.

185B. Public Access

DESCRIPTION: This park, located on the East Branch, offers parking for several cars, as well as access to a millpond and the young, brook-sized river below the dam.

DIRECTIONS: From its intersection with NY 46 in Booneville, take NY 294 west for 6.8 miles to its end in the hamlet of West Leyden, turn left on NY 26, and travel for 0.1 mile to the bridge.

185C. Public Access

DESCRIPTION: This informal site offers parking for about 10 cars.

DIRECTIONS: From the heart of the hamlet of Westernville, head north on Main Street for several hundred yards, take a left onto Stokes-Western Road (CR 53), and travel 0.2 mile to the bridge.

ADDITIONAL INFORMATION: A mudflat skirts the bank just below the parking area. Avoid it by taking the trail in the corner of the parking lot to the bridge. Here the stream resembles a trout creek more than a river, offering long runs and pools punctuated with ripples.

185D. Delta Lake Dam Access

DESCRIPTION: At press time there is no official public access to the pool at the foot of the dam, and the NYS Canal System would prefer anglers not fish there— but the spot is so productive, many still do. Word has it a new power generating facility is being planned and a fishing access site is being considered.

DIRECTIONS: From its intersection with NY 69 in Rome, head north on NY 46 (Black River Boulevard) for about 4.8 miles, turn left (west) on Golf Course Road just below the dam, and travel 0.1 mile to the shoulder parking site on the left.

185E. Public Access

DESCRIPTION: Located across the street from the state fish hatchery, this site boasts handicapped access and parking for 100 cars.

DIRECTIONS: On NY 46, 4.5 miles north of Rome.

186. DELTA LAKE

KEY SPECIES: Northern pike, chain pickerel, walleyes, black bass, black crappies, and panfish.

DESCRIPTION: This 2,500-acre reservoir averages 22 feet deep and has a maximum depth of 60 feet.

TIPS: From opening day through June, drift the shoreline and swim or jig (yo-yo) spinnerbaits for monster northern pike.

THE FISHING: This reservoir has a reputation for huge northern pike over 40 inches long. Most are taken on large minnows suspended below bobbers. However, flatlining with Challenger and Bass Pro Shops XPS Minnows also works, especially in May and again in October. Pickerel are abundant, averaging a solid 20 inches, and strike just about any lure, but especially jigs and crankbaits. Walleyes range from 2 to 6 pounds and are taken with jigs, grubs, and crankbaits like Rat-L-Traps and Smithwick Rogues. Smallmouth bass in the 1- to 3-pound range are common in the main lake and take worms, minnows, and crayfish. Largemouths from 1 to 4 pounds rule the "back sets" (shallow bays and flats) around the mouth of the Mohawk River and respond to topwater lures and spinnerbaits. Perch ranging from 6 to 12 inches and black crappies from 9 to 12 inches are plentiful and take small minnows and 2-inch scented, curly-tailed grubs. Bullhead up to 14 inches are abundant and take worms fished on bottom in the backwaters, primarily in spring. Pumpkinseeds averaging 5 inches thrive along the shoreline and in the backwaters along NY 46, and hit flies, poppers, and worms fished below tiny bobbers.

DIRECTIONS: Head north out of Rome for about 5 miles on NY 46.

ADDITIONAL INFORMATION: Delta Lake State Park, a fee area, offers a paved double-lane ramp, parking for about 25 rigs, 101 campsites, hot showers, playgrounds and playing fields, picnic facilities, and hiking trails. The campground is open mid-May through Columbus Day; free day use permitted off-season.

CONTACT: New York State Department of Environmental Conservation Region 6 and Oneida County Convention and Visitors Bureau.

TUG HILL
PLATEAU REGION

*Author's note: Only the upper reaches of the Salmon River are covered in this book.
The world famous lower river is covered in my previous book,*
Fishing the Great Lakes of New York.

Christian Snyder, a professional
Tug Hill fishing guide, deciding
what fly to use.

187. MAD RIVER (SALMON RIVER DRAINAGE)

KEY SPECIES: Brook trout.

DESCRIPTION: Springing out of the wilds of western Lewis County, a few miles
east of the tri-county line, this stream crosses into Jefferson County, then
heads south through Oswego County. Picking up numerous feeders along
the way, it grows into a small river by the time it feeds the North Branch of
the Salmon River in Battle Hill State Forest, north of Redfield.

TIPS: After a rain, drift a worm on bottom, tight to submerged logs and boulders.

THE FISHING: The state stocks around 400 brookies annually into this stream's upper reaches in Lewis County. The rest of the river hosts wild brookies that outgrew their home range in the Mad River's tiny tributaries and headed downstream in search of larger haunts. Ranging from 4 to 12 inches, they are partial to worms, salted minnows, flies, small spoons, and spinners. Some browns are available in the lower reaches below Mad River Falls.

DIRECTIONS: CR 17 parallels the river.

ADDITIONAL INFORMATION: Primitive camping is permitted in Battle Hill State Forest. The state owns 6.6 miles of public fishing rights to this stream.

CONTACT: New York State Department of Environmental Conservation Region 7.

187A. Otto Mills State Fishing Access Site

DESCRIPTION: This site is on the edge of state land and has parking for about four cars. Otto Mills Road ends a few hundred yards later at a private, barricaded suspension footbridge crossing the river; no shoulder parking. This site is a few hundred yards west of the stream, so you'll have to park and hike the distance through the woods.

ADDITIONAL INFORMATION: The state owns public fishing rights for a couple of miles upstream and downstream of the bridge. Cold Brook and Beaver Creek feed the river about 0.5 and 1 mile, respectively, upstream of the bridge, and offer about a mile of public fishing rights.

DIRECTIONS: Head north out of Redfield on CR 17 for about 3 miles. Turn east onto Otto Mills Drive and travel for a little over a mile.

188. NORTH BRANCH SALMON RIVER

KEY SPECIES: Brook trout.

DESCRIPTION: Gurgling out of the woods of the Tug Hill Plateau's Little John Wildlife Management Area, this stream runs south for about 15 miles and pours into the northeastern corner of the Salmon River Reservoir.

TIPS: Cast black, all-purpose nymphs into the heads and tails of pools.

THE FISHING: Each year, the state releases in excess of 3,000 brook trout averaging 9 inches. Combined with the stream's natives, they make this one of Oswego County's most productive streams. The fishing is best from late April through May, when the trout hit worms and salted minnows. Come summer, terrestrials, nymphs, caddis, emergers, and moth patterns work well.

ADDITIONAL INFORMATION: From May through mid-June, the blackflies are thick enough to drive you off the stream. The easiest way to deal with them is to douse yourself with insect repellent. However, health-conscious anglers find mesh garments only slightly less convenient and a lot healthier. The state owns 8.9 miles of public fishing rights to this stream.

CONTACT: New York State Department of Environmental Conservation Region 7.

188A. Public Access

DESCRIPTION: This paved site has parking for about four cars.

DIRECTIONS: Head north out of Redfield on Harvester Mill Road for about a mile, to the first bridge.

188B. Public Access

DESCRIPTION: This site has parking for about eight cars.

DIRECTIONS: Head north out of Redfield on Harvester Mill Road for about 2 miles, to the second bridge.

188C. Public Access

DESCRIPTION: This site has parking for five cars.

DIRECTIONS: At the CR 17 bridge, about 3.5 miles north of Redfield.

188D. Public Access

DESCRIPTION: This site has parking for five cars.

DIRECTIONS: Head north out of Redfield on CR 17 for about 5 miles and turn west on Caster Drive.

188E. Public Access

DESCRIPTION: This site has parking for about three cars.

DIRECTIONS: Head north on CR 17 out of Redfield for about 5.5 miles, turn left on Abes Drive, and travel about 0.5 mile.

189. SALMON RIVER

KEY SPECIES: Brook trout and rainbow trout.

DESCRIPTION: This stream flows off the Tug Hill Plateau and drains into the Salmon River Reservoir.

TIPS: The best fishing is in May.

THE FISHING: The state stocks about 900 brookies averaging 9 inches and 1,800 rainbows averaging 8 inches annually. Most are caught by local meat anglers early in the season. Still, some survive, and 12-inchers—some even bigger— are available by late summer. Both species hit worms and salted minnows in spring, nymphs in summer, and Woolly Worms in autumn.

DIRECTIONS: Waterbury and Osceola (CR 46) Roads parallel the River east of Redfield.

ADDITIONAL INFORMATION: Camping is permitted on the state land a few hundred yards upstream of the bridge. Blackflies often get so thick from May through mid-June that they can run unprotected anglers off the stream.

CONTACT: New York State Department of Environmental Conservation Region 7.

190. SALMON RIVER (REDFIELD) RESERVOIR

KEY SPECIES: Black bass, walleyes, black crappies, sunfish, rock bass, brown bullheads, and brown, brook, and rainbow trout.

DESCRIPTION: Created in 1914 when a power dam was built on the Salmon River, this reservoir covers 3,379 acres, averages 20 feet deep, and has a maximum depth of 57 feet.

TIPS: Cast a weightless stickworm tight to emergent vegetation for bucketmouths.

THE FISHING: This is primarily a warmwater fishery. Largemouth bass ranging from 1 to 5 pounds are plentiful and strike crayfish, minnows, and soft Berkley PowerBaits cast into any vegetation you can find. Smallmouths found their way into the system a little while back and are gaining a foothold. Averaging about 13 inches, they're targeted mostly by drifting minnows and crayfish. Rick Miick of Dream Catcher Charters likes to fish for them on the surface: "When you see a lot of rings on the water, walk the dog with a darter or twitch a floating minnowbait," he advises. Walleyes aren't plentiful, but their numbers are growing. Mostly they're targeted with bucktail jigs on the rocky drops around the islands, and by drifting night crawlers on harnesses. Crappies are abundant, and highly prized by locals who would rather keep their presence in the reservoir a secret. While they average a whopping 10 inches, many over 14 inches are taken each year, primarily on buckeye and flathead minnows. Bluegills and pumpkinseeds averaging 6 inches are common and take poppers, flies, worms, and spikes. Rock bass averaging a solid 7 inches are abundant over the impoundment's numerous rock fields. They hit worms and minnows. Bullheads range from 8 to 14 inches and are a popular rite of spring for locals bank fishing with worms at night. A few large trout (brown, rainbow, and brook), migrants from tributaries like the Salmon River, are available. Indeed, there are enough 20-inchers of each species to attract locals who still-fish for them in the early spring, off points, with worms. In addition, a dedicated following targets these trout in warm weather by trolling small spoons in open water by day, or casting crankbaits along the shoreline around dawn and dusk.

DIRECTIONS: Head east out of Pulaski on CR 2 for about 10 miles.

ADDITIONAL INFORMATION: Most of this reservoir's east bank, about 0.5 mile, is open to the public and is easily accessible from CR 17 on the south side of Redfield. Two bridges carry the road over the Salmon River onto Redfield Island. The island offers a paved launch, parking for about 15 rigs, and a handicapped fishing platform on its northwestern corner; there's a gravel launch with parking for six cars on CR 17, just beyond the southern bridge. Trout season is open year-round. Primitive camping is permitted on the state land off CR 2, in Hall Island State Forest on the south shore, and on the islands.

CONTACT: New York State Department of Environmental Conservation Region 7 and Oswego County Tourism.

190A. Jackson Road Fishing Access Site

DESCRIPTION: This site has a double-wide concrete launch, parking for about 20 rigs, and shore-fishing access.

DIRECTIONS: Jackson Road is about 9.5 miles east of Pulaski, off CR 2.

ADDITIONAL INFORMATION: The lower half of Jackson Road isn't plowed in winter.

190B. CCC Road (Little America) Fishing Access Site

DESCRIPTION: This site has parking for about 15 cars and shore fishing access.

DIRECTIONS: Take CR 2 east out of Pulaski for just under 11 miles, turn right on CCC Road, and travel for about 0.5 mile.

ADDITIONAL INFORMATION: This site's steep banks make launching even small canoes difficult. Camping is allowed in the surrounding Salmon River State Forest. The lower portion of CCC Road isn't plowed in winter.

190C. Salmon River Project Falls Road Day Use Area

DESCRIPTION: This site, maintained by Brookfield Renewable Power, has a beach launch, picnic facilities, parking for about 25 cars, and shore-fishing access.

DIRECTIONS: Head east out of Pulaski on CR 2 for about 9 miles and turn right on Dam Road. Travel for 1.2 miles and turn left at the four-corners.

ADDITIONAL INFORMATION: Dam Road isn't plowed in winter.

190D. Hall Island State Forest Fishing Access Site

DESCRIPTION: This site has upper and lower parking lots that accommodate a total of 40 cars. If the upper barrier is closed, you have to park and walk 0.8 mile to the reservoir.

DIRECTIONS: Head south on NY 13 from Pulaski for about 6.5 miles to Altmar. Turn left on Cemetery Road (at the SALMON RIVER FISH HATCHERY sign) and continue straight (the road turns into CR 22 north) for 3.2 miles to CR 30. Turn south and travel for 0.3 mile, bear left on Pipe Line Road, and travel 2.2 miles to the parking area and access road on the left.

ADDITIONAL INFORMATION: This is a popular night-fishing spot for early-season bullheads. Primitive camping is allowed in the surrounding state forest.

191. SALMON RIVER BETWEEN THE RESERVOIRS

KEY SPECIES: Rainbow trout and brown trout.

DESCRIPTION: This portion of the river spills out of the Salmon River Reservoir, runs through a 2-mile gorge, tumbles over spectacular Salmon River Falls about midway, and feeds Lighthouse Hill Reservoir.

TIPS: The best trout fishing is downstream of the Salmon River Falls, especially early in the season.

THE FISHING: The stretch above Salmon River Falls has poor habitat and is best suited for anglers more interested in pristine scenery and solitude than trout. Still, a few wild brookies, and some browns and rainbows that went over the dam, are available. Below the falls is a different story. The plunge pool is massive and deep, home to numerous undersized smallies and a few trout. They respond enthusiastically to live bait, streamers, and lures. During the spring thaw and after autumn rains, the rapids draw spawning browns and rainbows from Lighthouse Hill Reservoir. Some end up staying, but life ain't easy in the old riverbed (about 95 percent of the stream is diverted through a pipe to the power plant at Bennetts Bridge). The water that escapes man's grasp and makes it into the river's ancient course is wide and shallow, nothing more than a blanket of shallow ripples creeping over a smooth riverbed punctuated with fractures. But don't let those cracks fool ya; they're ideal trout habitat. Watered by cool springs, this ancient riverscape's pools, runs, and rifts are the ticket to some decent fishing embraced by the looming cliffs of a spectacular gorge. The fish range from 8 to 20 inches and respond to worms after a rain, and to expertly presented flies the rest of the time.

DIRECTIONS: Head east out of Altmar on CR 22 for 3.4 miles to Bennetts Bridge (the double white bridges). Pipeline Road parallels the south bank; Falls Road runs along the north bank.

ADDITIONAL INFORMATION: The bank on both sides of the tailrace between the bridge and powerhouse is posted.

CONTACT: New York State Department of Environmental Conservation Region 7 and Oswego County Tourism.

191A. Salmon River Falls Unique Area

DESCRIPTION: This 112-acre preserve has parking for 30 cars and a wide, hardened trail to the scenic falls punctuated with scenic overlooks. The 150-foot descent to the river below the cataract is primitive, steep, and difficult.

DIRECTIONS: Continue north on CR 22 from Bennetts Bridge for about a mile to Falls Road. Turn right and travel for 1.5 miles.

Salmon River Falls.

192. LIGHTHOUSE HILL (LOWER) RESERVOIR

KEY SPECIES: Rainbow trout, brown trout, largemouth bass, sunfish, yellow perch, and brown bullheads.

DESCRIPTION: This 164-acre impoundment averages 25 feet deep and has a maximum depth of 50 feet. Its only development is powerhouses on the east and west ends.

TIPS: From May through mid-July, swing white nymphs through the rapids at the mouth of the power company's tailrace.

THE FISHING: The state stocks about 4,000 rainbow trout averaging 9 inches annually. While a day of trout fishing will load your creel with stockies, fish stretching 18 inches and more are fairly common. They respond to worms, Berkley Trout Bait, and spinners in the spring, and dry flies fished at dusk and dawn in summer. Brown trout, descendants of former stocking programs, range from 6 to 20 inches and are usually caught incidentally by guys targeting rainbows at Bennett Bridges, or drifting minnows and casting minnow-imitating crankbaits for largemouth bass. Bucketmouths range from 1 to 4 pounds and take spinnerbaits and Carolina-rigged worms fished in 5 to 20 feet of water. Yellow perch up to 10 inches, bluegills and pumpkinseeds between 4 and 7 inches, and brown bullheads averaging 10 inches hit worms fished on bottom.

DIRECTIONS: Head south out of Pulaski on NY 13 for 6.8 miles to Altmar. Turn left on Cemetery Road (at the SALMON RIVER HATCHERY sign) and continue straight (it turns into CR 22) for 3.4 miles to the double bridges.

ADDITIONAL INFORMATION: The Salmon River Project Bennett Bridges Day Use Site has parking for about 30 cars, a beach launch, and several hundred yards of shore-fishing access on the reservoir, at the mouth of the old Salmon River and the power company canal. Electric motors only.

CONTACT: New York State Department of Environmental Conservation Region 7 and Oswego County tourism.

192A. Salmon River Project Picnic Area and Canoe Launch

DESCRIPTION: This spot offers loads of bank fishing, a picnic table, a beach launch, and parking for about 10 cars.

DIRECTIONS: From the Bennett Bridges access site above, continue north on CR 22, cross the second bridge, turn left on Hog Back Road, and travel a few hundred feet.

193. MAD RIVER (OSWEGO RIVER DRAINAGE)

KEY SPECIES: Brown trout and brook trout.

DESCRIPTION: This fast-flowing stream is the West Branch Fish Creek's largest tributary, feeding it on the southern outskirts of Camden.

TIPS: Wear a head net from mid-May through mid-June.

THE FISHING: This river gets stocked with roughly 5,300 8.5-inch browns annually. They end up ranging from 8 to 14 inches and take worms and spinners. Wild book trout up to 12 inches are available in the upper reaches and take the same baits.

DIRECTIONS: River Road crosses the stream a couple of times and parallels it in several spots between Camden and Florence.

ADDITIONAL INFORMATION: Access and parking for 10 cars is at the Church Street (NY 69) bridge in Camden. Primitive camping is allowed in the Mad River State Forest, about 5 miles north of Camden on River Road.

CONTACT: New York State Department of Environmental Conservation Region 6 and the Oneida County Convention and Visitors Bureau.

193A. Quarry Road

DESCRIPTION: Running for only about 0.5 mile, this hard-surface road skirts the stream—coming within eyeshot a good part of the way—offering access from the shoulder.

DIRECTIONS: Head north out of Camden on NY 13 for a little over 0.5 mile, turn right onto Lovers Lane, and travel 0.7 mile to stop sign. Cross the highway to Quarry Road.

193B. Mad River Road Access

DESCRIPTION: Mad River Road skirts the stream for about a mile—coming to within easy view in spots—offering access at the shoulder.

DIRECTIONS: Continue east from **site 193A** for a few hundred yards to the stop sign. Quarry Road turns into Mad River Road on the other side of the highway.

194. WEST BRANCH FISH CREEK

KEY SPECIES: Brown trout, brook trout, and walleyes.

DESCRIPTION: Pouring out of Kasoag Lake, this stream runs over the southern edge of the Tug Hill Plateau. Tamed by several dams, it flows south for 25 miles on a relatively gentle course of mild rapids and long pools, and joins the East Branch in Blossvale. Wide, flat, and deep, the place is ideal for fly fishing from a canoe.

TIPS: Most any white fly catches trout all summer long.

THE FISHING: About 5 miles shorter than the East Branch, but far more accessible, this stream gets stocked annually with about 13,000 brown trout averaging 8.5 inches and a couple hundred 12- to 15-inchers. Life is decent, and quite a few reach the 12- to 16-inch range—and even larger. Wild brook trout ranging from 4 to 12 inches move into the creek from tributaries. Both species respond to flies, worms, minnows, spoons, and in-line spinners. Postspawn walleyes ranging from 18 to 21 inches can be caught below the dam in McConnellsville for most of May on minnowbaits, jigs, and worms. The daily limit for walleye is three.

DIRECTIONS: NY 13 parallels the stream from the hamlet of McConnellsville to its source.

ADDITIONAL INFORMATION: This creek's trout season extends to November 30. From the mouth upstream to the McConnellsville dam, fishing is prohibited from March 16 through the first Saturday in May to protect spawning walleyes.

CONTACT: Oneida County Convention and Visitors Bureau and New York State Department of Environmental Conservation Region 6.

194A. Public Fishing Access Site

DESCRIPTION: This site is located at a dam. Above the barrier there is a canoe launch, a manicured lawn suitable for the handicapped, and parking for about 50 cars. Below the dam, a set of rapids runs about 100 yards before the creek comes to rest in a pool.

DIRECTIONS: Take NY 13 north out of Camden for 3.5 miles into Westdale, turn right (east) on Cemetery Road, and travel a few hundred yards to the bridge.

194B. Public Access

DESCRIPTION: Situated at the bridge just upstream of a dam in the village of Camden, the west bank's Freedom Park offers handicapped-accessible fishing in the millpond and rapids below the dam; there's parking for about 25 cars. The east bank is also accessible but stairs prevent easy wheelchair access to the rapids.

DIRECTIONS: On NY 69, less than a block west of the intersection with NY 13.

194C. Forest Park

DESCRIPTION: This sprawling facility has a long winding road that comes right to the creek's bank in a couple of spots.

DIRECTIONS: Located on Ripley Road, on the southern edge of the village of Camden.

ADDITIONAL INFORMATION: This village park is dedicated to local folks. It has numerous shelters with picnic tables and grills; many have swing sets.

194D. Brewer Road Access

DESCRIPTION: Located at a bridge, this site offers shoulder parking for about five cars and primitive trails down to the creek.

DIRECTIONS: Take NY 13 south out of Camden for about 0.5 mile; the bridge is 0.8 mile down the road.

194E. Blakesley Road Access

DESCRIPTION: Informal access at the bridge and shoulder parking for about 10 cars.

DIRECTIONS: Blakely Road is 1.1 miles south of Camden off NY 13. The bridge is 0.7 mile down the road.

194F. Buell Road Access

DESCRIPTION: A bridge used to cross the creek here. There's shoulder parking for about six cars.

DIRECTIONS: Buell Road is off NY 13, 1.2 miles south of Camden. The creek is 0.8 mile down the road.

194G. Trestle Road Access

DESCRIPTION: Formal state access site on the east side of the bridge and parking for 10 cars.

DIRECTIONS: Trestle Road is off NY 13, 2.4 miles south of Camden.

ADDITIONAL INFORMATION: The mouth of the Little River is within casting distance of the southwestern corner of the bridge. Slow and deep, sporting heavy growth on its banks, it's tough to fish but its wild browns and brookies can make the trouble worthwhile.

194H. McConnellsville Access

DESCRIPTION: A dam at the Harden Furniture Factory forms a long, quiet pool above, a staircase of rapids and pools down below. Shoulder parking for about three cars.

DIRECTIONS: Head south out of Camden on NY 13 for 4.4 miles, turning east on McConnellsville Road then immediately left at the post office.

ADDITIONAL INFORMATION: No trespassing on the dam.

195. EAST BRANCH FISH CREEK

KEY SPECIES: Brown trout, rainbow trout, brook trout, and Atlantic salmon.

DESCRIPTION: Pouring out of the high reaches of the Tug Hill Plateau, East Branch Fish Creek drops about 1,600 feet on its circuitous, 30-mile trip to its juncture with the West Branch, a mile south of the village of Blossvale. Fast, wide, relatively shallow, punctuated by countless pools and channels, this freestone stream resembles a western river more than an eastern creek. Tirelessly running through the "Hill," it cuts Central New York's most spellbinding gulf, a druidic setting where sheer cliffs tower anywhere from 20 to 90 feet above the water, offering a truly wild fishing experience.

TIPS: Nymphs and streamers help prevent the heartbreak of rough fish.

THE FISHING: The upper section above the Rome Reservoir (**site 196**) is stocked yearly with about 4,000 browns, 1,500 brookies, and 870 rainbows averaging 8.5 inches. Most are caught the first few weeks of the season. Browns enjoy the greatest rate of survival, followed by the rainbows, primarily because they find their way into the relatively safe reservoir. They return to the creek to spawn—browns in the fall, rainbows in the spring.

Below the impoundment, the creek becomes the size of a small river. The state stocks this stretch each year with about 9,100 8.5-inch browns. They hit worms, tiny spinners, and spoons. Most of the stockies are like the majority of anglers, sticking close to the road. There's always a few that beat fins deep into the woods where fishing pressure is light, giving ambitious anglers the opportunity to catch better-than-average-sized fish on flies.

ADDITIONAL INFORMATION: Downstream of Rome Reservoir, trout season is open from April 1 through November 30. Fishing is prohibited from the mouth to the NY 69 bridge in Taberg from March 16 to the first Saturday in May to protect spawning walleyes. Since the 1990s, the Fish Creek Atlantic Salmon Club has been raising 20,000 Atlantics annually at their hatchery in McConnellsville and stocking them into the creek and its tributaries. Recently, kids at Camden Middle School have been raising trout and salmon and stocking them, too. Returns are spotty, but anglers increasingly report catching homeward-bound 20-something-inch Atlantics in the Oswego and Oneida Rivers and Oneida Lake in late summer and early autumn.

CONTACT: Oneida County Convention and Visitors Bureau, New York State Department of Environmental Conservation Region 6, and the Tug Hill Commission.

Bridgeport resident Jack Zasada fishing the East Branch Fish Creek (site 195F) below the CR 67A bridge.

195A. Junction Road Bridge Access

DESCRIPTION: Alder Creek pours into the East Branch Fish Creek about 100 yards downstream of the bridge. Shoulder parking for 10 cars.

DIRECTIONS: Head north out of the hamlet of West Leyden on Fish Creek Road (CR 47) for about 5 miles, turn left on Kotary Road, travel about 0.5 mile, turn right on Junction Road, and travel 0.6 mile.

ADDITIONAL INFORMATION: The state stocks Alder Creek with 2,500 yearling brown trout annually, and its upper reaches contain wild brookies. This stream offers 4.85 miles of public fishing rights, with bridge access at Meyer Road (continue north on Junction Road for about a mile, turn right, and travel another mile) and Sweeney Road (at the intersection of Junction and Meyer Roads, bear left onto Meyer, travel about a mile, turn right on Sweeney, and continue for about 2 miles).

195B. Kotary Road Bridge Access

DESCRIPTION: This New York State Department of Environmental Conservation fishing access site offers a trail down to the creek and parking for about five cars.

DIRECTIONS: This site is at the intersection of Junction and Kotary Roads, 0.6 mile south of **site 195A**.

195C. Osceola Road (CR 46) Bridge

DESCRIPTION: This bridge crosses the creek a few hundred feet upstream of its mouth on the East Branch Reservoir; there's parking for about 10 cars.

THE FISHING: Above the bridge, the water goes through a system of deep pools, fast chutes, and shallow ripples. Most of the trout are browns and rainbows ranging from 8 to 10 inches, but some wild brook trout running from 3 to 12 inches are also present. They hit worms, nymphs, and spinners.

DIRECTIONS: Head north out of Taberg on Coal Hill Road for about 7.5 miles (it turns into CR 67A). A few hundred feet after going through the sharp curve, turn left on Creek Road (turns into Swancott Mill Road at the Jefferson County line). Travel for about 5 miles to the stop sign on CR 46, turn right, and continue for a couple hundred yards.

195D. Public Fishing Access

DESCRIPTION: A single-lane blacktop road leads to a small parking area at the foot of the ruins of an ancient bridge; parking for about five cars.

THE FISHING: Upstream of this site, the creek flows through the heart of the Tug Hill Plateau wilderness, picking up numerous tributaries. Brook trout become more common the deeper you go into the woods.

DIRECTIONS: The 0.5-mile-long access road is off CR 46, 0.2 mile east of **site 195C**.

195E. East Osceola State Forest

DESCRIPTION: Primitive camping is allowed in this 1,974-acre state forest.

DIRECTIONS: From its intersection with Swancott Mill Road (see **site 195C**), head west on CR 46 (Osceola Road) for about 8 miles.

195F. E. Frederick W. Parker Jr. (CR 67A) Bridge Access

DESCRIPTION: This site has shoulder parking and stone steps leading down to the river.

THE FISHING: Deep within the canyon, this site's rapids and deep pools hold good numbers of browns in the 10- to 14-inch range. They take emergers, terrestrials, and streamers in the quiet water, nymphs in the pocket water.

DIRECTIONS: Head north out of Taberg on Coal Hill Road (it turns into CR 67A) for about 7.5 miles.

195G. Point Rock Creek Access

DESCRIPTION: Access and shoulder parking at the bridge. Anglers can access a remote section of the gorge by wading—and fishing—Point Rock Creek for 0.5 mile to its mouth.

THE FISHING: The state stocks about 3,000 8-inch brown trout annually into this tiny, freestone stream. They respond to nymphs and worms.

ADDITIONAL INFORMATION: This is one of the tributaries the Fish Creek Atlantic Salmon Club stocks with landlocked salmon.

DIRECTIONS: Continue east on CR 67A from **site 195F** for about 0.25 mile to the stop sign, turn right on Point Rock Road (CR 67), and travel about 0.5 mile to the bridge.

195H. Old Coal Hill Road Access

DESCRIPTION: This informal access site is on private property directly across from the southern terminus of Old Coal Hill Road. You'll have to hike about 0.25 mile due south to get to the water.

DIRECTIONS: Head north out of Taberg on Coal Hill Road for just under 3 miles, park at the guardrail across from Old Coal Hill Road, and hike in.

ADDITIONAL INFORMATION: Jack Zasada, an old-timer who's been fishing the creek for years, says, "This spot is off the beaten path. The hike is long but worth it, ending in pools and pocket water that hold big browns." (A lot of locals consider this their secret spot, so if you try it and like it, don't tell anyone about it—Author.)

195I. Palmer Road Access

DESCRIPTION: Just upstream of the bridge, the creek barrels west out of the hills, slams into a cliff, and banks hard to the south, offering anglers a deep pool and nice rapids. Shoulder parking.

DIRECTIONS: Take Coal Hill Road north out of Taberg for about a mile, turn right on Palmer Road, and continue a few hundred yards to the bridge.

195J. Stone Wall Access

DESCRIPTION: A popular put-in site for spring kayakers, this shoulder access point is on private property that wasn't posted at press time.

DIRECTIONS: From NYS Thruway exit 34 in Canastota, head north on NY 13 for about 12 miles to NY 49 and turn east. About 5.5 miles later, turn north on Herder Road. Roughly 4.3 miles later, a farmer's field will appear on the right. About 100 yards beyond its north end you'll find a slot in the woods. Park on the shoulder, walk down the dip into the forest, and follow the creek downstream to an old stone wall where the cliff is low enough to descend to the water.

196. EAST BRANCH FISH CREEK RESERVOIR (ROME RESERVOIR)

KEY SPECIES: Brown trout and black bullheads.

DESCRIPTION: Formed in 1960 when the city of Rome dammed the East Branch of Fish Creek for an additional water supply, this 400-acre impoundment is ringed by woods.

TIPS: Right after ice-out, suspend minnows about 3 feet below bobbers for brown trout.

THE FISHING: Annually, the state stocks 4,000 6.5-inch browns. They end up ranging from 8 to 12 inches, but 4-pounders are caught regularly. They are mostly targeted with worms, minnows, and Rooster Tail spinners. Some rainbows are also available and reach the same size as the browns. The bullheads average 6 inches and respond to worms fished on bottom, especially in the spring.

DIRECTIONS: From NYS Thruway exit 34 in Canastota, head north on NY 13 for about 12 miles to NY 49 and turn east. About 5.5 miles later, turn north on Herder Road (which turns into Blossvale Road) and follow it for about 5 miles to Taberg. Turn left at the stop sign, then right onto Coal Hill Road several hundred yards later. After about 8 miles, the road banks a sharp right and turns into Yorkland Road (CR 67A). Continue for a few hundred feet, turn north on Creek Road (it turns into Swancott Mill Road at the county line), and continue for about 4 miles.

ADDITIONAL INFORMATION: The state owns public fishing rights to the southern half of the reservoir's west bank, and to the entire east bank. A fishing access site on Swancott Mill Road has parking for about 20 cars. Gas-powered motors aren't permitted on the reservoir. Camping isn't allowed in Swancott Mill State Forest, to protect Rome's water supply. However, primitive camping is allowed in nearby East Osceola State Forest (**site 195E**), a 1,974-acre woods accessible off Osceola Road (CR 46), 8 miles west of the Osceola Road and Swancott Mill Road intersection.

CONTACT: Tug Hill Commission and New York State Department of Environmental Conservation Region 6.

196A. Powlish Pond Brook

DESCRIPTION: Feeding the northwestern corner of the East Branch Fish Creek Reservoir, this small stream offers wild brook trout throughout its length, and reservoir-run brown and rainbow trout near its mouth. The state owns 2.4 miles of public fishing rights.

DIRECTIONS: On Swancott Mill Road, a few hundred feet south of its intersection with Osceola Road.

197. POINT ROCK CREEK

KEY SPECIES: Brook trout, brown trout, and Atlantic salmon.

DESCRIPTION: This tributary of East Branch Fish Creek is pretty skinny, but its numerous holes, runs, and rapids offer loads of ideal trout habitat.

TIPS: Use large, woolly streamers.

THE FISHING: The upper reaches of this creek are prime wild brook trout water. The state stocks the lower stretch with 3,000 browns annually, all close to the road. Survivors of the opening weeks of the season get smart quick, developing a knack for detecting human offerings, clamming up whenever something unusual occurs, like a worm dropping into the water noisily on a sunny afternoon. But they'll hit a juicy crawler after a rain, and large flies imitating minnows, leeches, or caterpillars anytime. Additionally, the Fish Creek Atlantic Salmon Club stocks the place with Atlantics, and each autumn sees a few return to spawn. They'll take anything from a naturally presented dry fly to a streamer swung through the current.

DIRECTIONS: West Ava Road (CR 67) parallels the lower third of the creek upstream of the hamlet of Point Rock, offering access at the bridge in the village, at the next bridge 1.5 miles up the road, and at the formal state public access site 0.3 mile beyond that.

ADDITIONAL INFORMATION: The state owns public fishing rights to 20 miles of stream.

CONTACT: New York State Department of Environmental Conservation Region 6.

197A. Statzer Road Public Fishing Access

DESCRIPTION: The creek is pretty skinny and rocky here, offering wild brookies to stealthy anglers who know how to dip flies into pockets and around windfalls, and dead-drift nymphs along undercut banks and limestone outcrops.

DIRECTIONS: From the hamlet of Point Rock, head north on West Ava Road for about 3 miles, bear left on Kessler Road at the bend (it turns into Kirk Road), travel for 0.8 mile, turn left onto Statzer, and continue for a little over a mile to the bridge; parking for about four cars.

THOUSAND ISLANDS REGION

While the Thousand Islands are generally considered a feature of the St. Lawrence River, the outcrops responsible for this geological wonderland stretch south to a point midway between the river and the Tug Hill Plateau. This rugged area is studded with lakes. All but five—Lakes Bonaparte, Perch, Star, and Sylvia, plus Sixtown Pond—belong to the Indian River Lakes group, 18 glacial gems set dead center on the southern edge of the St. Lawrence lowlands. Their close proximity to one another, coupled with their diverse physical characteristics, offer time-strapped anglers a wide variety of habitats containing every species indigenous to the state. Set in an economically depressed area, many Indian River Lakes are subject to heavy ice fishing, with locals singling out certain lakes in a given year, depleting the yellow perch and sunfish. As a rule, game fish numbers aren't fazed, however.

198. PERCH LAKE

KEY SPECIES: Northern pike, yellow perch, black crappies, and sunfish.

DESCRIPTION: Fed by Gillette Creek and a couple of springs, this 545-acre lake's average depth is 4 feet, and its maximum depth, a small hole out in the middle, drops to 12 feet. Totally surrounded by the Perch River Wildlife Management Area, its shoreline is undeveloped.

TIPS: Use a shelter to protect yourself from the wind.

THE FISHING: This lake is only open to fishing from December 1 through March 1. Yellow perch averaging 8 inches long and northern pike ranging from 18 to 40 inches long are its most popular game. The perch respond to small minnows and ice jigs tipped with grubs; the northerns prefer large minnows. Pumpkinseeds and bluegills ranging between 5 and 8 inches and black crappies up to 12 inches are also available. The crappies take minnows, and they, along with the sunfish, respond to ice jigs tipped with grubs.

DIRECTIONS: From Watertown, take NY 12 north for about 3 miles and turn right onto Mustard Road. At its end, about 1 mile later, bear left onto Perch Lake Road and follow it for about 5 miles to the access road on the left.

ADDITIONAL INFORMATION: The wildlife management area surrounding this lake is a nesting site for bald eagles, and the lake is closed to fishing from March 2 to November 30 to protect them. The access road is plowed, and ends in a parking lot big enough for about 50 cars. You must sign in at the unmanned station located in the parking lot. Access is restricted to the upper lake.

CONTACT: New York State Department of Environmental Conservation Region 6.

199. SIXTOWN POND (CRYSTAL LAKE)

KEY SPECIES: Largemouth bass, walleyes, northern pike, yellow perch, and brown bullheads.

DESCRIPTION: This 169-acre lake averages 14 feet deep and has a maximum depth of 24 feet. Ringed almost entirely by reeds, its shoreline is lightly developed with private residences.

TIPS: Work Texas-rigged worms along the edges, and in the openings, of vegetation.

THE FISHING: Largemouth bass average 14 inches, and northern pike range from "pin pike" (18- to 20-inchers) to respectable 32-inchers. Both hit minnows, darters, and floating and suspending minnowbaits. "As of 2012," according to the state, "walleye fishing was supported by annual stocking of over 500,000 walleye fry." Anglers typically catch 18- to 20-inchers by drifting and trolling worms on harnesses (spinner-rigged and plain), bouncing bucktail jigs and scented curly-tailed grubs on bottom, and casting minnowbaits. Yellow perch average 7 inches and respond to small lures, worms, and minnows; bullheads ranging from 8 to 12 inches respond to worms fished on bottom.

The minimum length for walleyes is 18 inches, and the daily limit is three.

DIRECTIONS: A public access site is off NY 178, 5.4 miles west of Adams (I-81 exit 41).

ADDITIONAL INFORMATION: The state access site off NY 178 offers shore fishing, a beach launch suitable for cartop craft, and parking for 20 cars.

CONTACT: New York State Department of Environmental Conservation Region 6.

200. INDIAN RIVER

KEY SPECIES: Brook trout, brown trout, walleyes, northern pike, black bass, channel catfish, and black crappies.

DESCRIPTION: Stretching over 100 miles, this stream grows quickly, from creek-sized in the village of Indian River to a respectable river by the time it feeds the Oswegatchie River, 2 miles downstream of Black Lake. Although it has some killer drops, like the falls in the villages of Theresa and Rossie, it's generally a mild-mannered stream slicing through pasture, marsh, and forest. And while it drains the Indian River Lakes (**sites 201–215**), the only one it feeds is Black Lake.

TIPS: Drift live bait.

THE FISHING: The state annually stocks roughly 300 brook trout averaging 9.5 inches and 1,000 brown trout averaging 8 inches into the upper reaches, around the villages of Indian River and Natural Bridge. The water is creek-sized here and largely posted. Anglers access the stream at crossroads and walk the bank, working worms, salted minnows, in-line spinners, or nymphs for brookies ranging from 4 to 13 inches and browns up to 18 inches long.

Below Natural Bridge the river becomes a warmwater fishery. Walleyes generally run less than 22 inches. Most locals catch them by drifting worms (plain or on spinner harnesses) or casting bucktail jigs and crankbaits. Both species of black bass are well represented. Smallmouths range from 12 to 15 inches, and largemouths can go as large as 6 pounds, particularly downstream of Rossie. Drift with minnows and crayfish, or work Carolina- or Texas-rigged worms around structure for both species. Northern pike usually run from 18 to 30 inches, but lunkers pushing 40 inches are caught

Indian River Falls (site 200), Rossie, New York.

each year in the lower reaches below Rossie. They respond to spinnerbaits, rubber-skirted jigs tipped with stickworms, and large minnows drifted or fished below bobbers. The pool below the falls in Rossie is famous for black crappies in the 9- to 12-inch range, especially in the spring. Fish buckeye or flathead minnows below bobbers or jig 2-inch scented tubes and grubs. There are enough monster channel catfish up to 20 pounds in the lower river to attract dedicated followers who still-fish for them on bottom in deep holes and channels with clumps of worms, minnows, shrimp, cut bait, even chicken parts.

The minimum length for black bass is 10 inches from the source to the falls in Rossie. Downstream of the cataract to the Oswegatchie River, the minimum size for black bass is 15 inches. In addition, downstream of Rossie Falls the minimum length for walleyes is 18 inches, and the daily limit is three.

DIRECTIONS: The river is paralleled in spots by US 11, NY 37, CR 21, CR 3, CR 6, and CR 4.

CONTACT: New York State Department of Environmental Conservation Region 6, Fort Drum, Indian River Lakes Chamber of Commerce, and St. Lawrence County Chamber of Commerce.

200A. Fort Drum Public Access

DESCRIPTION: Home of the army's 10th Mountain Division, this 100,000-something-acre military base has 25 miles of Indian River running through it. Most of it is in the "high impact area" and off-limits to civilians. Still, over "400 acres of open water and at least 39 miles of streams"—highly productive resources containing trout, walleyes, northern pike, smallmouth bass, and largemouth bass—are open to the public.

ADDITIONAL INFORMATION: Along with all of the state regulations, you'll be expected to abide by Fort Drum Regulation 420-3 (mostly commonsense stuff like no fishing downrange during target practice). The regulations are posted online (www.fortdrum.isportsman.net), and recreational maps are available at building S-2509. You must possess a Fort Drum Access Pass (available online) at all times. Primitive camping is allowed but you need a Fort Drum Nighttime Recreation Pass and you must "check in and check out at Range Branch (315-772-7152), building P-4855."

CONTACT: Fort Drum Fish and Wildlife Program Manager (315-772-9636), fortdrum@isportsman.net.

200B. Antwerp Public Access

DESCRIPTION: This small, grassy landing on the southeast corner of Antwerp's Main Street bridge is suitable for bank fishing and launching cartop craft onto the long, narrow impoundment between two dams. Parking for about three cars is available.

DIRECTIONS: From Watertown, take US 11 north for about 20 miles to Antwerp, then turn right (east) onto CR 194 and follow it for about 0.25 mile.

200C. Public Access

DESCRIPTION: A popular bank-fishing spot, this site has parking for 10 cars and is suitable for launching cartop craft.

THE FISHING: Located on a slow-moving portion of the river, this site is popular with canoe anglers targeting walleyes, smallmouth bass, northern pike, and panfish.

DIRECTIONS: Two miles south of Theresa on CR 46.

200D. Theresa Public Access

DESCRIPTION: This town-owned site has a paved ramp, parking for three cars, and a picnic table.

THE FISHING: The site is on an especially scenic flat stretch known for bass, walleyes, and northerns.

DIRECTIONS: At the NY 26 bridge in Theresa.

ADDITIONAL INFORMATION: In late summer the river often drops to about a foot below the ramp. This leaves a foot or so drop at the end of the asphalt, making it unsuitable for launching large, trailered craft—unless, of course, you have a monster truck with really high clearance.

200E. Indian River Wildlife Management Area Public Access

DESCRIPTION: This site has a beach launch for small trailered craft and parking for five cars.

THE FISHING: A mild-mannered, fairly straight stretch of river runs through the wildlife management area. Marsh borders much of this section, making it a productive northern pike, largemouth bass, and panfish spot.

DIRECTIONS: Head north out of Theresa on Red Lake Road for 3.7 miles, turn left on Nelson Road, and travel 0.2 mile to the gravel launch.

200F. Public Access

DESCRIPTION: A manicured lawn gently slopes down to the river, providing easy launching of cartop craft and about 500 feet of open bank-fishing access suitable for safe family outings.

THE FISHING: This site's still water surrenders walleyes, northerns, and bass to folks casting crankbaits and spinnerbaits.

DIRECTIONS: On CR 3, about 1 mile south of the hamlet of Rossie.

201. RED LAKE

KEY SPECIES: Walleyes, northern pike, black bass, black crappies, yellow perch, bluegill, and brown bullheads.

DESCRIPTION: At 366 acres, this lake is one of the largest in the Indian River chain. It's also one of the deepest, averaging 27 feet and dropping to 47 feet in the middle. Its habitats range from undercut marsh mats to steep drop-offs at the bases of scenic cliffs.

TIPS: Cast curly-tailed grubs and soft plastic minnows rigged on spinner forms.

THE FISHING: The state maintains a walleye presence by stocking fry or finger-lings (depending on what's available) regularly. They end up ranging from 15 to 25 inches and respond to minnowbaits like ThunderSticks, lipless rattling crankbaits, and worms trolled or drifted on spinner harnesses. This lake is loaded with northern pike. Unfortunately, the only ones that seem to hit in summer are "ax handles," a couple of inches on each side of the minimum length. They like live minnows, Rat-L-Traps, minnowbaits, and spinner-baits. Still, 15-something-pound pike are available, appearing like magic after first ice. They like large minnows fished below tip-ups. Smallmouths range from 1 to 4 pounds, and largemouths often run a couple of pounds heavier. Work rattling crankbaits along drop-offs for bronzebacks, and rip soft plastic worms and jerkbaits through the surface film around vegetation and timber for bucketmouths. Black crappies range from 9 to 12 inches, and yellow perch go 6 to 12 inches. Both are plentiful and take small minnows, Beetle Spins, and Berkley Atomic Teasers. Bluegills running 5 to 8 inches and brown bullheads up to a staggering 16 inches are plentiful. Both take worms, and the sunnies have a taste for poppers and wet flies, as well.

Yellow perch and sunfish can be taken in any number.

DIRECTIONS: Head north out of Watertown on I-81 for about 15 miles to exit 49 (La Fargeville) and head east on NY 411 (it turns into NY 26). In the heart of Theresa, take a left onto Bridge Street, then a quick left onto Red Lake Road; continue for about 4 miles.

ADDITIONAL INFORMATION: The state fishing access site at the end of Red Lake Road has a beach launch and parking for about 10 rigs. The fish, especially yellow perch, tend to be grubby. While they don't affect the fish's flavor or food value, they're unsightly enough to ruin your appetite.

CONTACT: New York State Department of Environment Conservation Region 6 and Indian River Lakes Chamber of Commerce.

202. MOON LAKE

KEY SPECIES: Tiger muskies, northern pike, walleyes, largemouth bass, and black crappies.

DESCRIPTION: This 243-acre lake averages 12 feet deep and has a maximum depth of 20 feet. Half the shoreline is developed with summer cottages; the other half is a scenic mixture of marsh, forest, and outcrops.

TIPS: Work tiny jigs and tubes around brush and sunken timber for crappies.

THE FISHING: Best known as a crappie hot spot, Moon Lake gets heavy ice-fishing pressure. Still, every winter sees enough 9- to 12-inchers taken on minnows and grubs to draw anglers back year after year. Northerns up to 30 inches are plentiful and respond to spinnerbaits and large minnows. The state has been stocking 8- to 9-inch tiger muskies for years. Those that avoid the jaws of their larger kin generally end up running from 30 to 40 inches. They are mostly taken incidentally by anglers casting crankbaits for northerns and bass. Largemouth bass typically range from 1.5 to 5 pounds and hit buzzbaits and jerkbaits. While walleyes have always been present, they've been relatively rare. The state increased their numbers by stocking some in 2012. Ranging from 15 to 22 inches, they'll hit jigs, crankbaits, and worms drifted on harnesses.

Motors over 10 horsepower are prohibited.

DIRECTIONS: From Theresa, take Red Lake Road for about 3 miles, hook a right onto Moon Lake Road, and travel for 1.4 miles.

ADDITIONAL INFORMATION: A fishing access site on Moon Lake Road offers a beach launch and parking for 10 cars.

CONTACT: New York State Department of Environmental Conservation Region 6 and Indian River Lakes Chamber of Commerce.

203. MUSKELLUNGE LAKE

KEY SPECIES: Largemouth bass, northern pike, muskellunge, black crappies, bluegills, and brown bullheads.

DESCRIPTION: Blanketing 275 acres, this lake averages 11.5 feet deep, and its maximum depth is 25 feet. Set deep in spectacularly rugged country, shaped like a medieval battle-ax, its largely undeveloped shoreline is ringed by cliffs. Two scenic islands rise out in the middle.

TIPS: Cast spinnerbaits and buzzbaits for largemouths and northerns.

THE FISHING: Bucketmouths in the 15- to 20-inch class are common and respond to crayfish, minnows, stickworms, jerkbaits, spinnerbaits, and poppers. Northern pike typically range 18 to 22 inches, but 3-footers are available. Most are taken through the ice on large shiners. Devoid of free public access, this lake doesn't get the heavy ice-fishing pressure its sister lakes do. Crappies ranging from 9 to 12 inches and bluegills up to 10 inches are plentiful. The crappies take small minnows suspended below pencil floats and marabou jigs fished plain or tipped with soft plastic grubs or tubes. The sunnies like worms, flies, poppers, Berkley Power Wigglers, and 1-inch Power Grubs.

Brown bullheads range from 10 to 14 inches and, incredibly, are popularly taken in broad daylight with worms still-fished on bottom. While muskellunge are few, they have a knack for tearing into baits intended for bass and pike. They like large minnows and big lures.

DIRECTIONS: Take CR 22 east out of Theresa for about 5 miles. Turn left on New Connecticut Road and travel 2.4 miles, then turn left at the sign reading, GENE'S FISHING CAMP, MUSKELLUNGE LAKE, NATURE'S FISH BOWL. Continue on the potholed road for just under 1 mile to the boat launch at Gene's Fishing Camp.

ADDITIONAL INFORMATION: Gene's Fishing Camp (315-287-3418), a privately owned commercial operation offering the only public access to the lake, is open from May 1 through October 24 and allows launching for a fee. Ice fishing is generally reserved for family, but the owner has been known to grant permission to folks who ask during the camp's open season.

CONTACT: New York State Department of Environmental Conservation Region 6 and Indian River Lakes Chamber of Commerce.

204. PAYNE LAKE

KEY SPECIES: Tiger muskies, northern pike, walleyes, largemouth bass, yellow perch, black crappies, bluegills, and brown bullheads.

DESCRIPTION: This 150-acre lake averages 6.6 feet deep and has a maximum depth of 15 feet. A spectacular cliff runs along most of its west bank.

TIPS: Use jigs tipped with grubs or perch eyes immediately after first ice.

THE FISHING: This shallow lake is a local favorite for panfish. Yellow perch averaging 8 inches, black crappies up to 12 inches, bluegills ranging from 5 to 10 inches, and brown bullheads up to 14 inches are plentiful. Ice fishing with live grubs is the most popular method of taking the perch, sunfish, and crappies. Bullheads are primarily targeted in spring with nightcrawlers fished on bottom. Massive quantities of largemouth bass running from 12 to 20 inches, with a few even larger, are available. They respond to spinnerbaits, rattling crankbaits, minnow-imitating crankbaits, poppers, crayfish, minnows, you name it. Northern pike usually run from 18 to 25 inches and like large minnows and spinnerbaits. Tiger muskies are stocked regularly. Most end up about 36 inches, but fish over 40 inches are caught all the time. They like large in-line bucktail spinners and hard jerkbaits. Walleyes are available but they're relatively rare. Ranging from 15 to 20 inches, they are taken every now and then with minnowbaits, especially around dusk and dawn.

Motors over 10 horsepower are prohibited.

DIRECTIONS: Head north out of Theresa on CR 22 for about 8 miles.

ADDITIONAL INFORMATION: The state access site on CR 22 offers a concrete ramp, parking for 30 rigs, and bank fishing. Primitive camping is permitted in the 1,600-acre Pulpit Rock State Forest, on the west shore opposite the launch.

CONTACT: New York State Department of Environmental Conservation Region 6 and Indian River Lakes Chamber of Commerce.

205. SIXBERRY LAKE

KEY SPECIES: Lake trout, walleyes, smallmouth bass, bluegills, yellow perch, and landlocked salmon.

DESCRIPTION: Largely undeveloped, this 123-acre lake is ringed by a forest of evergreens and white birch clinging to steep, rugged banks sporting striking granite outcrops. Triangular in shape, it averages 45 feet deep and has a maximum depth of 90 feet.

TIPS: Drift over deep water and vertically jig spoons for lakers.

THE FISHING: According to the DEC, "As of 2012, the lake has been stocked with at least 300 lake trout and 500 Atlantic salmon annually." Survival and growth are good, and they join fish that were stocked in earlier years, offering exciting angling with a good chance of catching a trophy. Lakers typically run between 4 and 8 pounds and are eagerly targeted by locals with spoons and minnows trolled deep behind Christmas tree and Seth Green rigs. The salmon usually go 15 to 20 inches and take flatlined streamers, small spoons, and crankbaits. Walleyes generally run between 2 and 5 pounds but trophies up to 11 pounds are caught regularly. They take minnows through the ice, diving crankbaits in spring and fall, and floating minnowbaits trolled 10 to 20 feet deep off downriggers in summer. Smallmouth bass average 1.5 pounds and take minnows and crayfish drifted on bottom along breaks, as well as tubes and curly-tailed grubs jigged over the same habitat. Bronzebacks will also take streamers, small spoons, and crankbaits worked around windfalls, and over 5 to 20 feet of water in the north and south bays. Bluegills ranging from 5 to 8 inches and yellow perch averaging 9 inches are commonly taken during warm weather by bottom-fishing with worms. The perch will also take streamers and wet flies, while the sunfish will rise to tiny poppers worked in 3 to 10 feet of water.

Lake trout and landlocked salmon can be taken year-round. Motors exceeding 10 horsepower are prohibited.

DIRECTIONS: Take Main Street west out of Theresa. A few hundred yards out of town, turn north on Aex Bay Road, then right onto CR 21 (English Settlement Road), travel for about 4 miles, then turn west on Sears Road and continue for about 0.25 mile.

ADDITIONAL INFORMATION: The state access site on Sears Road has a single-lane paved ramp, parking for about 10 cars, and shore-fishing access. A private campground is next to the boat launch.

CONTACT: New York State Department of Environmental Conservation Region 6, 1000 Islands International Tourism Council, and Indian River Lakes Chamber of Commerce.

206. LAKE OF THE WOODS

KEY SPECIES: Lake trout, lake whitefish, northern pike, smallmouth bass, bluegills, rock bass, landlocked salmon, and rainbow trout.

DESCRIPTION: Lightly developed, this 166-acre lake is more than it seems. Indeed, it's only about 1,500 feet wide, but it averages 43 feet deep and drops to a maximum depth of 80 feet in the middle. Its wooded shoreline is steep, and branches of submerged timber reach out of the waves like phantom limbs.

TIPS: Ice fish with minnows on bottom for lake trout.

THE FISHING: The state stocks about 2,900 6.5-inch lakers annually. They pig out on the lake's freshwater shrimp and end up averaging a very respectable 5 pounds. Locals go after them by deep-trolling minnowbaits like Red Fins and Jr. ThunderSticks and small spoons behind wobblers. About 2,000 landlocked salmon are stocked regularly. Typically running from 15 to 20 inches, they respond to flatlined streamers and freelined garden worms drifted over deep water. Rainbow trout averaging 9 inches are also released regularly. Survival is decent, and "bows" running up to 20 inches are available. They take worms, dry flies cast along the shoreline at dusk and dawn, Berkley Trout Bait suspended about 18 inches off the floor, and flatlined streamers and spoons. This is one of the few lakes around that still has whitefish. They range from 16 to 22 inches and are targeted, mostly in winter, with ice-fishing flies tipped with a kernel of corn. Northern pike range from 18 to 25 inches and take minnows, jerkbaits, and Rat-L-Traps. Smallmouth bass in the 12- to 16-inch range are common and respond to spinnerbaits retrieved slowly, or yo-yoed and allowed to occasionally bounce bottom. Sunfish and rock bass up to 0.75 pound can be counted on to hit worms and surface poppers anytime.

Lake trout and landlocked salmon can be taken year-round. Motors over 10 horsepower are prohibited.

DIRECTIONS: Take CR 21 (English Settlement Road) north out of Theresa. About 7.5 miles later, at the stop sign in Chapel Corners, turn left on Cottage Hill Road. Take the next right, 0.4 mile later, onto Burns Road and follow it for 0.8 mile; turn right on the dirt road at the FISHING ACCESS SITE sign.

ADDITIONAL INFORMATION: The fishing access site has a beach launch and parking for about 20 rigs.

CONTACT: New York State Department of Environmental Conservation Region 6, Indian River Lakes Chamber of Commerce, and 1000 Islands International Tourism Council.

207. GRASS LAKE

KEY SPECIES: Black bass, northern pike, walleyes, bluegills, black crappies, brown bullheads, and tiger muskies.

DESCRIPTION: This 324-acre lake averages 15 feet deep and drops to a maximum depth of 55 feet. Paradoxically, its southern half only averages 3 feet deep. Its surroundings range from pristine marsh to steep, forested hills lightly developed with environmentally sensitive seasonal residences.

TIPS: Work weedless floating lures around vegetation.

THE FISHING: State fisheries biologist Frank Flack considers this the best Indian River lake for autumn bass, "mainly because it's the least fished." Bronzebacks typically range from 12 to 20 inches, and bucketmouths can reach 6 pounds. Both wantonly strike spinnerbaits and buzzbaits early in the season but wise up quickly and, come fall, respond best to gentle presentations like drifting minnows and crayfish, gently dragging Carolina-rigged finesse worms, and delicately bouncing bucktail jigs tipped with worms or minnows. Northern pike do well in this food-rich habitat, averaging a cool 24 inches. Twenty-eight-inchers are common, and pikeasauruses stretching over 36 inches are available. They like minnows, rattling crankbaits, and spinnerbaits. DEC stocks massive quantities of walleyes periodically: 960,000 0.5-inchers in 2014. Survival is decent and they can grow to anywhere from 15 to 24 inches. They take minnowbaits worked along the shore from dusk to dawn, spring through fall; vertically jigged bladebaits and scented grubs bounced on bottom in summer, and minnows fished on bottom below tip-ups at ice time. Bluegills running up to 10 inches and crappies averaging 11 inches are abundant. Calicoes hit streamers, minnows, and small lures; the sunfish like worms and tiny poppers; both take marabou jigs and wet flies. Bullheads ranging from 8 to a whopping 14 inches respond enthusiastically to worms, especially during a light rain or at night. The state regularly stocks the place with norlunge, 1,600 8-inchers in 2014. Many reach 30 to 36 inches. Go for them with large bucktail spinners and shallow-running minnowbaits.

The minimum length for walleyes is 18 inches, and the daily limit is three. Motors over 10 horsepower are prohibited.

DIRECTIONS: From **site 206**, continue north on Burns Road for about 2 miles to the county line. Turn right on the single-lane dirt road, travel for 0.4 mile, bear left, drive for 0.2 mile, then bear right and travel for 0.1 mile.

ADDITIONAL INFORMATION: The state fishing site off Butler Road offers a beach launch and parking for three rigs.

CONTACT: New York State Department of Environmental Conservation Region 6 and 1000 Islands International Tourism Council.

208. CRYSTAL LAKE (INDIAN RIVER CHAIN)

KEY SPECIES: Northern pike, black bass, black crappies, bluegills, yellow perch, brown bullheads, and walleyes.

DESCRIPTION: Spilling over only 88 acres, this lake offers a lot for its small size. It averages 21 feet deep and drops to a maximum depth of 40 feet; only about 30 percent of its scenic shoreline is developed. The remainder is either striking cliffs crowned in forest or bottomland woods.

TIPS: Work deep-diving lures like Wally Divers along drop-offs.

THE FISHING: Northern pike ranging from 18 to 22 inches are plentiful and respond to minnows and soft jerkbaits. Smallmouth bass commonly go between 12 and 15 inches. They like freelined minnows fished around weeds and shoreline structure like docks and windfalls; and live crayfish, scented 3-inch grubs and tubes, and Carolina-rigged 4-inch worms dragged slowly on bottom in 10 to 30 feet of water. Largemouth bass running from 1.5 to 3 pounds hang out wherever they can find shallow structure and respond to scented tubes and Texas-rigged worms. Black crappies only average 8 inches, but enough keepers are available to make crappie dinners for two a realistic goal. Most anglers target them with minnows and grubs, primarily in the spring and through the ice. Yellow perch up to 9 inches, sunnies from 5 to 8 inches, and bullheads up to 12 inches are abundant and respond to worms. Up until recently, the state stocked 4,000 walleyes annually. Currently, they run up to 23 inches and respond to bucktail jigs and worms drifted on harnesses.

DIRECTIONS: Head south out of Redwood on NY 37 for 0.7 mile, turn left on Crystal Lake Road, and travel for 0.4 mile.

ADDITIONAL INFORMATION: Currently, there is no public access on the lake. The Crystal Lake Campground used to offer launching for a fee but it was sold recently and it's unclear what the new owners plan to do.

CONTACT: New York State Department of Environmental Conservation Region 6 and Indian River Lakes Chamber of Commerce.

209. MILLSITE LAKE

KEY SPECIES: Lake trout, northern pike, largemouth bass, smallmouth bass, yellow perch, rainbow trout, and landlocked salmon.

DESCRIPTION: This 469-acre lake averages 42 feet deep and dives to a maximum depth of 75 feet. Its clear, cold water is splattered with islands and ringed largely by a wooded shoreline.

TIPS: Cast minnowbaits parallel to shore in the spring.

THE FISHING: Millsite is notorious for cisco-fed pike in the 30- to 40-inch range. While you can catch numerous legal-sized northerns on any given day by casting lures over weed beds and working jigs in the openings of bays and island drop-offs, the really big pikeasauruses prefer large minnows freelined or fished below bobbers. Smallmouth bass usually run 1 to 2.5 pounds and hit crayfish, salted tubes, and bucktail jigs. Pillars of the bucketmouth community up to 6 pounds lurk around shallow structure and weedy bays, and can't resist slamming buzzbaits, Zara Spooks, and other noisy offerings disturbing the peace. Yellow perch up to 13 inches long thrive in shoreline habitats and take worms, small minnows, and 2-inch curly-tailed grubs. Natural lake trout typically run from 8 to 13 pounds and respond to spoons trolled deep behind downriggers. The state regularly stocks 8-inch rainbow trout (500 in 2015) and Atlantic salmon (almost 2,000 ranging from 2 to 7 inches in 2014). Rainbows and salmon typically reach 15 to 20 inches and respond to spoons and minnowbaits fished close to shore in spring and fall, and flatlined in open water in summer. Come winter, they're partial to minnows suspended a few feet below the ice.

Minimum size for rainbows is 12 inches, and the daily limit is three. Landlocked salmon and rainbow trout can be taken year-round. Motors exceeding 10 horsepower are prohibited.

DIRECTIONS: From the south side of Redwood, head east on Cottage Hill Road for about 1 mile.

ADDITIONAL INFORMATION: The state fishing access site on Cottage Hill Road has a hard-surface ramp and parking for 10 cars.

CONTACT: New York State Department of Environmental Conservation Region 6 and Indian River Lakes Chamber of Commerce.

210. BUTTERFIELD LAKE

KEY SPECIES: Walleyes, northern pike, largemouth bass, smallmouth bass, yellow perch, black crappies, bluegills, and bullheads.

DESCRIPTION: This 962-acre body of water is the second largest Indian River lake. Averaging 14.4 feet deep, it has a maximum depth of 50 feet, boasts numerous islands, and has a largely forested shoreline accented in outcrops and cliffs.

TIPS: In spring, work bucktail jigs, plain or tipped with 3-inch Power Grubs or minnows, along weed edges and drop-offs for northerns and walleyes.

THE FISHING: A winding coastline and numerous islands stretch this 2-plus-mile-long lake's shoreline to over 13 miles. Combined with the lake's relatively shallow water, all this edge habitat makes for a highly productive warmwater fishery. The state has been stocking about 300,000 walleye fry annually since 2012. Many survive to range between 15 and 23 inches, and have a taste for worms trolled deep on spinner harnesses, bucktail jigs, bladebaits jigged on bottom, and minnowbaits like ThunderSticks and Bass Pro Shops XPS Minnows worked parallel to shore around dawn and dusk. Northern pike grow from 18 to 30 inches and strike spinnerbaits, silver and perch-colored spoons, and large minnows. Bucketmouths up to 6 pounds like Texas-rigged worms dragged on bottom along weed edges, and 4-inch tubes pitched into weed openings and edges. Bronzebacks up to 4 pounds prowl the drop-offs on the south end and strike bucktail jigs tipped with Berkley's Power Honey Worms, Carolina-rigged 4-inch worms, and fat-bodied crankbaits. Black crappies in the 9- to 14-inch range and yellow perch up to 12 inches take small minnows, Berkley Atomic Teasers tipped with a Berkley Honey Worm, and 2-inch scented curly-tailed grubs jigged or worked on spinner forms. Bluegills the size of cup saucers hit garden worms in early spring, wet flies and poppers in summer, night crawlers in autumn, and mousies and spikes through the ice. Bullheads up to 16 inches swarm into the shallows in spring and can't resist a juicy worm squirming on a muddy floor.

The minimum length for walleyes is 18 inches, and the daily limit is three.

DIRECTIONS: Set into the hamlet of Redwood's east side, the southern half of the lake's west bank is paralleled by Stine Road.

ADDITIONAL INFORMATION: The state launch at the end of Butterfield Lake Road (off Stine Road) in Redwood has a concrete ramp, parking for 50 rigs, and toilets.

CONTACT: New York State Department of Environmental Conservation Region 6 and Indian River Lakes Chamber of Commerce.

Cliffs, like this one on Butter-field Lake (site 210), punctuate the shorelines of the Indian River Lakes.

Working the docks at Butterfield Lake (site 210).

211. HYDE LAKE

KEY SPECIES: Tiger muskies, walleyes, northern pike, crappies, sunfish, and largemouth bass.

DESCRIPTION: This 179-acre lake averages 11.5 feet deep and drops to a maximum depth of 25 feet. A spectacular cliff towers over most of the east shore. The north and south basins are shallow, with the south basin averaging 3 feet deep for about 100 yards out. The east and west sides, however, drop quickly to 15 feet deep.

TIPS: Work large bucktail spinners over the gentle drops on the north and south ends for norlunge.

THE FISHING: This is the best bet in the Indian River lakes for catching a keeper norlunge. The state stocks them annually (1,000 8-inchers in 2014), and anglers take tigers ranging from 30 to 40 inches with surprising regularity. Northern pike in the 18- to 25-inch range are common. Both of these members of the pike family respond to large noisy offerings like Bass Pro Shops XPS Pro Series Minnows and Mepps Musky Killers. The state maintains a walleye presence by stocking roughly 4,000 fingerlings annually. Those that survive their first year stand a good chance of making it to 20 inches, and better. They take jigs, minnowbaits, and, surprisingly, 4-inch finesse worms tipped on jigheads and dragged on bottom. The lake has good populations of largemouth bass in the 12- to 18-inch range, with many growing larger. They're partial to shallow water and hit darters and poppers on the surface, spinnerbaits and soft jerkbaits worked just below the waves, Texas-rigged worms and 4-inch tubes dragged on bottom around structure. Black crappies over 9 inches and perch reaching up to 12 inches are relatively plentiful and strike minnows and curly-tailed grubs worked on spinner forms. Bullheads from 10 to 14 inches and bluegills over 5 inches are typical and take worms.

The minimum length for walleyes is 18 inches, and the daily limit is three. Motors over 10 horsepower are prohibited.

DIRECTIONS: From the village of Theresa, take NY 26 north for about 4 miles to Funda Road and turn left.

ADDITIONAL INFORMATION: The state fishing access site on Funda Road, off NY 26, has a beach launch and parking for about 15 rigs.

CONTACT: New York State Department of Environmental Conservation Region 6 and Indian River Lakes Chamber of Commerce.

212. CLEAR LAKE

KEY SPECIES: Northern pike, black bass, walleyes, black crappies, yellow perch, sunfish, and bullheads.

DESCRIPTION: This 157-acre lake averages 24 feet deep and has a maximum depth of 44 feet. Its shoreline is largely developed with private residences. Oxygen levels are poor in the deeper sections during deep summer.

TIPS: Work soft jerkbaits like YUM Houdini Shads through the northern shallows for postspawn pike and black bass.

THE FISHING: This popular warmwater fishery boasts good numbers of northern pike. Most go around 2.5 pounds, but 10-pounders—and even better—are available. They hit live minnows and minnow-imitating crankbaits such as Bomber Long A's. Largemouth bass ranging between 1.5 and 3 pounds and smallmouths in the 1- to 2-pound class are well represented. While the bucketmouths tend to gravitate toward the shallows and the bronzebacks prefer drop-offs, either one can be caught in both places. They share a common taste for crayfish, spinnerbaits, 3- and 4-inch tubes, and 3-inch Berkley Power Grubs. Though not overly abundant, walleyes running from 18 to 22 inches are present and like Rat-L-Traps and Sonars retrieved steadily or yo-yoed in anywhere from 10 to 20 feet of water. Black crappies averaging 9 inches and yellow perch ranging between 7 and 10 inches are plentiful and strike minnows and curly-tailed grubs. Numerous bluegills between 5 and 8 inches long and bullheads stretching up to 14 inches thrive in this habitat. Both take worms; and the sunnies like poppers and flies, too.

The minimum length for walleyes is 18 inches, and the daily limit is three.

DIRECTIONS: Head south out of Alexandria Bay on NY 26 for 6.6 miles, turn left on Clear Lake Road, and continue for 0.8 mile.

ADDITIONAL INFORMATION: A hard-surface public launch is at the end of Clear Lake Road. There is no formal parking lot, but shoulder parking is permitted a couple hundred yards up the road.

CONTACT: New York State Department of Environmental Conservation Region 6 and Indian River Lakes Chamber of Commerce.

213. BLACK LAKE

KEY SPECIES: Black bass, walleyes, northern pike, muskellunge, black crappies, yellow perch, rock bass, bluegills, bullheads, and channel catfish.

DESCRIPTION: Covering over 10,980 acres, Black Lake is the largest in the highly productive Indian River Lakes group. Roughly 20 miles long, averaging 8 feet deep, dropping to a maximum depth of 29 feet, and punctuated with scenic islands, its warm, clean, weedy water makes it the most fruitful largemouth bass and crappie fishery in the state.

TIPS: In spring and autumn, drift worms around the causeway for walleyes.

THE FISHING: The largemouth bass fishing is legendary—5-pounders are common. They respond to everything from Texas-rigged worms pitched into windfalls and weed openings, to crankbaits and spinnerbaits worked around docks, bass bugs and Mann's Goblins bounced off lily pads, and jig-n-pigs worked in slop. Smallmouths aren't as plentiful, but there's still a lot of them. They like minnows and crayfish, as well as scented curly-tailed grubs and finesse worms and tubes dragged on bottom, especially in channels and around island drop-offs. After being all but wiped out in the last century, allegedly by crappies feeding on their fry, walleyes are staging a comeback—with human intervention. Over the past several years, the state has stocked a total of a couple hundred thousand fry and tens of thousands of fingerlings—30,000 and 22,400 respectively in 2002. While there's no proof it's "payback time," crappie numbers are down slightly, and the eyes seem to be thriving. Indeed, 2- to 3-pounders are becoming so plentiful, word is getting out and anglers are increasingly targeting them, with good results, on crankbaits, jigs, and worms.

Northern pike easily reach 10 pounds and are mostly caught with large minnows. Muskies, though few, average about 30 pounds. Troll for them with large crankbaits. This lake is considered one of the best crappie waters in the Northeast. Slabs typically range from too short to 11 inches, with some 15-inchers available. They like minnows, 2-inch Berkley Power Grubs, YUM Wooly Beavertails, and small hard lures like Cotton Cordell's Spot Minnows and ¼-ounce Silver Buddies. Perch ranging from 6 to 12 inches are common and hit the same baits the crappies like. Bluegills reaching 10 inches and bullheads up to 16 inches like worms. Catfish up to 20 pounds hug the lake's channels and deep holes and hit large minnows, clumps of worms, cut bait, and shrimp.

This lake has sturgeon, a protected species in New York. If caught, they must be released immediately, with no unnecessary injury.

The minimum length for walleyes is 18 inches, and the daily limit is three. The minimum length for black bass is 15 inches.

DIRECTIONS: Head south out of Morristown on NY 58 for about 6 miles.

ADDITIONAL INFORMATION: Black Lake Boat Launch, on CR 6, offers two double-wide paved ramps and parking for 50 rigs. There are several private campgrounds on the lake.

CONTACT: New York State Department of Environmental Conservation Region 6, Black Lake Chamber of Commerce, and St. Lawrence County Chamber of Commerce.

Gary Fischer of Central Square, New York, holding a bucketmouth he caught in Black Lake (site 213).

213A. Eel Weir State Park

DESCRIPTION: Located on the Oswegatchie River, about 2 miles downstream of Black Lake's outlet, this fee area offers 38 campsites, hot showers, a picnic area, a playground, a paved ramp, and 600 feet of shore-fishing access. Open Memorial Day through Columbus Day; free day use is allowed off-season.

DIRECTIONS: From Edwardsville, head east on CR 6 for 8 miles and turn right on CR 4. The park is 2 miles down the road on the right.

214. PLEASANT LAKE

KEY SPECIES: Walleyes, northern pike, black bass, yellow perch, bluegills, and brown bullheads.

DESCRIPTION: This 210-acre lake averages 22 feet deep and has a maximum depth of 32 feet.

TIPS: Drag 4-inch worms rigged on jigheads on bottom along gently sloping drop-offs.

THE FISHING: Pleasant Lake offers above-average warmwater habitat. The state maintains a walleye presence by stocking several thousand fingerlings most years and up to 600,000 fry some years. Life for these small guys in this predator-rich environment is tough, but enough make it to the minimum 18-inch length to make pursuing them worthwhile. Walleyes typically run from 18 to 22 inches and are mostly targeted with bucktail jigs, fished plain or tipped with a worm or scented grub, or lipless crankbaits like Rat-L-Traps and minnowbaits. Jigs worked on the drop-offs, in 15 to 30 feet of water, produce eyes even in daytime. At night they come close to shore, in anywhere from 3 to 10 feet of water, and strike minnowbaits. Northern pike averaging 22 inches are common. Mostly hanging out in relatively shallow water, especially in the north and south bays, they respond to minnows and jerkbaits, particularly about an hour on either side of dawn and dusk. Populations of smallmouth and largemouth bass are pretty equal. Bronzebacks generally run between 12 and 15 inches and prefer soft plastics like curly-tailed grubs and finesse worms fished on bottom, but will also strike hard crankbaits worked in deep water. What's more, they come to the surface on calm days and strike darters and poppers. Bucketmouths like soft plastic jerkbaits, 7- to 10-inch Texas-rigged worms, and snakes worked over and around structure like windfalls, weed edges, and docks. The lake's yellow perch easily reach 10 inches, its bluegills average 7 inches, and its bullheads go anywhere from 8 to 14 inches. The perch hit small jigs, in-line spinners, and minnows; the sunnies like worms, wet flies, and 1-inch curly-tailed grubs; and the bullheads respond to worms and cut bait still-fished on bottom.

DIRECTIONS: Head east out of Rossie on CR 8 for 3.2 miles. Turn right on Pleasant Lake Road and travel 0.2 mile, then turn right on Pleasant Lake Road Number 2 and travel 0.2 mile to the launch at the bend in the road.

ADDITIONAL INFORMATION: The town launch isn't marked and only has room for launching, not bank fishing. Parking for several rigs is at the shoulder along the guardrail.

CONTACT: New York State Department of Environmental Conservation Region 6 and St. Lawrence County Chamber of Commerce.

215. YELLOW LAKE

KEY SPECIES: Northern pike, largemouth bass, black crappies, sunfish, yellow perch, and bullheads.

DESCRIPTION: This 364-acre lake is prime warmwater habitat. Averaging about 4 feet deep, it drops to a maximum depth of 13 feet in a couple of spots in the deep channel running up the middle of its northern half. Less than 10 percent of its shoreline is developed, making it one of the best spots in the state for solitary fishing experiences framed in scenic granite outcrops crowned with precariously perched timber.

TIPS: Cast large plugs along the drop-off in the deep center for pike.

THE FISHING: Relatively isolated, hard to get to, rich in marsh and weeds that minnows love, this place boasts great populations of northern pike and largemouth bass. Pike usually run from 18 to 26 inches, with some stretching the tape to 36 inches. Bucketmouths normally range from 2 to 4 pounds, with a lot of bigger ones around. Both take large minnows, jerkbaits, buzzbaits, spinnerbaits, and surface lures imitating swamp critters like snakes, ducklings, and frogs. Bluegills and pumpkinseeds normally run from 5 to a whopping 10 inches, crappies up to 15 inches have been reported, and yellow perch and bullheads go 8 to 14 inches. Fly fish for the sunfish crappies, and perch with tiny streamers and poppers. Bullheads hang out in the shallows and take worms still-fished on bottom, especially in the spring and on hot summer nights; bring lots of insect repellent.

DIRECTIONS: From the NY 26/CR 22 intersection in Theresa, take CR 22 north for 9.5 miles to CR 25 and turn left (north). At the Y in the road 1 mile later, continue straight on CR 10 for 4 miles, then bear right onto Liscum Road, which turns into Hall Road. The state's fishing access site is on the right, several hundred yards later.

ADDITIONAL INFORMATION: The fishing access site is separated from the parking area by about 0.25 mile of pasture on which the state owns easement rights. You'll have to walk, going through two S-shaped openings (designed to block cattle) in fences, so make sure the craft you bring can be lifted about 5 feet. The access site itself is just a narrow channel through marsh, unsuitable for bank fishing most of the time. Primitive camping is allowed in the Yellow Lake State Multiple Use Area hugging the southeastern half of the lake. Completely surrounded by private land, state land is reachable only by boat.

CONTACT: New York State Department of Environmental Conservation Region 6 and Indian River Lakes Chamber of Commerce.

216. STAR LAKE

KEY SPECIES: Rainbow trout, lake trout, brown trout, Atlantic salmon, largemouth bass, and smallmouth bass.

DESCRIPTION: Spread over 213 acres, this lake averages 21 feet and drops to a maximum depth of over 60 feet. Its shoreline is heavily developed with private residences.

TIPS: Flatline tandem streamers like Gray Ghosts for Atlantic salmon.

THE FISHING: Located close to the road, this two-story fishery gets a lot of attention. The state stocks the place annually with varying numbers of salmonids (300 lake trout averaging 7 inches, almost 5,000 Atlantic salmon ranging from 2 to 8 inches, and 1,580 9-inch rainbow trout in 2014; brown trout have been stocked in the recent past). The salmon, rainbows, and browns typically go 16 to 20 inches, while the lakers can go up to 15 pounds. In late fall and early spring, the salmonids move close to shore and respond to spoons and minnowbaits flatlined in 5 to 15 feet of water. In summer, they move deeper, mostly into the eastern half of the lake, and respond to the same lures trolled 25 to 50 feet down off downriggers. Come winter, the lakers and a few browns hug bottom, striking minnows fished on the floor; while the rainbows and the majority of browns suspend, hitting minnows lowered a few feet below the ice. Dotted with islands, boasting an irregular shoreline punctuated with countless bays and points, you'd think this was dynamite bucketmouth territory. But it's not. Oh, there's a few around in the 12- to 20-inch class, primarily in the shallow bays. And while they'll take a spinnerbait or jerkbait, they gotta go through a bunch of smallmouth to get to it. Bronzebacks outnumber largemouths five to one. Running anywhere from 12 to 18 inches, the smallies primarily hang out off the points and drop-offs, gobbling up every moving object they can fit in their mouths. They're especially fond of minnows, crayfish, tubes, Flukes, and bucktail jigs tipped with a Berkley Power Honey Worm or similar flavored plastics.

Trout and salmon can be taken year-round. The minimum length for brown and rainbow trout is 12 inches, and the daily limit is three. Electric motors only.

DIRECTIONS: On the south side of the hamlet of Star Lake.

ADDITIONAL INFORMATION: A NYSDEC launch site suitable for cartop craft is off NY 3 in the village of Star Lake.

CONTACT: New York State Department of Environmental Conservation Region 6 and St. Lawrence County Chamber of Commerce.

217. SYLVIA LAKE

KEY SPECIES: Rainbow trout, lake trout, smallmouth bass, largemouth bass, yellow perch, and sunfish.

DESCRIPTION: Its shoreline half developed with residences, this 313-acre lake averages 70 feet deep and has a maximum depth of 142 feet.

TIPS: Troll spoons in deep areas.

THE FISHING: Managed as a coldwater fishery, this place has natural populations of lake trout ranging from 2 to 5 pounds. In addition, each year the state stocks anywhere from 3,000 to 5,000 rainbows averaging 9.5 inches. They respond to spoons: flatlined for the rainbows, trolled deep for the lakers. Smallmouth bass range from 0.5 to 3 pounds. Fish for them along drop-offs in 10 to 25 feet of water by dragging jig worms and Carolina-rigged 4-inch worms. Largemouths averaging 2 pounds are abundant and like all the usual suspects: spinnerbaits, buzzbaits, rubber worms . . . Yellow perch range from 6 to 12 inches, and bluegills and pumpkinseeds average 7 inches. They all take worms, and the perch hit small lures and minnows, too.

Trout season is year-round, the minimum length is 12 inches, and the daily limit is three. Lake trout can be taken year-round, too.

DIRECTIONS: Head north on NY 3/NY 812 out of the hamlet of Harrisville. Less than a mile out of town, stay on NY 812 when it veers off on its own. About 8.4 miles later, turn left at the NYSDEC access sign, go through the Vanderbilt Minerals LLC facility, and continue for 0.6 mile to the primitive access site.

ADDITIONAL INFORMATION: The fishing access site has a few hundred feet of shore access and parking for about 10 rigs. There is no formal launch, but the beach drops quickly and locals launch trailered craft here.

CONTACT: New York State Department of Environmental Conservation Region 6 and St. Lawrence County Chamber of Commerce.

218. SUCKER LAKE

KEY SPECIES: Black bass, rock bass, and pumpkinseeds.

DESCRIPTION: Covering 98 acres, this lake averages about 6 feet deep and drops to a maximum depth of 10 feet in a relatively small hole in its south end. Its north shore sports all the development, while the rest of the shoreline is mostly lowland punctured with nooks and crannies bass love to hide in.

TIPS: Rip frog, duckling, and snake imitations near shore in early evening and an hour on both sides of sunup.

THE FISHING: This little pond has some pretty big bucketmouths for its size. But human activity like swimming and boating sends them deep for most of the day. Reaching up to 16 inches—even better if you're really lucky—they're always looking toward the surface for something good to drop out of the sky. While they'll readily hit a spinnerbait, it's a lot more thrilling to watch them engulf a popper or darter. Small numbers of bronzebacks are also available. Typically running too small to just big enough, these scrappy fighters are a lot of fun on ultralight tackle. They'll take worms, crayfish, bucktail jigs, spinners, and spoons. Rock bass and pumpkinseeds ranging from 5 to 7 inches are present and strike worms, flies, and small poppers.

DIRECTIONS: From its intersection with NY 3 just south of the hamlet of Fine, head down Ridge Road for a little under 3 miles, take a right at the T onto Briggs Switch Road, and continue about 0.4 mile to the launch.

CONTACT: New York State Department of Environmental Conservation Region 6.

219. LAKE BONAPARTE

KEY SPECIES: Lake trout, brown trout, walleyes, smallmouth bass, largemouth bass, northern pike, yellow perch, and burbot.

DESCRIPTION: Covering 1,248 acres, this lake averages 31 feet deep and has a maximum depth of 75 feet. Its shoreline is heavily developed with private residences.

TIPS: In the spring, run spoons parallel to shore for trout and northern pike.

THE FISHING: Bonaparte is managed as a two-story fishery. The state usually stocks about 800 lake trout averaging 7 inches and 2,800 brown trout averaging 8.5 inches annually. Survival isn't great, but the lucky ones that make it reach between 1 and 4 pounds, with some going over 10 pounds. Lakers are targeted with silver spoons trolled deep. Browns respond best, especially in the spring, to silver and perch-colored crankbaits like Rapala Minnows and ThunderSticks trolled close to shore. In 1997 the state started a five-year walleye stocking program calling for 25,000 fingerlings to be stocked annually. By 2001 creel surveys showed keeper walleyes were available. Still, fry weren't appearing in surveys, possibly because of predation by crappies and bass, so the state started managing the fishery with regular stocking. Ghost eyes in the 2- to 5-pound range are common, and whoopers up to 10 pounds are netted often. They hit worms drifted on harnesses, curly-tailed grubs, and crankbaits. Largemouth bass range from 1.5 to 5 pounds and are normally taken in the bays with Texas-rigged worms and soft jerkbaits. The best bucketmouth habitat is Fort Drum's Mud Lake and around the channel connecting it to the west side of Lake Bonaparte. Back in the main lake, smallmouths range between 1 and 2.5 pounds and can be taken on drop-offs with crayfish, minnows, and jigs. Northern pike run from 18 to 36 inches and are targeted with large minnows and spoons. Perch range from 6 to 12 inches and take worms, minnows, and 2-inch curly-tailed grubs during warm weather, minnows and live grubs tipped on jigs when the place is sealed in ice. Winter sees a lot of burbot averaging 2 pounds caught incidentally on minnows targeting walleyes, northerns, and perch.

The minimum length for trout is 9 inches, and their season is open year-round. A pass is needed to fish on Fort Drum property.

DIRECTIONS: Head east out of Watertown on NY 3 for about 11 miles and bear left (east) on NY 3A. Continue for about 4 miles, get back on NY 3 east, travel for 15.4 miles, and turn left onto North Shore Road. At the T in the road 0.2 mile later, turn left and continue for 3.5 miles.

ADDITIONAL INFORMATION: The day-use area off North Shore Road has a concrete launch, parking for 20 rigs, several hundred feet of shore-fishing access, and a toilet. There are three no-frills campsites along the access road just before the launch; a permit, available from the local forest ranger, is needed to use them.

CONTACT: New York State Department of Environmental Conservation Region 6, Fort Drum, and Lewis County Chamber of Commerce.

Kayak anglers setting out on Lake Bonaparte (site 219).

220. ST. LAWRENCE RIVER (ST. LAWRENCE COUNTY)

KEY SPECIES: Muskellunge, black bass, northern pike, walleyes, carp, yellow perch, black crappies, sunfish, rock bass, and brown bullheads.

DESCRIPTION: The outlet for the Great Lakes system (the world's greatest freshwater reservoirs—combined, they cover fully 1 percent of the planet's landmass), the St. Lawrence is the world's 14th largest river. Its New York section stretches for over 100 miles, from Cape Vincent to the St. Regis Mohawk Indian Reservation east of Massena.

TIPS: Muskies are biggest and hungriest in autumn.

THE FISHING: Big water like this produces big fish. Arthur Lawton's 69-pound, 15-ounce muskie—a fish that held the world record until being dethroned in the 1990s on a technicality (by an only slightly less controversial fish, incidentally)—came out of this river. Their numbers nose-dived in the 1960s and 1970s, but catch-and-release practices, along with increased minimum lengths, allowed muskellunge to bounce back. Currently 20-pounders are common, 40-pounders are very possible, and 50-pounders are caught each year. Most are taken by trolling large crankbaits like Cisco Kids, Swim Whizzes, and Buchertail Depth Raiders. Good numbers are also taken on topwater lures like Jitterbugs and buzzbaits.

Northern pike are the river's most popular game. Averaging 4 pounds, there are enough in the 10- to 15-pound range to make targeting trophies a reasonable bet. While a skillful guide can still get his clients 25 pike a day, their numbers are down significantly from 20 years ago. Scientists trace the problem to the construction of the Seaway Trail, whose flow regime prevents extreme fluctuations in river levels, destroying marshes northerns need for spawning. Others blame the drop in pike numbers on shrinking weed beds, the result of strict anti-pollution laws that reduce nutrients discharged into the river by municipalities and industry. On the bright side, pike are larger, healthier, and a lot more challenging to catch because greater visibility requires you fish farther from the boat. The largest pikeasauruses are most successfully targeted with live minnows. However, scrappy northerns in the 22- to 26-inch range love buzzbaits, spinnerbaits, and jigheads tipped with minnow/tube combinations.

There's a great population of largemouth bass in the 3- to 6-pound range. Crayfish, minnows, crankbaits, Texas- and Carolina-rigged worms, and loud surface baits all produce. The river is loaded with roving schools of smallmouth bass averaging 1.5 pounds. Find a school and you can catch them till your arms hurt. They respond to crayfish, shiners, spinnerbaits, crankbaits, and Carolina-rigged worms and craws dragged on bottom. Walleyes weighing over 10 pounds are caught so frequently, they rarely raise an eyebrow anymore. Troll for them with Krocodile spoons and crankbaits like Red Fins and Rapalas, or drift and bounce jigs tipped with worms, minnows, or soft plastics like tubes and 3-inch scented curly-tailed grubs on bottom.

The state's greatest concentration of really huge carp, ranging from 20 to 50 pounds, is found here. Most are taken by bow fishing. However, anglers are learning the thrill of monster carp on light tackle and are increasingly going after them with kernel corn, bread balls, baked potato, a mash composed of various grains, even peanut butter. Yellow perch ranging from 7 to 12 inches, sunfish 5 to 7 inches, and rock bass averaging 0.5 pound can be found in shallow water anytime. Black crappies up to 1.5 pounds roam around the bays, particularly around submerged timber. Perch, crappies, and rock bass love small minnows, wet flies, and 2-inch curly-tailed grubs and tubes. All but the crappies have a taste for worms. Sunfish and rock bass provide explosive summertime action on ⅟₃₂-ounce Hula Poppers. In spring bullheads ranging from 8 to 16 inches congregate on muddy bottoms in bays and are taken by still-fishing with worms on bottom.

The St. Lawrence River is governed by the special Great Lakes Regulations found in the New York State Department of Environmental Conservation *Fishing Regulations Guide*. The minimum length for muskies is 54 inches, and the daily limit is one. Minimum length for northern pike is 22 inches, and the daily limit is five. Minimum length for walleyes is 18 inches, with a daily limit of three. Fishing for black bass out of season, even catch and release, is prohibited.

DIRECTIONS: Take I-81 north out of Watertown for approximately 30 miles to exit 50. NY 12 and NY 37 parallel the eastern half of the river, and NY 12, NY 12E, and CR 6 parallel its western half.

ADDITIONAL INFORMATION: All river villages offer municipal docks and boat launches. The north half of the river is Canadian, and you need a province of Ontario license to fish there. Many fishing derbies are held here annually, including qualifying events for major tournaments (check tourism offices for details).

CONTACT: 1000 Islands International Tourism Council, St. Lawrence County Chamber of Commerce, and New York State Department of Environmental Conservation Region 6.

220A. Cedar Island State Park

DESCRIPTION: Nestled on an island that is half private and half state-owned, this fee area offers day-use and camping sections. The day-use area boasts a pavilion, picnic facilities, hiking trails, and shore fishing. The campground has 18 lightly wooded sites, toilets, and two floating docks.

THE FISHING: This island sits on the outer edge of Chippewa Bay, a traditional hot spot for northern pike ranging from 22 to 36 inches. They can be found virtually anywhere in the bay from October through spring, around tributaries in May, and at the drop-offs around Cedar Island all summer long. The channel running the length of the bay's mouth is a productive trolling area for muskies in autumn. Largemouth bass up to 6 pounds thrive in the bay's massive weed beds. Smallmouth bass averaging 1.5 pounds always mill around Chippewa Point and the numerous rocky shoals surrounding it. Brown bullheads up to 14 inches literally invade the bay from April through May. Yellow perch ranging from 7 to 11 inches, black crappies up to 14 inches, and rock bass, pumpkinseeds, and bluegills from 5 to 10 inches live in the bay year-round.

DIRECTIONS: Cedar is the large island at the entrance to Chippewa Bay, midway between Chippewa Point and Oak Island. The quickest way to get there is to launch from the hard-surface public ramp at the end of Denner Road, in the hamlet of Chippewa Bay.

220B. Jacques Cartier State Park

DESCRIPTION: This 463-acre fee area offers 124 campsites (34 with electric hookups), a flat rock launch ramp with parking for 10 rigs, a swimming beach, hot showers, and picnic facilities. The campground is open from mid-May through Columbus Day. A day-use fee is charged from Memorial Day through Labor Day.

THE FISHING: This section of the St. Lawrence River gives up numerous muskies in the 20- to 30-pound range and several 40-pounders every year. The local hot spot is around American Island, about 1 mile upstream of the park. Northern pike range from 22 to 30 inches and occupy the outside edges of weedy bays, tributary mouths, island drop-offs, and deep weed beds out in the main river. Walleyes ranging from 6 to 10 pounds hang out on rocky shelves at the heads and tails of islands and along drop-offs. Locals go for them by flatlining diving lures or by drifting worms and minnows. Smallmouth bass ranging from 1 to 2.5 pounds are plentiful off points from opening day through the second week of July and around rocky shoals for the remainder of the season. They like live minnows fished on bottom or freelined. Yellow perch generally run from 7 to 11 inches and are found in weeds, on shoals, at drop-offs—you name it. They respond to minnows, grubs, worms, and tiny jigs.

DIRECTIONS: Off NY 12, 2 miles west of Morristown.

220C. Morristown Municipal Boat Ramp and Dock

DESCRIPTION: This facility offers a two-lane paved ramp, parking for 10 rigs, overnight docking for a fee, and ice-fishing access.

THE FISHING: The islands out in front of the village hold good numbers of northern pike in the 22- to 28-inch range. They like tube jigs tipped with minnows. Area shoals and drop-offs are prime smallmouth habitat and contain good numbers of bronzebacks in the 1.5- to 2.5-pound class. They like live crayfish and their imitations. Yellow perch from 6 to 12 inches can be found anywhere there are rocks or weeds and respond to 2-inch scented YUM Wooly Curltails.

DIRECTIONS: On Water Street in Morristown.

220D. Ogdensburg Municipal Boat Launch

DESCRIPTION: This site has two double-lane paved ramps, parking for 30 rigs plus overflow parking, and a long stretch of shore-fishing access.

THE FISHING: Drift worms, minnows, or crayfish over the sandbar located due north of the boat launch for yellow perch from 8 to 12 inches. Northern pike in the 22- to 36-inch range are taken by trolling Ripplin' Red Fins and ThunderSticks around the mouth of the Oswegatchie River. Smallmouth bass ranging from 12 to 16 inches are so plentiful around shoals, folks fishing on bottom with crayfish or minnows expect 50-fish days. The rocky shoal just upstream of the international bridge draws schools of bronzebacks. Walleyes ranging from 5 to 10 pounds also like this shoal and respond to crankbaits like Bomber A's and ThunderSticks. The deep water between the red-and-white buoys directly in front of the boat launch is a traditional muskie spot. Some claim this is where Arthur Lawton caught his 69-pound, 15-ounce world record. Most are taken on large crankbaits trolled against the flow. Wheathouse Bay, just downstream from the launch, is a popular ice-fishing spot for yellow perch, northerns, and walleyes.

DIRECTIONS: At the end of Paterson Street in the city of Ogdensburg.

220E. Ogdensburg City Boat Launch

DESCRIPTION: This park-like site has a double-wide paved ramp, parking for about 10 rigs, picnic facilities, and shore-fishing access.

DIRECTIONS: Riverside Avenue in Ogdensburg.

220F. Waddington Boat Launch

DESCRIPTION: Open year-round, this facility offers a double-wide paved ramp and parking for 25 rigs. Overflow parking is available in the adjacent park.

THE FISHING: The bay at the mouth of Sucker Brook holds perch ranging from 6 to 10 inches, largemouth bass up to 6 pounds, and northern pike in the 22- to 27-inch range. Smallmouths up to 2.5 pounds thrive in the weed lines and drop-offs. They all take minnows and jigs. Walleyes up to 12 pounds are taken by flatlining deep-diving crankbaits like Heddon Hellbenders over the shelves skirting the drop-off paralleling the north side of Ogden Island (the big island due north).

DIRECTIONS: Head north on NY 37 out of Ogdensburg for about 15 miles to Waddington, turn left on Pine Street, then right on Park Lane.

220G. Brandy Brook Boat Launch

DESCRIPTION: This site offers a hard-surface ramp and parking for 10 rigs.

DIRECTIONS: The launch is about 3 miles north of Waddington on NY 37.

220H. Coles Creek State Park

DESCRIPTION: This 1,800-acre fee facility offers 228 primitive campsites, 147 campsites with electricity, hot showers, picnic facilities, a swimming beach, and shore-fishing access. The campground is open from mid-May through Labor Day. A day-use fee is charged from Memorial Day through Labor Day.

THE FISHING: The park is on the shores of Lake St. Lawrence, the massive impoundment created by the Robert Moses Power Dam. The weedy shallows in Coles Creek's mouth and the area's countless weedy bays hold largemouth bass ranging from 2 to 6 pounds and yellow perch from 8 to 12 inches year-round. Northerns up to 40 inches, smallmouth bass ranging from 1 to 3 pounds, and walleyes up to 10 pounds hang out around the drop-offs paralleling the main river channel and its islands.

DIRECTIONS: Take NY 37 north out of Waddington for about 3 miles.

220I. Wilson Hill Public Access

DESCRIPTION: This site offers a paved launch ramp and parking for 50 rigs.

THE FISHING: The site is located on the eastern border of the Wilson Hill State Wildlife Management Area. Northern pike from 22 to 40 inches and largemouth bass over 6 pounds rule the weedy bays, growing big and fat on a generous supply of perch and sunfish. Smallmouth bass from 1 to 2 pounds and walleyes up to 8 pounds lurk along the drop-offs and shelves hugging the ancient river channel. This is the best spot on the river for trophy carp over 40 pounds. Fishing is prohibited in the wildlife management area.

DIRECTIONS: Head west out of Massena on NY 37 for about 4 miles, then turn right on Willard Road and travel about 1 mile.

220J. Robert Moses State Park

DESCRIPTION: An arm of the St. Lawrence River runs through this 2,322-acre fee area. Built half on the mainland and half on Barnhart Island (constructed from river rubble brought up during construction of the St. Lawrence–FDR Power Project), this park offers 130 campsites without hookups, 38 campsites with electricity, two boat launches with paved ramps, miles of shore-fishing access, a marina with 42 slips, hot showers, picnic areas, playgrounds, hiking trails, and a pump-out station. The park is open year-round, and camping is allowed from mid-May through Columbus Day. A day-use fee is charged from mid-June through Labor Day.

THE FISHING: The dams here block muskie and walleye migrations. The fish find the pickings pretty good below the barriers and always stick around for a while before heading back downstream. Muskies ranging from 20 to 40 pounds are commonly taken in autumn by trolling crankbaits through the heavy current. Walleyes ranging from 3 to 12 pounds share this habitat with the muskies; however, they also run up the southern arm of the river below the Long Sault Spillway dam. They respond to crankbaits. Smallmouths up to 3 pounds can be taken in the fast water on crayfish, jigs, and crankbaits.

DIRECTIONS: Take NY 37 east out of Massena for about 2 miles. Turn north on NY 131, travel about 1 mile, then continue north on Barnhart Island Road for 0.5 mile to the park.

ADDITIONAL INFORMATION: Barnhart Island Road goes under the Eisenhower Lock, and ocean freighters are often visible in the channel above the road.

APPENDIX

NEW YORK STATE DEPARTMENT OF ENVIRONMENTAL CONSERVATION REGIONAL OFFICES

Fisheries Office
NYSDEC Region 5
PO Box 296
Ray Brook, NY 12977-0220
(518) 897-1200

Fisheries Office
NYSDEC Region 6
State Office Bldg.
317 Washington Street
Watertown, NY 13601-3787
(315) 785-2261

STATE PARKS

Cedar Island State Park
County Route 93
Hammond, NY 13646
(315) 482-3331

Coles Creek State Park
NY Route 37
Waddington, NY 13694
(315) 388-5636

Jacques Cartier State Park
PO Box 380
Morristown, NY 13664
(315) 375-6371

Moreau Lake State Park
605 Old Saratoga Road
Gansevoort, NY 12831
(518) 793-0511

Pixley Falls State Park
11430 State Route 46
Boonville, NY 13309
(315) 337-4670

Robert Moses State Park
19 Robinson Bay Road
Massena, NY 13662
(315) 769-8663

PUBLIC CAMPGROUNDS
Alger Island
303 Petrie Road
Old Forge, NY 13420
(315) 369-3224

Ausable Point
3346 Lake Shore Road
Peru, NY 12972
(518) 561-7080

Brown Tract Pond
Uncas Road
Raquette Lake, NY 13436
(315) 354-4412

Buck Pond
1339 County Route 60
Onchiota, NY 12989
(518) 891-3449

Caroga Lake
3043 State Highway 29A
Caroga Lake, NY 12078
(518) 835-4241

Cranberry Lake
243 Lone Pine Road
Cranberry Lake, NY 12927
(315) 848-2315

Crown Point
742 Bridge Road
Crown Point, NY 12928
(518) 597-3603

Eagle Point
8448 State Route 9
Pottersville, NY 12860
(518) 494-2220

Eel Weir
RD #3
Ogdensburg, NY 13669
(315) 393-1138

Eighth Lake
1353 NY 28
Inlet, NY 13360
(315) 354-4120

Fish Creek Pond
4523 State Route 30
Saranac Lake, NY 12983
(518) 891-4560

Forked Lake
381 Forked Lake Campsite Lane
Long Lake, NY 12847
(518) 624-6646

Golden Beach
NY Route 28
Raquette Lake, NY 13436
(315) 354-4230

Hearthstone Point
3298 Lakeshore Drive
Lake George, NY 12845
(518) 668-5193

Higley Flow
442 Cold Brook Drive
Colton, NY 13625
(315) 262-2880

Indian Lake Islands
State Route 30
Sabael, NY 12864
(518) 648-5300

Lake Durant
Routes 28 & 30
Blue Mountain Lake, NY 12812
(518) 352-7797

Lake Eaton
HC01 Route 30
Long Lake, NY 12847
(518) 624-2641

Lake George Islands
232 Golf Course Road
Warrensburg, NY 12885
(518) 623-1200
Glen Island (518) 644-9696
Long Island (518) 656-9426
Narrow Island (518) 499-1288

Lake Harris
291 Campsite Road
Newcomb, NY 12852
(518) 582-2503

Lewey Lake
4155 NY Route 30N
Lake Pleasant, NY 12108
(518) 648-5266

Limekiln Lake
Limekiln Lake Road
Inlet, NY 13360
(315) 357-4401

Lincoln Pond
4363 Lincoln Pond Road
Elizabethtown, NY 12932
(518) 942-5292

Little Sand Point
CR 24 Old Piseco Road
Piseco, NY 12139
(518) 548-7585

Meacham Lake
119 State Camp Road
Duane, NY 12953
(518) 483-5116

Moffitt Beach
Page Street
Speculator, NY 12164
(518) 548-7102

Moreau Lake
605 Old Saratoga Road
Gansevoort, NY 12831
(518) 793-0511

Northampton Beach
328 Houseman Street
Mayfield, NY 12117
(518) 863-6000

Paradox Lake
897 NYS Route 74
Paradox, NY 12858
(518) 532-7451

Point Comfort
1365 CR 24
Old Piseco Road
Piseco, NY 12139
(518) 548-7586

Poplar Point
CR 24
Old Piseco Road
Piseco, NY 12139
(518) 548-8031

Putnam Pond
763 Putts Pond Road
Ticonderoga, NY 12883
(518) 585-7280

Rogers Rock
9894 Lake Shore Drive
Hague, NY 12836
(518) 585-6746

Rollins Pond
4523 State Route 30
Saranac Lake, NY 12983
(518) 891-3239

Sacandaga
1047 State Route 30
Northville, NY 12134
(518) 924-4121

Scaroon Manor
8728 State Route 9
Pottersville, NY 12860
(518) 494-2631

Sharp Bridge
4390 US Route 9
North Hudson, NY 12855
(518) 532-7538

Taylor Pond
1865 Silver Lake Road
Ausable Forks, NY
(518) 647-5250

Wilmington Notch
4953 NYS Route 86
Wilmington, NY 12997
(518) 946-7172

INDIAN NATIONS
Mohawk Council of Akwesasne
Conservation Department
PO Box 489
Hogansburg, NY 13655
(613) 575-2250, ext. 2412

CHAMBERS OF COMMERCE AND TOURISM OFFICES
Adirondack Regional Tourism Council
PO Box 911
Lake Placid, NY 12946
www.visitadirondacks.com

Black Lake Chamber of Commerce
P.O. Box 12
Hammond, NY 13646
(315) 375-8640

Franklin County Tourism
193 River Street
Saranac Lake, NY 12953
(888) 577-6678
www.adirondacklakes.com

Indian River Lakes Chamber of Commerce
Town Clerks Office
Commercial and Main Streets
Theresa, NY 13691
(315) 628-5046

Plattsburgh–North Country Chamber of Commerce
7061 State Route 9
Plattsburgh, NY 12901
(518) 563-1000
www.goadirondack.com

Saranac Lake Chamber of Commerce
193 River Street
Saranac Lake, NY 12983
(518) 891-1990
www.saranaclake.com

St. Lawrence County Chamber of Commerce
101 Main Street
Canton, NY 13617-1248
(877) 228-7810
www.northcountryguide.com

1000 Islands International Tourism Council
Box 400
Alexandria Bay, NY 13607
(800) 847-5263
www.visit1000islands.com

Warren County Tourism Department
1340 State Route 9
Lake George, NY 12845
visitlakegeorge.com
(800) 958-4748

OTHER CONTACTS

Fort Drum
(315) 772-6283
www.fortdrum.isportsman.net

Brookfield Power
(877) 856-7466

For information on water releases at power plants contact:
Waterline
(800) 452-1742
www.h2oline.com

Paul Smiths College VIC
8023 State Route 30
Paul Smiths, NY 12970
(518) 327-6241

Tug Hill Commission
Dulles State Office Bldg.
317 Washington Street
Watertown, NY 13601-3782
(888) 785-2380

INDEX